Public Lies
and other plays

Detaining Mr. Trotsky • Public Lies
Borderline • The Dershowitz Protocol

Public Lies

and other Plays

Detaining Mr. Trotsky
Public Lies
Borderline
The Dershowitz Protocol

Robert Fothergill

Playwrights Canada Press
Toronto • Canada

Public Lies and Other Plays © copyright 2007 Robert Fothergill
Introduction © copyright 2007
Detaining Mr. Trotsky © copyright 1987 • *Public Lies* © copyright 1993
Borderline © copyright 2004 • *The Dershowitz Protocol* © copyright 2003
The author asserts moral rights.

Playwrights Canada Press
The Canadian Drama Publisher
215 Spadina Avenue, Suite 230, Toronto, Ontario CANADA M5T 2C7
416-703-0013   fax 416-408-3402
orders@playwrightscanada.com • www.playwrightscanada.com

CAUTION: The works in this book are fully protected under the copyright laws of Canada and all other countries of The Copyright Union. No part of this book, covered by the copyright hereon, may be reproduced or used in any form or by any means – graphic, electronic or mechanical – without the prior written permission of the publisher except for excerpts in a review. Rights to produce, film, or record, in whole or in part, in any medium or any language, by any group, amateur or professional, are retained by the author, who has the right to grant or refuse permission at the time of the request. For amateur or professional production rights please contact Playwrights Canada Press at the above address.

Any request for photocopying, recording, taping or information storage and retrieval systems of any part of this book shall be directed in writing to Access Copyright,
1 Yonge St., Suite 800, Toronto, Ontario CANADA M5E 1E5 416-868-1620.

This book would be twice its cover price were it not for the support of Canadian taxpayers through the Government of Canada Book Publishing Industry Development Programme, Canada Council for the Arts, Ontario Arts Council, and the Ontario Media Development Corporation.

 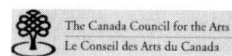 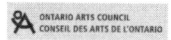 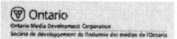

Front cover images: © 2007 JupiterImages Corporation
Production editor/cover design: JLArt

Library and Archives Canada Cataloguing in Publication

Fothergill, Robert A.
    Public lies and other plays / Robert Fothergill.

Contents: Detaining Mr. Trotsky -- Public lies -- Borderline --
    The Dershowitz protocol.
ISBN 978-0-88754-743-0

    I. Title.

PS8561.O82P82 2007   C812'.6   C2007-903943-X

First edition: July 2007.
Printed and bound by Canadian Printco Ltd. at Scarborough, Canada.

Every best effort was made to locate the actors listed below. Anyone knowing their whereabouts is encouraged to contact the publisher.
    Andrew Akman
    James D. Mitchell
    Karen Kenedy
    Paula Grove

Especially for Eleanor, who had the original idea.

Table of Contents

Introduction	iii
Detaining Mr. Trotsky	1
Public Lies	71
Borderline	145
The Dershowitz Protocol	189
About the Author	218

INTRODUCTION

Plays are conceived out of the oddest conjunctions. Quite a few years ago, in a bookstore on the Charing Cross Road in London, my wife looked up from what must have been the Isaac Deutscher biography to ask, "Did you know that Trotsky spent a month in Canada? You should write a play about that." Which was odd in itself, because I wasn't particularly "into" writing plays at that time. Nevertheless, when looked at, it did seem like a godsend of an idea. In April 1917, world-historical figure Leon Trotsky had indeed spent several weeks in Canada, in quite remarkable circumstances. On his way from New York to Petrograd with his wife and two sons following the fall of the Tsar, he was taken off a ship bound for Norway and sent from Halifax to the internment camp in Amherst, Nova Scotia. There he found himself up against the very epitome of reactionary imperialism in the person of Colonel Arthur Henry Morris (British army, retd.), commandant of the camp, who detested everything Trotsky was and stood for. Held incommunicado, seething with impatience to get to Russia where Lenin was already seizing control of the Petrograd soviet, Trotsky spent his time fomenting rebellion among the German internees and captured sailors, and provoking Morris to murderous fury. The catalyst for the actual play came with the invention of the young Canadian lieutenant, part of the guard contingent in the camp, who finds himself caught between his conventional loyalties and the slightly demonic appeal of the charismatic revolutionary.

In the course of researching the subject, I drove to Amherst, encountering a man who remembered as a child meeting Colonel Morris, inspecting the remains of the camp, including the cement floor of the commandant's office, where Trotsky himself would have stood, and interviewing an old soldier who had actually spoken with the mysterious Russian prisoner. Unfortunately his recollections were faint and confused, to the point where he appeared to be mistaking Trotsky for Stalin. Nevertheless, he seemed to recall that Trotsky spoke English "well enough," and that he had piercing black eyes! I was able to tell myself that I was looking into the eyes of a man who had looked into the eyes of Leon Trotsky.

The play as it began to emerge was a sprawling thing, a mix of documentary and drama calling for up to twenty actors. These included a number of German prisoners and a German-Canadian trade union leader – a character who was more of a concept than a person, and who didn't survive into later drafts. After a couple of early expressions of interest – one from Stratford, no less – the play languished for several years, until the Toronto Free Theatre undertook to workshop it in December 1985, following which Guy Sprung indicated that if the cast could be cut to eight, he might be interested. This drastic pruning proved easier than expected and (I think) constituted a considerable improvement. Richard Greenblatt – a "red-diaper baby" – and hence sympathetic – was assigned to direct it and together we wrestled it into its final shape in the summer of 1987. The rehearsal process, with what seemed to me an ideal cast, was immensely enjoyable, and we opened on October 21. The show got quite good notices and received some unexpected attention. At the end of one of the performances, several elderly men in the front row got to their feet, turned to the audience, and raised their fists in salute to the Leon Trotsky who had been resurrected for them by actor Angelo Rizacos!

The genesis of *Public Lies* was of a very different kind, beginning actually as a sort of commission. In 1988, someone at the National Film Board of Canada apparently had the rather perverse notion that its fiftieth anniversary (1989) might be celebrated by some kind of theatre piece, featuring its founder and first Commissioner, John Grierson. A small amount of money was advanced to the Canadian Stage Company (into which the TFT had been absorbed) to commission a workshop of something suitable. What was envisaged, I think, was a solo impersonation of Grierson, of a generally worshipful nature, to be performed at a ceremonial occasion. Several writers were approached and turned it down, but I found the challenge intriguing, having some knowledge of the history of Canadian cinema and some experience of making 16mm films. I had even attended a speech by Grierson in 1969, of which all I can recall is the scathing phrase (in derisive Scottish accent), "eight millimetre films for eight millimetre minds." So I wrote some scenes, not the monologue initially envisaged, situating Grierson at the height of his power in the early 1940s as Mackenzie King's "propaganda maestro," and again in the fall of 1970, on his return to Canada as a guest lecturer at McGill University, during the October Crisis. These scenes were workshopped by CanStage, under the direction of Miles Potter, with R.H. Thomson, Diana Belshaw, John Jarvis, David Fox and Karen Kenedy. As can be imagined, the workshop was very stimulating and enjoyable, but I was slow to capitalize on the stimulus to further development, and after another brief workshop a year later, CanStage decided not to pursue it. (The NFB's fiftieth anniversary had come and gone anyway.)

But in the interim I had had the opportunity to track down and interview some "Old Griersonians" from the 1940s, some of whom were quite touchingly eager to share their recollection of the most exciting years of their lives. Out of these encounters came some more substantial character material, and a sense of the complexity of the man. When I reported to one of them that a former colleague had insisted that I must convey that Grierson was "lovable," she replied witheringly, "Well, he... *wasn't!*" In the fall of 1992, I submitted the script to Urjo Kareda at the Tarragon, who agreed (with surprising promptness) to include it in the 1993–94 season, with Richard Greenblatt, once again, to direct. This time the dramaturgical and rehearsal process was rather more turbulent, with some energetic disagreement over issues of structure (the 1940s/1970 alternation) and details of Grierson's behaviour. But consensus was achieved, and in the event a number of the O.G.s, including one who, whether he knew it or not, had served as a component of one of the composite characters, felt they had seen their old boss alive and well in Layne Coleman's impersonation.

Borderline, rather incongruously (given its final shape), began as a vaguely conceived musical. In the summer of 1994, Marty Bell of Livent Inc. was workshopping elements of *Ragtime* in the studios at York University. In an introductory talk to cast, crew and guests, he had asked rhetorically, "Why should these characters be made to *sing?*" There and then I had the notion of a play about refugees and family reunification in war-torn Africa, which might feature the powerful cadences and rhythms of African music. The idea for a musical didn't last long, but the conception of a play set in Africa continued to develop, with the still-current events in Rwanda demanding attention. The genocide itself seemed altogether too vast and appalling to attempt to put in a play. Only movies can tackle events on that scale, and several have done so. So the situation which began to take shape was between a Canadian relief worker and a refugee in one of the camps, after the capture of Kigali by the Tutsi RPF had sent the Hutu population fleeing.

Entered in the biennial Herman Voaden competition for new Canadian plays, it won second prize and was workshopped in Kingston, Ontario, in the fall of 1999, directed by Bill Glassco, with Laurel Paetz, Nigel Shawn Williams, Matthew Gibson and Mo Bock. Two or three more drafts followed, but failed to attract any interest, so in 2004 I entered a condensed version in the Toronto Summerworks festival, where it was directed by Mark Cassidy. In addition to Niki Landau and Marvin Hinz, who had appeared in *The Dershowitz Protocol* the previous summer, I was fortunate to find in Lucky Ejim and Ayodele Adewumi two African actors who could bring an indispensable authenticity to their roles. (Though they agreed that my assumption that Nigerians can play Rwandans was like an African assuming that – what shall we say? – Danes can play Italians.) Some Rwandans who saw the show professed to be painfully moved by Lucky's performance as Patrice Umbiwimana, and he played the role again in the CBC Radio version in 2005.

The Dershowitz Protocol had the simplest, and by far the shortest, gestation period of the four. In the fall of 2002, I heard a CBC Radio interview with the Harvard law professor Alan Dershowitz, about his suggestion that the interrogation under torture of so-called "ticking bomb terrorists" should be conducted accountably and under judicial warrant, rather than secretly farmed out to foreign states under special "rendition." The idea came immediately of attempting to dramatize the first actual implementation of such a proceeding. Accepted into Summerworks 2003, it was presented in August, directed by Mark Cassidy, in a very small and very hot venue in the Artword Theatre premises. People who saw it, then and later, disagreed quite vehemently as to what the play seems to "say" about the practice it displays. The play has had a couple of limited productions since that time, including one by the Downstairs Cabaret Theatre in Rochester, NY, and at the time of writing there are plans for an off-off-Broadway production in November 2007.

The four plays in this volume all sit pretty squarely at the public-historical – as opposed to the private-fictitious – end of the dramatic spectrum. The actions that the characters are caught up in, and the contentions that engage them, are precipitated by events in the real world where history is being made, rather than by eruptions in their own domestic-romantic environments. I hesitate to call them "political plays," if that implies plays which seek to propagate or reinforce an explicit ideological position, or to incite mobs to storm the nearest barricade. Of course any play will exhibit certain general sympathies and biases, some of them relatively unexamined, but I would like to hope that the contentions among my characters leave the issues in question to some extent unresolved. I cannot see the point of writing a play which clearly endorses a particular point of view, articulated by ventriloquists' dummies who are unambiguously right. On the other hand, if political plays are those in which issues of social and ethical concern are wrangled over by characters for whom, to reverse the popular adage, the political is personal, then these may qualify. None of them, I hope, offers The Answer which the spectator is supposed to take home and display with a fridge magnet.

In conclusion, I would like to thank most sincerely the many people who have generously helped to push and pull these plays into the shapes which, for better or worse, they take in this book. In response to your many suggestions, I put things in, changed things, moved things around, and took things out – though one or two of the latter I did sneak back in again, when you weren't looking!

Robert Fothergill
May 2007

DETAINING MR. TROTSKY

Passport photograph of Leon Trotsky
public domain – picture circa 1917

Detaining Mr. Trotsky was first produced by the Toronto Free Theatre, at the Berkeley Street venue of what is now CanStage, in October 1987, with the following company:

LEON TROTSKY	Angelo Rizacos
COLONEL ARTHUR MORRIS	Graeme Campbell
LIEUTENANT PHILIP WHITMORE	Ross Manson
NATALYA SEDOVA-TROTSKY	Karen Kenedy
DAVID MENDEL	David Bolt
SOPHIE MENDEL	Paula Grove
SERGEANT OGILVIE	Stephen Walsh
KAPITÄN VON PLAMBECK	Derek KeurVorst
PRIVATE BAXTER	James D. Mitchell
Direction	Richard Greenblatt
Set and Costume Design	John Ferguson
Lighting Design	Steven Hawkins
Sound Design	Sound Beginnings Ltd.
Stage Management	Louise Currie

Colonel Morris and his staff.
courtesy of Cumberland County Museum and Archives

CHARACTERS

LEON TROTSKY, age 37.
COLONEL ARTHUR HENRY MORRIS, CMG, DSO, age 56. Retired British professional soldier, living in New Brunswick, appointed by the Canadian government to command Amherst Internment Camp.
LIEUTENANT PHILIP WHITMORE, age 21, Canadian volunteer officer.
SERGEANT OGILVIE, age 35, Scottish migrant, wounded in France, left arm amputated.
KAPITÄN HEINZ VON PLAMBECK, age 45, Prussian professional naval officer.
DAVID MENDEL, age 45, Russian-Jewish translator for Halifax Naval Police.
SOPHIE MENDEL, age 18, his daughter.
NATALYA IVANOVNA SEDOVA-TROTSKY, age 35.
PRIVATE BAXTER, clerk-secretary to Colonel Morris.
YOUNG LADY TO RECITE POEM (doubles with Natalya).
VOICES OF TELEGRAPH OPERATORS.

SETTINGS

Amherst Camp, Naval Control Office in Halifax, David Mendel's home.

TIME

April, 1917.

Natalya Ivanovna Sedova as a young woman in Paris.
public domain – picture circa 1910

DETAINING MR. TROTSKY

Part One: Prelude

At the head of a ship's gangway, TROTSKY and NATALYA Sedova are waving farewell to a crowd of well-wishers. The flicker of a strobe light converts the scene into a silent newsreel. A couple of other passengers hover about; a woman puts a bouquet of flowers into NATALYA's hands; TROTSKY waves and gives a revolutionary salute. Faintly there can be heard the sound of "The Internationale" in Russian. TROTSKY gives a final salute and turns as if to enter the ship. Light of newsreel fades. Fade in the sound of Morse telegraph, and over it the sound of a woman's VOICE.

VOICE Naval Control Office, Halifax, Nova Scotia, to Admiralty, London, April 2nd, 1917. Stop. Suspected German agent Leon Bronstein embarked New York to Petrograd on board steamship *Christianafiord*, registered Bergen. Stop. Removed from ship, Halifax, as per your instruction, also wife, two children. Stop. Wait your further instruction. Stop.

Morse telegraph continues a few seconds longer, then fades.

Scene One

An early morning bugle-call brings up the dawn light over Amherst camp. In the small camp office, lit by a single bulb, sits Private BAXTER at his desk. BAXTER is bespectacled and ferrety, and displays towards Colonel MORRIS a barely perceptible vein of mockery. Colonel MORRIS limps in briskly with a walking cane, hangs up his cap, and warms his hands at a pot-bellied stove with a chimney pipe going through the roof.

MORRIS Good morning, Baxter. Chilly morning.

BAXTER A bit chilly, sir. *(He has risen at MORRIS's entrance.)*

MORRIS Sit, sit, Private. At ease, what?

BAXTER Thank you, sir.

MORRIS Everything in order in the barnyard? No disturbances? Nobody flew the coop in the night?

BAXTER The night duty report is on your desk, sir. Shall I be making tea?

MORRIS *(putting on spectacles)* Thank you, Baxter, very good of you. *(BAXTER goes to prepare tea.)* Blasted foggy morning. Spring very late this year.

BAXTER   Oh, April's still pretty cool in Nova Scotia, sir. Why, just a couple of years ago...

MORRIS   I suppose it is. Keep thinking of England, you know. We'd have daffs and tulips and what-not all over the place by now. Nodding and dancing in the breeze, what?

BAXTER   Would that be poetry, sir?

MORRIS   Tennyson, Baxter, Tennyson. *(stamps his feet)* So bloody damp here. Murder on the old gammy leg.

BAXTER   Is it giving you trouble, Colonel?

MORRIS   What? Aches like the dickens! Old spear wound, you know.

BAXTER   Yes sir.

MORRIS   Tell you how I got it, did I?

BAXTER   It was when you were cutting your way out of Kumasi...

MORRIS   *(in unison)* Africa. Cutting our way out of Kumasi, we were...

BAXTER   In 1899.

MORRIS   *(drily)* What a wonderful memory you have to be sure, Private Baxter! Well. Why don't you get on with that tea?

BAXTER   Right you are, sir.

MORRIS   Morning paper here yet?

BAXTER   On your desk, sir. *(As MORRIS opens the* Halifax Herald, *the phone rings.)* Amherst. Yes sir. Just one moment. *(He gives the receiver to MORRIS.)* Naval Control Office, sir. Halifax.

MORRIS   *(taking phone)* Colonel Morris. Captain Makins? Good morning.... Yes indeed, I'm just reading it.... What can I do for you?... Do you know how many prisoners I've got up here now? Eight hundred and fifty! Facilities barely adequate for half that number.... Of course it's only one more. It's always only one more.... Damn it, Makins, spies are your business. My business is prisoners of war.... I see. Well, what else can I say? It's bloody presumptuous, that's all.... I'll send one of my officers down today. What?... Don't mention it. Just don't send me any more! *(hangs up)* Damnation. *(knock at the door)* Yes? *(enter OGILVIE)* Four minutes past seven, sergeant. I was afraid you had deserted, what?

OGILVIE   *(He has closed the door smartly, snapped to attention, and saluted.)* No fear of that, sir. Spot of trouble in the bunkhouse. Another of the Boches gone a bit loony in the night – yelling and carrying on like a sinner in hell.

MORRIS   *(whistling kettle boils)* Dangerous, was he?

OGILVIE Oh not at all, sir. Just troublesome, disturbing the others. So I put him in the dungeon, to simmer down a bit.

MORRIS Dungeon, sergeant?

OGILVIE One of the old coke-ovens, sir; walls are five foot thick. He can howl bloody murder in there, and nobody'll hear a thing.

MORRIS Very good. Work parties today?

OGILVIE Yes sir. Detail of a hundred and fifty going over to the experimental farm.

MORRIS To dig 'til they gently perspire…

OGILVIE Excuse me, sir?

MORRIS Kipling, sergeant.

OGILVIE Exactly sir. And forty more working on the hospital grounds. Five men sick, only one serious. Roll call taken this morning. All present and correct.

MORRIS Splendid. Anything else?

OGILVIE Captain von Plambeck wants to see you, sir.

MORRIS What does he want this time?

OGILVIE Don't know, sir.

MORRIS Well you'd better fetch him in, I suppose.

OGILVIE goes out. BAXTER comes in with a tray of tea.

BAXTER (*bringing tea-tray to MORRIS's desk*) Excuse me, sergeant. There you are, sir. No biscuits, I'm afraid.

OGILVIE returns with Kapitän von PLAMBECK, the senior officer among the German internees. PLAMBECK conducts himself very stiffly and correctly, as one officer to another, with much bowing and heel-clicking. MORRIS is disdainfully courteous towards him. OGILVIE stands aloof.

PLAMBECK Kolonel Morris, good morning.

MORRIS Captain Plambeck?

PLAMBECK Kolonel Morris, on behalf of the officers and men, I am requesting the honour of your presence at a performance of our choir-of-the-camp on Friday, of sacred music.

MORRIS A concert is it, Captain? For Good Friday. Yes, well, what time would that be? I shall be leaving here around tea-time on Friday.

PLAMBECK Let us name a time to suit you, Kolonel. Fourteen hours?

MORRIS Two o'clock? Yes, splendid. I shall be very glad to attend. Thank you, Captain Plambeck.

PLAMBECK Thank *you*, Kolonel. We shall be honoured.

MORRIS Sacred music, do you say? Very suitable notion.

PLAMBECK I believe we shall be hearing music of Bach.

MORRIS Really? Bach, eh? Well. All things considered, don't you think you might have found something English?

PLAMBECK Would Herr Kolonel be so good as to propose something?

BAXTER What about Handel's "Messiah," sir?

MORRIS When I want a suggestion from you, Private Baxter, I'll ask for it. Thank you, Captain. That will be all.

PLAMBECK Kolonel Morris. *(Clicks heels and exits. MORRIS nods.)*

MORRIS Bach, indeed! *(looking at his pocket watch)* Damn it all, where's Lieutenant Whitmore? He should be in here by now!

OGILVIE 'Fraid I don't know, sir.

MORRIS It's no way to run an army!

OGILVIE No sir.

MORRIS You're a judge of men, sergeant. What do you think of Whitmore?

OGILVIE Sir?

MORRIS What's your opinion of him?

OGILVIE *(carefully)* He's very young, sir.

MORRIS My Harry was nineteen, sergeant. Question is, has he got what it takes?

OGILVIE A bit wet behind the ears, if I might put it that way. I've seen a lot of them like that at first.

MORRIS Yes. Well. Keep an eye on him, will you? *(showing OGILVIE the newspaper)* Now then, sergeant, what do you say to this?

OGILVIE Well that's grand news, sir. About time too! Be over by Christmas now – what do you say, sir?

MORRIS I don't know that I'd be too sure of that, sergeant. We'll see how long it takes the Americans to get into the line, shall we, before we count our chickens?

Lieutenant WHITMORE enters the office, salutes.

WHITMORE Good morning, sir. Very fresh morning. Good morning, sergeant.

OGILVIE Sir.

MORRIS Good morning, lieutenant. *(ironically)* These early mornings too much for you? Not getting enough rest?

WHITMORE Oh yes, sir. As a matter of fact, I was…

MORRIS Well, you can catch up on your sleep on the train.

WHITMORE Sir?

MORRIS I'm sending you down to Halifax. Naval Control's got hold of some kind of a German agent. Rather a hot potato, apparently, so they're tossing him up to us, to cool him off a bit. Go down with him, Sergeant, see he doesn't make a mess of things.

WHITMORE They caught him in Halifax?

MORRIS Took him off a boat, I understand. Got a tip-off from London to be on the lookout. Scuttling back to Europe before the Yankees declared war, most likely. They're in at last, by the way. The sergeant and I were just discussing the news. Did you see this? *(indicates newspaper)*

WHITMORE Yes sir. I was reading it in the orderly room. Very encouraging.

BAXTER Might I have a look, sir?

MORRIS *(tossing paper to BAXTER)* Better be getting over there yourself pretty quick, lieutenant, or it'll be all over, bar the shouting.

WHITMORE Very true, sir. Soon as we reach battalion strength, we'll be shipping over. Recruiting's not as brisk as it was.

MORRIS Well, we'll be sorry to see you go, eh, sergeant?

OGILVIE Certainly will, sir.

MORRIS Keen to be off?

WHITMORE Oh yes indeed, sir. One feels very helpless and ashamed, kicking one's heels over here, while so many men are… well, you know what I mean, I'm sure.

MORRIS Yes, it's hardly the place for a brave young fellow like you to spend the war. Eh? Only for old fogeys, and chaps who've done their bit already, like the sergeant here. Well. Your father has mixed feelings, I expect? Goodness me, when I sent my son off to fight, I was as proud as Punch. Proud of him! I wouldn't have had it any other way. *(MORRIS gets up, stumps around to WHITMORE, and starts to fuss at his uniform in a parental sort of way.)* Yes, indeed. Well, I'm sure you're going to be a credit to us – credit to the colonies eh? Show you're as good as the best of our lads at home, and twice as keen. Smartly now, attenSHUN! Ah ha! Not smart enough, lieutenant. Once again. At ease. AttenSHUN! *(MORRIS humorously makes as if to pin a medal on WHITMORE's chest.)* "For exemplary valour in the face of the enemy." My heartiest congratulations, young man. *(MORRIS salutes, then shakes*

WHITMORE's hand. *End of this little charade.*) Damn it, I envy you young men. Be glad to get over there myself, to be in for the kill. Never once had a crack at the Boche, you know. Spent my entire life chivvying Wogs of one sort or another. Not the same. Well. Got a brother over there, haven't you?

WHITMORE   That's right, sir. Captain in the Cumberlands.

MORRIS   Good show! Soon be fighting side by side, eh?

WHITMORE   I hope so, sir.

MORRIS   That's the spirit. Yes indeed, sergeant, it might just be over by Christmas. Eh? So long as the bloody damn Russians don't pull out. (*MORRIS raps the paper, which BAXTER is reading.*) Bad business, that business in Russia. What do you say, sergeant?

OGILVIE   I'm sure you're right, sir.

MORRIS   Of course I'm right! Eh, Whitmore? Chucking out their king in the middle of a war? What kind of a thing do you call that?

WHITMORE   (*tentatively*) Well, it might be for the best in the long run, sir. Democracy, you know. The papers are calling their man Kerensky "the Lloyd George of Russia."

MORRIS   Oh come now, lieutenant – you're not going to swallow all that radical humbug! Democracy? Good Lord, their discipline's all gone to hell. They're dropping their rifles and running away like flies. Democracy be damned! I'm telling you, if the Ruskies collapse, and old Fritz can throw his whole weight against us in France... by God, things could look pretty black! (*The lighting changes to isolate MORRIS and OGILVIE at a recruiting meeting, played directly to the audience. WHITMORE exits. MORRIS's final lines are almost drowned out by the singing of a vigorous chorus of "Rule Britannia."*) No more excuses, then! *Men* is what old England needs. Men with pride in themselves, and love for the mother country, ready to shoulder arms and brave the foe! England has sent her best, and now she calls on you! And now we're going to hear from a true hero, a man who has answered the call and given his best! Sergeant Ogilvie! (*MORRIS leaves the stage.*)

OGILVIE   (*stepping forward and addressing the audience*) Now there's a song to stir your hearts, lads! There's a song to get your courage up, eh? "Rule Britannia, Britannia rule the waves. Britons never will be slaves!" Well, is that true, or isn't it? Because when the song says "Britons," it doesn't just mean Englishmen – it means you and me. Now I'm a Scot, as you can tell, and I'm proud of that. And you know, in the days gone by, there's been no love lost between the Scots and the Sassenachs. But when old Kaiser Bill starts rattling his sword, I reckon we're all on the same side! And now it's time to stand up and show what you're made of! Time to show that there isn't one among you that we call "the shirker." Do you know who I mean? We don't want any of that sort here, eh? They can go back where they came from – for they're mostly foreign – and good riddance!

And if it's those Frenchies down in Quebec, eh? If it's those Froggies down there in Quebec, well, we've got one thing to say to them, loud and clear. "You refuse to serve your country? You want yourselves a republic? Well, by God, you just go ahead and try! We may have sent our best lads over to France, but we've enough left behind to lick the lot of you Froggies before breakfast!" *(OGILVIE has been isolated by the lighting. In the transition to the next scene, fog-horns from Halifax harbour can be heard offering a dismal commentary on his speech. Suddenly, WHITMORE's voice interrupts OGILVIE's tirade, summoning him into the naval control office.)*

Scene Two

Lights up on the Naval Control Office, Halifax. WHITMORE is preparing to interrogate TROTSKY, which he will do somewhat uncomfortably, with an attempt at officiousness, referring to notes and documents which have been passed to him by the Navy. David MENDEL is on hand to act as official interpreter. N.B. When TROTSKY is speaking in Russian with MENDEL his accent should change from stage Russian to normal, and his speech, which in English is marked by many minor errors – not typos – should become fluent.

WHITMORE *(to OGILVIE, still in his recruiting tirade)* Sergeant! Sergeant Ogilvie!

OGILVIE Sir!

WHITMORE The prisoner, please, sergeant. Mr. Mendel? You will supply translation as required.

MENDEL Yes sir.

To WHITMORE's surprise and consternation, OGILVIE escorts TROTSKY and NATALYA Sedova into the office area.

WHITMORE Who is this person, Sergeant?

OGILVIE Wife of the prisoner, sir. There are two boys outside as well.

WHITMORE Two boys? *(addressing NATALYA awkwardly)* You may sit please. Sit? Sit down? *(clears throat, shuffles documents)* Now. Your name is Bronstein. That's a German name is it not? Mr. Mendel, would you…?

TROTSKY *(He is angry and impatient.)* It is the name of a Russian Jew. My name is Trotsky.

WHITMORE Why do you travel under a false name, Mr. Bronstein?

TROTSKY Trotsky is my name. You understand? It is like Voltaire; a nom-de-guerre, nom-de-plume, what you call it?

WHITMORE *(casually, making a note)* I see. And this, er, Walther, is he one of your associates?

TROTSKY He is French writer. You have not hear of him in the Canada?

WHITMORE Oh, Voltaire. I see. *(embarrassed)* Now, er, what are your full Christian names?

TROTSKY I do not understand.

WHITMORE Your Christian names! Mr. Mendel, translate please.

MENDEL *(to TROTSKY, in "Russian")* He asks your "Christian names" – your given name and patronymic.

TROTSKY *(in "English")* Ah, Christian! I have no "Christian" names.

WHITMORE Your names, what are your names?

TROTSKY My given name is Lev, which you will call in English, Leon. My patronymic is Davidovich. I am Leon Trotsky.

WHITMORE And when did you leave Russia, Mr. Bronstein?

TROTSKY Since nineteen hundred seven. Before you are asking: I was living in Vienna until nineteen hundred fourteen. When war started I must fly from Vienna to Paris, with my wife and children, or Austrian police will arrest me. As enemy spy.

WHITMORE I see. And what work did you do in Vienna?

TROTSKY Journalist.

WHITMORE Really! Do you speak German?

TROTSKY Journalist for Russian newspapers.

WHITMORE But you do speak German?

TROTSKY *(impatiently)* Yes, I speak German. Also French. And, as you see, a little English, not so good. So I am French spy and English spy, yes?

WHITMORE You were expelled from France. Why was that?

TROTSKY Why? Because police of the Tsar make slanders to French police. Now I ask to *you* – who gives you your informations? Who has told you to arrest me here?

WHITMORE I'm asking the questions…

TROTSKY You do not know?

WHITMORE *(He has a list to get through.)* Er, what are your religious convictions? *(TROTSKY doesn't understand the question.)* Mr. Mendel, please.

MENDEL He asks your religion.

TROTSKY *(He is trying to pump MENDEL for information, under cover of a pretence at translation.)* You are Russian? When did you come here?

MENDEL Nine, ten years ago. I came to…

TROTSKY Did you leave for political reasons?

MENDEL I am Jewish.

TROTSKY You were in trouble with the police?

WHITMORE I must ask you not to speak more Russian than is absolutely necessary. Please simply answer the question.

TROTSKY I do not tell you of religion. What religion have *you*?

WHITMORE I see. And what is your purpose in returning to Russia? *(TROTSKY again appears not to understand the question.)* Mr. Mendel.

MENDEL I was accused of keeping liberal literature. I was a teacher.

TROTSKY In October nineteen-o-five, were you in Petrograd?

MENDEL I was in Odessa.

TROTSKY But you heard about the revolution?

WHITMORE That's enough. You surely don't need to hold a conference!

TROTSKY Please explain me your question.

WHITMORE Do you propose to assist the new government in St. Petersburg?

TROTSKY again feigns incomprehension.

MENDEL Of course I heard about it! The General Strike, the Workers' Soviet. In Odessa...

TROTSKY Yanovsky. You remember the man called Yanovsky? President of the Petrograd Soviet?

MENDEL He was sent to Siberia. A bold young man. And Jewish!

NATALYA *(indicating her husband)* He is Yanovsky.

MENDEL *(in dismay)* Oy, gevalt!

TROTSKY *(to WHITMORE)* I welcome the downthrow of the Tsar Nicholas, and of the Tsarina. The new government has give me passport to return to Russia. Do you see that? *(He indicates the paper which WHITMORE has in front of him, then turns to address MENDEL, in "Russian.")* You must send a telegraph for me to the Russian consul in New York. Yes, I demand it. Also to the nearest Russian consul in Canada. Do you know where he is?

MENDEL In Montreal.

WHITMORE What about Montreal? What are you discussing?

MENDEL He asks me from where I come in Canada.

WHITMORE There must be no private conversation! Mr. Bronstein, it seems that before you left New York the sum of ten thousand dollars was given to you by

Germans living in the United States. What was that money to be used for? And where is it now?

TROTSKY (*in English, but partly to MENDEL*) Ten thousand dollars give to me? What is he dreaming?

NATALYA What does he say?

TROTSKY He says that in New York we were given ten thousand dollars to take to Petrograd. How much did the comrades give us?

NATALYA Three hundred and ten dollars – to pay for our passage on the ship.

TROTSKY Well you see how it has multiplied! We should go to sea more often. (*to WHITMORE*) Our comrades in New York collected for us three hundred dollars, three hundred ten dollars. Some of them who gave were Germans. Some were Russians, Ukrainians, Polish, Finnish, Litauen. Some were Americans. Not many. (*to MENDEL*) You must do what I ask you. It is absolutely necessary.

WHITMORE I have very good information that you were given ten thousand dollars, and I want to know…

TROTSKY But you are wrong! Your information is a liar, or a stupid.

WHITMORE Mr. Bronstein, I'm simply trying to understand your case more clearly.

TROTSKY Why are you ask foolish questions, of which you have no right? I do not discuss these things. I will tell to you everything of my identity, otherwise nothing. (*to MENDEL, urgently*) Do you understand what you have to do?

WHITMORE Very well. You'd better get ready to leave.

TROTSKY This is all? We are going back to ship?

WHITMORE Ah, no, I'm sorry. You're going to Amherst. It's been decided.

TROTSKY What is Amherst?

WHITMORE Oh, you'll find out soon enough.

TROTSKY How many days I am there, at Amherst?

WHITMORE I don't know I'm afraid. It's not up to me.

TROTSKY How many days?

WHITMORE Well, 'til the end of the war, I should think.

TROTSKY Until end of war? Until end of war? It is a prison, this Amherst, yes?

WHITMORE Well, it's a, er, camp.

TROTSKY A prison camp. I am sending to prison, without accusation, without trial?

Angelo Rizacos and Karen Kenedy
photo by Michael Cooper

WHITMORE You will be given fair treatment, according to law.

TROTSKY And my wife, my boys? Prison also for them? They are also criminals? Prisoners of war?

WHITMORE I don't know exactly. Sergeant, has any provision been made? What is usually done…?

OGILVIE The woman could go to the Salvation Army hostel, sir. It's been done before. I don't know about the boys.

TROTSKY Listen me! Separate mother from the child is crime against the Red Cross code. You understand that? *(to NATALYA, simply)* He proposes to separate you from the boys. I will not permit it.

NATALYA Where are you going? What are these vermin trying to do?

TROTSKY They are sending me to prison somewhere...

NATALYA To prison? This is outrageous!

WHITMORE Mr. Bronstein! Please do not speak in Russian...

TROTSKY I speak to my wife! She speaks no English.

NATALYA This is the filthy Tsarist police still at their work. *(to WHITMORE, who doesn't understand)* The Tsar has been overthrown. We are free citizens. You have no right to interfere with our journey. *(WHITMORE waves his hands uncomprehendingly.)* Speak you French?

WHITMORE A little...

NATALYA *Ecoutez, nous sommes des citoyens Russes, légitimement munis de passeports Russes!*

TROTSKY Natalya Sedova, this will do no good. This one decides nothing.

NATALYA You must utterly refuse to go. Let them drag you away by force.

TROTSKY They dragged me from the ship, they will drag me to their prison. I have no choice. I cannot resist. When our revolution has just begun, am I to let myself be shot by some imbecile of an English soldier, as a gift for M'sieur Kerensky? No. We must have diplomatic intervention. Mendel, you must send a telegraph to...

WHITMORE Mr. Bronstein, I must repeat...

TROTSKY Alexandra Kollontai, at *New World* in New York.

WHITMORE You are to speak only to me. And Mr. Mendel, you are obliged to repeat to me any, er, seditious remarks expressed by the prisoner.

TROTSKY *(to MENDEL)* You understand?

WHITMORE Do you hear what I say?

MENDEL Yes sir.

NATALYA Lev Davidovich, tell this wretched puppy that if he tries to take the boys away he will have to chain me up and stuff my mouth and drag me like an animal from here. Does he want that?

TROTSKY *(to WHITMORE)* You will not separate the mother from the children. Absolutely.

OGILVIE   The boys could go to the orphanage, I suppose, sir.

TROTSKY   *(to MENDEL)* What is he saying?

MENDEL   He suggests putting them in a home for orphans.

TROTSKY   *(to WHITMORE)* Ah, this is very good! When you come to Russia, bring your children who speak no Russian, and we will find for them orphan home, because we say their father is Turkish spy. Yes? You admire to this?

MENDEL   *(as WHITMORE seems confused and uncertain)* Captain, sir...

WHITMORE   *(correcting)* Lieutenant.

MENDEL   Perhaps, the woman and the boys, perhaps they can stay in my house?

WHITMORE   Well, I don't know if...

MENDEL   I live only with my daughter, Sophie. Eighteen years old. My wife is dead. I could make a place for them. You would perhaps pay me something, only for their food.

WHITMORE   Sergeant, do you think...?

OGILVIE   It's up to you, sir. I don't know as how I'd trust him myself.

MENDEL   All the work I have is for the Navy. Interpreter. It is all my living – I have everything to lose. You can trust me.

WHITMORE   *(considers uneasily)* All right. I'll try it. But listen to me, Mr. Mendel. The responsibility is on you. You must see that they report every day to this office. Their papers will be kept here. And they must not communicate with *anyone*, anyone at all. Do you understand what you are undertaking?

MENDEL   Yes lieutenant. I give my word.

TROTSKY   *(to NATALYA)* They have agreed that you shall stay in the home of Mr. Mendel, together with the boys. He has made the request himself.

MENDEL   You will pay me something for my trouble?

WHITMORE   That will be decided later. Mr. Bronstein, please take personal necessities only from your luggage. Sergeant, would you make an inspection?

TROTSKY selects a few items of clothing from one of the bags. OGILVIE checks each one, not really knowing what to look for.

NATALYA   *(taking MENDEL's hand)* Comrade Mendel, you are a good friend. You will not be sorry for your kindness to us.

MENDEL   *(withdrawing his hand nervously)* No, no, not comrade. Please understand. I have to obey them. This is my only livelihood. You must do everything I say, and ask nothing difficult of me.

TROTSKY Send the telegraph to New York – that is all I ask of you. Tell them we are here, illegally detained by the British. You need not use your own name. Natalya Sedova will pay you.

WHITMORE *(as TROTSKY begins to select books)* Ah, personal necessities only, I'm afraid. No books or printed material. That all has to stay here.

TROTSKY Books are personal necessity to me!

WHITMORE I'm sorry. It's a rule.

TROTSKY To Siberia, you know, I could take my library!

WHITMORE I'm sorry. Well, are you ready, then?

TROTSKY *(taking NATALYA by the arms)* Patience, comrade. It cannot be long, if we can get word to New York. Keep the boys safe. Trust our friend. *(to WHITMORE)* We are ready.

> *MENDEL ushers NATALYA Sedova out of the office. OGILVIE follows. WHITMORE takes TROTSKY tentatively by the arm, and the lights narrow to a spot on WHITMORE and TROTSKY, marching in place facing the audience. The sound of Morse telegraph comes up, and an English VOICE recites over.*

VOICE Foreign Office, London, to Sir George Buchanan, Minister Plenipotentiary of the Government of Great Britain in Petrograd. Stop. Suspected agent Lev Davidovich Bronstein, alias Leon Trotsky, travelling from New York to Russia, arrested and detained in Canada. Stop. Advise Foreign Minister Miliukoff, British Government requests instruction on disposition of prisoner. Stop.

> *There is the sound of trains shunting.*

Scene Three

> *Lights change to indicate the main bunkhouse area at Amherst where the prisoners are housed. It is the inside of an old factory building, roughly suggested by beams, corners of bunks, high dirty windows, etc. A placard in large Gothic script reads "Von Hindenburg Platz," and another "Unter den Linden." Against the back wall there is a large hand-drawn map of Europe on a stretched sheet, with the battle-lines, as of April 1917, indicated by lines of string around pins. To one side there is a fenced enclosure, which serves Kapitän von PLAMBECK as semi-private quarters. Trains can be heard shunting immediately outside the building. As the scene begins, PLAMBECK crosses the stage, pausing in the middle to acknowledge a salute from the direction of the audience by clicking his heels and saluting with a curt bow. He then proceeds to enter his enclosure through a little gate. WHITMORE and TROTSKY remain frozen to one side. OGILVIE marches in aggressively, turns smartly to the*

front, and addresses first PLAMBECK, then the audience as if addressing the inmates of the internment camp.

OGILVIE   Captain Plambeck – work roster for tomorrow. Work parties fall in at oh-seven-hundred hours: groups three and four to the farm; group six to the gravel pit; group eight, latrine duty; group ten, kitchen and clean-up. *(to the audience)* All right, do you want to hear some good news? Are you listening to me? The Yankees have come into the war – and they're not on your side, I can tell you that!

At this point, TROTSKY and WHITMORE appear in the lighted area of the bunkhouse. WHITMORE exchanges salutes with PLAMBECK.

WHITMORE   Sergeant Ogilvie?

OGILVIE   Oh, beg pardon sir. *(to PLAMBECK)* Captain Plambeck, I've got another guest for your hotel. He wants a room with a bath and a view of the promenade.

PLAMBECK   Sergeant Ogilvie, you see we have no more room here! How can a place be found?

OGILVIE   You've got five men in the infirmary, and one of them won't be coming back, the M.O. says.

WHITMORE   Pretty filthy in here, isn't it sergeant! The place stinks.

OGILVIE   It does get very stale in the winter, sir, with the men cooped up so much. And they're not a very sweet-smelling bunch of violets to begin with, that's the truth.

PLAMBECK   *(inspecting TROTSKY)* What is this one, Herr Leutnant? He is not German, I think?

WHITMORE   Well no, he isn't actually, but apparently he's doing some kind of spy work for Germany.

PLAMBECK   Leutnant Vitmore, I must protest! We are in here only serving officers and men, also reservists and men of the merchant Navy. For spies there is no place.

WHITMORE   It's not my decision, I'm afraid.

PLAMBECK   You will speak to Kolonel Morris? Say to him that this is most unsuitable, and dangerous to the morale of the men. He is also Jewish, I think?

WHITMORE   I'll tell him what you have said.

OGILVIE   *(to WHITMORE)* It's not a private club we're running here, sir.

WHITMORE   Sergeant?

OGILVIE   I'd tell him to take what he's given, and make no bones about it, if I were you, sir.

WHITMORE   Thank you, sergeant, that will do. Captain Plambeck, I will pass on your objection.

PLAMBECK   *(clicking his heels)* Leutnant Vitmore.

WHITMORE   *(saluting)* Captain Plambeck. Carry on, sergeant. *(WHITMORE and OGILVIE exit.)*

PLAMBECK   *(to TROTSKY, who observes him frostily)* You! *Kommen Sie hier!* I wish to speak with you. Do you understand that, as senior German officer, I am in authority here? I shall require from you the same respect and obedience that I require from all the men under my command, by virtue of an authority deriving from his Imperial Majesty.

TROTSKY   I am a free Russian citizen and a civilian. I do not recognize that authority.

PLAMBECK   Your reply is insolent and of no importance. As long as you remain in this camp, you are subject to German military discipline. A bunk will be assigned to you. *(PLAMBECK retires to his own quarters.)*

TROTSKY   *(coming to the front and contemplating the audience)* Comrades! *Meine Kameraden!* *(He pauses.)* Long live the international working class! Down with the capitalist war! Down with the Tsar Nicholas, the King George, and the criminal aggressor Kaiser Wilhelm! *(He pauses again, to judge the effect of this.)* Comrades, I have news for you. The emperors of Europe are falling from their thrones. Three weeks ago, in Petrograd, the reign of the Romanovs came to an end. The Tsar Nicholas and the Tsarina are under arrest. And the next to fall will be the Kaiser Wilhelm! *(getting into a harangue)* Comrades, twenty days ago the state power in Russia was shaken from the hands of the autocrats – the power to make the law, to direct the police, to rule between those who own and those who work, and the power to make war. You will ask, does this mean there will be peace? I ask *you*, into whose hands will that power fall? For the moment it has fallen into the plump white hands of the Liberal middle class. Do you know who I mean? Lawyers and doctors and professors, businessmen and stockbrokers and petty officials, ambitious and greedy and smug, with their well-groomed dogs and their well-groomed wives. Perhaps you have such people in Germany? Yes? And what is the war to them? The war is the way to extend the commercial interests of their class. This is called "patriotism." And even many of the working men and the peasants are infected with this disease of patriotism – as in Germany – and they dream of annexing Galicia and Constantinople for Russia. What does the annexation of Istanbul mean to the coal miner of the Donets? Does he expect to go there for a holiday? Yes, and even many of the workers' leaders, calling themselves Social Democrats, encourage this madness. They persuade themselves that, in return for their suffering and their blood and their hunger and their shattered limbs, the factory-owner will gratefully share with them the fruits of victory. The factory-owner will never share anything until he is compelled! And what are the fruits of victory, but the land and the labour of the defeated peoples – of working men and peasants as poor as themselves? Will there be peace? Only the Revolutionary Marxists, remaining true to the spirit of the Second International, insist on a peace without annexations or indemnities, concluded between popular democratic governments. *(He acknowledges applause.)*

PLAMBECK *(emerging from his quarters to address audience)* This is intolerable! I will not permit these seditious slanders. How do you dare to tolerate this outrage? Where is your patriotism? He speaks of peace with Russia? The Russians are hopeless soldiers, stupid and cowardly. Germany will smash them in the field. Your Kaiser will never make peace with Russia!

TROTSKY The Kaiser? Did I say the Kaiser?

PLAMBECK *(ignoring him)* The Germans are the most advanced people on earth. Germany has the highest culture, the best industry, the strongest armies, the finest social discipline. It is the law of history that the most advanced nation should command the others.

TROTSKY You are right, my friend! In 1914, Germany was more advanced than any country in Europe. We revolutionaries in Russia looked to Germany in envy and admiration. *There*, we said, is the vanguard of the Socialist movement. *There* is the largest mass organization, the most developed theory, the highest and broadest proletarian consciousness. Germany is our leader, we said. German Social Democracy will storm the Bastille, and we in Russia will be glad to emulate their example. So what *happened? (TROTSKY accuses the audience.)* You. You were there. You were a working man in Germany, yes? You – tell me what happened.

PLAMBECK I will tell you what happened. The Kaiser gave his call for men to serve in the armed forces, and as loyal sons of the Fatherland, these men obeyed that call!

TROTSKY Comrades, everybody obeyed that call. In every country in Europe, the leaders of the workers' movements had the power in their hands to cripple the war, to starve it into helplessness. War is a monster that must be fed with men and machines and materiel. The masters of war cannot feed their monster themselves. Yes, Germany was the leader of Europe until 1914, when the Socialists of Germany led the German workers into the mouth of the monster.

PLAMBECK *(He is trying to interrupt and silence TROTSKY. Their competing addresses to the audience begin to overlap.)* Enough now! I have heard enough!

TROTSKY That betrayal was the death of the Second International. But now Russia, poor, backward, suffering Russia, has come forward as the leader of Europe.

PLAMBECK What are you waiting for?

TROTSKY And yet, believe me, nothing would make us happier than to hand back the baton of revolutionary leadership to our German comrades.

PLAMBECK At a time when the men of Germany are shedding their blood for the glory of the Fatherland, this is a despicable treason!

TROTSKY He says the Kaiser will never make peace with Russia. No indeed, the Kaiser will never make peace.

PLAMBECK I absolutely forbid another word. Is that understood? I have given an order!

TROTSKY The revolutionary German people will make peace with Russia!

>*With a shrieking whistle and a deafening roar, an express train thunders through the theatre, as the lights go to black. Out of the darkness a WOMAN appears, dressed in the costume of Britannia, and declaims as many of the following verses as seem appropriate.*

"Last Call To Colours"
(*Winnipeg Post*, reprinted in *Halifax Herald*, 16 March 1917)

WOMAN *(as Britannia)* Wouldn't it be great if the country needn't wait
For conscription or compulsion, but, going its own gait,
Every Man should fall in line, and set out to conquer fate,
Daring death or winning glory, come it soon or come it late...

Say, wouldn't it be great?

Wouldn't it be great, since it's Canada's desire
To show the loyal legions she's the livest of live wire,
If we crumpled up the Kaiser's men and dumped them in the mire,
With their gassing and their Zepping and their samples of hell fire...

Say, wouldn't it be great?

Wouldn't it be great, as a sort of glad surprise,
Could we help the other peoples, both the foolish and the wise,
To hit the trail for freedom, life's first, last, and biggest prize,
As in the happy countries where the flag of England flies...

Say, wouldn't it be great?

Wouldn't it be great – you may call us mad or odd –
To try and right a world's wrong, we, where their gallant feet have trod,
Who played the game before us 'til they passed beneath the sod,
If *we* set the old ball spinning faster toward the goals of God...

Say, wouldn't it be great?

Wouldn't it be great – get a move or you'll be late!
Sign on and join the colours, fill the ranks at record rate,

To share the grandest fighting ever scored on history's slate!
If victory should follow at no very distant date...

Say, wouldn't it be great?

Scene Four

Morning. MORRIS, WHITMORE and OGILVIE are in the camp office. BAXTER will bring in tea, as usual. OGILVIE lays a file on MORRIS's desk.

MORRIS Thank you, Baxter. Very good, sergeant.

OGILVIE *(preparing to exit)* Sir.

MORRIS No working parties going out today?

OGILVIE No sir. Good Friday, sir.

MORRIS Of course. So no work. Just as I thought. They're all Christians, are they?

OGILVIE Pretty well all, sir. Protestants and R.C.'s both.

MORRIS Christians, my eye! They're about as Christian as Nebuchadnezzar, except when it suits their purposes, eh?

OGILVIE Yes sir. They've been practicing some singing all week, sir, that sounds quite religious, if you know what I mean.

MORRIS Yes indeed. Put 'em in a cage, and they'll sing like larks, I've no doubt. All right, sergeant, that's all, thank you.

OGILVIE Sir. *(salutes and exits)*

MORRIS Now, lieutenant?

WHITMORE It's about the Russian prisoner, sir. He's been demanding to see you for three days.

MORRIS Demanding, has he? Hah! We don't do anything in response to demands.

WHITMORE No sir. He's rather a high-handed sort of chap.

MORRIS Really? I can be pretty high-handed myself when I want to be, eh?

WHITMORE Yes sir.

MORRIS High-handed! Well. Ottawa seems to be in a bit of a flap about him. Making quite a fuss. No less than three telegraphs, telling me to keep him incommunicado, and not to talk to the newspapers – as if I'd talk to the damn papers! The only people who talk to the newspapers are politicians and divorcees. What's he like anyway? Is he a Russian, as he claims?

WHITMORE As far as I can tell, sir. Though he does speak German with the prisoners. He's been getting them quite excited. Captain Plambeck's very upset.

MORRIS German, eh? Doesn't look very good, does it? Does he speak English? Can you have a conversation with him?

WHITMORE Oh yes, sir. I talked with him a bit coming up here, on the train.

MORRIS Did you indeed? What about? You weren't indiscreet, I trust?

WHITMORE I hope not, sir. He was asking about Canada – not the sort of thing a spy would want to know. About the Liberals and the Tories, and Quebec, and that sort of thing.

MORRIS Well, see what you can get out of him. Get in his confidence, eh? *(There is a knock at the door, and OGILVIE looks in.)* Yes sergeant?

OGILVIE Sir. Captain Plambeck requests permission to speak with you again, sir.

MORRIS I might have guessed. Yes, Captain Plambeck? *(PLAMBECK enters.)* Oh, sergeant, I want to see the new fella, the Russian. March him over right away, would you?

OGILVIE Sir. *(exits)*

MORRIS Baxter, fetch me the new prisoner's card, will you? *(BAXTER brings a folder to MORRIS's desk.)*

PLAMBECK Kolonel Morris, good morning. May I remind you of your promise to us to attend our concert this afternoon?

MORRIS It's on the agenda, Captain. It's not forgotten.

PLAMBECK I am sure, Kolonel. But this is not all. Another thing, most important. The new prisoner...

MORRIS Yes, what about him? Lieutenant Whitmore said you weren't happy.

PLAMBECK I most strongly ask that he is moved to solitary quarters.

MORRIS Oh? Why is that, Captain?

PLAMBECK He is a most harmful disturbance to the men. He has been speaking against the monarchy and the Fatherland. He must be removed.

MORRIS Can you not exert your own authority, Captain Plambeck?

PLAMBECK Kolonel, he is arousing the men to insubordination with most provocative speeches. He is turning the whole camp into a political meeting. My own position, and that of my fellow officers, has been threatened. If I might advise you, he should be removed at once.

MORRIS I see. Well, I shall make my own decision about that, Captain, thank you.

PLAMBECK Kolonel Morris, I think you do not understand. He is provoking the men. I have been subject to insult.

MORRIS I've said I'll think about it, Captain!

PLAMBECK Kolonel Morris. I leave it to you. *(clicks heels and exits)*

MORRIS   Bloody Prussian jack-in-the-box! Waltzing in and out of here demanding this, that and the other thing. Do him good to be taken down a couple of pegs, what? *(knock at the door)* Yes, sergeant?

OGILVIE   Prisoner to see you, sir.

MORRIS   Bring him in.

OGILVIE   Sir. Advance, prisoner! Smartly, one-two, one-two, one-two, Halt! AttenSHUN!

> *TROTSKY walks in at his own pace, disregarding OGILVIE's quick-march.*

TROTSKY   Captain Morris…

MORRIS   *(studying the folder)* You'll speak when you're spoken to!

TROTSKY   From when is there war between the Canada and Russia?

MORRIS   *(peering through his glasses at the document)* "Trotsky, Leon, Bronstein… date of birth, October 26th, 1879." *(glances up)* Born at – where? I can't read this.

TROTSKY   You will explain me, please, why am I here.

WHITMORE   Cherson, sir.

MORRIS   Where's that?

WHITMORE   Somewhere near the Crimea, I believe, sir.

MORRIS   Is that so? Quite a well-travelled chap, what? And what brings you to this part of the world, Mr. Bronstein?

TROTSKY   You will call me Trotsky.

MORRIS   *(complacently)* I'll call you anything I damn well like, Bronstein. I'll call you Nebuchadnezzar, if I feel like it. The King of the Jews.

TROTSKY   Why am I here, Captain Morris?

MORRIS   Colonel Morris. Exactly – why *are* you here? Why aren't you back in Russia, fighting for your country? Eh? Like an honest man and a patriot?

TROTSKY   Are you commander here, Captain Morris?

MORRIS   *Colonel* Morris. Get that into your head and get it right, Bronstein.

TROTSKY   Are you commander here?

MORRIS   Yes, I am the commanding officer here.

TROTSKY   You will tell me why I am kept prisoner here. I am arrested as Prisoner of War. I ask you, what war?

MORRIS   What war? What war? Do you know what I saw the other week in Halifax? The Navy were bringing in survivors from a passenger steamer that

Angelo Rizacos, James D. Mitchell, Ross Manson and Graeme Campbell
photo by Michael Cooper

had been sunk by a German submarine. Not a British ship or a French ship, but a Danish ship – neutral, like the one you were on. And not content with sinking the ship and drowning scores of innocent people, the damned Germans surfaced and fired on the lifeboats – fired on women and children clinging to lifeboats. That's Kaiserism for you! That's what damned war we're fighting!

TROTSKY And as you say, I might be with my wife and children on this ship. So this is why you stop me to go to Russia?

MORRIS As far as I'm concerned, Bronstein, people like you are a danger and a threat to Russia. What? German sympathizers with German names, suddenly hurrying back like rats to a sinking ship!

TROTSKY I am a danger to Russia? We let government of Russia decide who is danger, yes? Here I have telegraph message you must send to Minister Miliukoff in Petrograd.

MORRIS Must send?

TROTSKY Also this to Minister Lloyd George in London. *(puts messages on table)*

MORRIS Must? There's no "must" about it, believe me!

TROTSKY Do you know better than government of Russia who is danger to Russia?

MORRIS Quite possibly, Bronstein, quite possibly. Frankly, I consider your sort to be a danger to the Allied cause in general. You sneak about the world like thieves; you've no real loyalties, no country… *(TROTSKY turns abruptly on his heel and heads for the door.)* Sergeant!

OGILVIE Now you hold it right there! *(OGILVIE seizes TROTSKY by the arm and wheels him around, back to MORRIS's desk.)*

MORRIS *(seizing his cane and beating on the desk)* God damn your insolence, man! By God, you'd better be thankful we're in a civilized country here, Bronstein. I'm telling you, if I had you on the Gold Coast, I'd have you strung up from the next tree, and no questions asked!

TROTSKY *(to WHITMORE)* Explain me, please, what he says.

WHITMORE He says in Africa he would, ah, hang you.

TROTSKY In Africa. I see. But in Canada he only keeps me in prison. So. I have the luck.

MORRIS Yes, you have the luck all right. By George you do. And if you want a bit of advice from me, I'd tell you to keep your nose very clean indeed, or you could find life extremely uncomfortable. I've dealt with tougher nuts than you, and I'm not going to have any aggravation from one beastly Russian. We'll find out in due course what's to be done with you, and until then, you watch your step. *(simmers down, pours more tea)* In the meantime, Easter is upon us. I don't imagine Easter means very much to you, Mr. Bronstein?

TROTSKY Eastern?

MORRIS Easter. The Feast of the Resurrection. After the Jews had executed the son of God. You know what I'm talking about, do you?

TROTSKY In Russia it is called "*Voskrisenya.*" It is popular time for pogrom. To greet the spring of the year, the Cossacks find some Jews, to beat them to death. It is well-loved feast.

MORRIS Well, you're in a civilized country now, thank your stars. All right, sergeant, thank you, take him away.

OGILVIE Keep him separate, sir?

MORRIS What? No, chuck him back in the pig-sty with the rest of them. Let Plambeck make the best of him.

OGILVIE *(marching TROTSKY out)* Let's be having you!

TROTSKY *(to WHITMORE)* You tell me, is this the fair treatment according to the law?

OGILVIE Smartly now! *(OGILVIE hustles TROTSKY out.)*

MORRIS *(complacently draining his cup of tea)* Aaah, very nice! Now then, lieutenant, get your coat on, and we'll put in an appearance at this bloody hymn-singing. I shall be leaving for Sackville right afterwards with Mrs. Morris. Colonel Black has very kindly invited us over for the Easter holiday. You're on duty this weekend?

WHITMORE Yes sir.

MORRIS Well, keep a close eye on our Russian friend, will you?

WHITMORE I'll do my best. What about the telegraphs, sir?

MORRIS What about them?

WHITMORE Aren't you going to send them?

MORRIS Certainly not! Why the blazes should I?

WHITMORE Well, sir, I…

MORRIS Eh? Why the blazes should I?

WHITMORE Well, just to… find out… you know…

MORRIS Go on, lieutenant.

WHITMORE He does have a right, sir. I mean, he's not technically a prisoner of war.

MORRIS Technically? Don't come to me with your "technically." He's a prisoner – sent here by the British authorities. And he's staying here until the British authorities say he can go. In the meantime I'll be damned if I'm running messages for him. Such gall! Coming in here, like Lord Muck of the Manor… *(MORRIS unfolds TROTSKY's messages, puts on glasses.)* "Lloyd George, Prime Minister, London. Mr. George…" Hah! Mr. George, indeed! "I protest with greatest strength illegal arrest of Free Russian citizens by British police, and criminal detention in the Canada. Demand immediate release and apology of British government…" Apology! Do you imagine, lieutenant, that I'm going to transmit that?

WHITMORE It is a bit…

MORRIS "High-handed" I think was your word. *(He tears the paper into pieces.)*

WHITMORE Yes sir. All the same…

MORRIS All the same nothing! I want nothing more said on the subject. Now then. Lead on, Macduff. Let's get it over with. *(German accent)* Der musik of Bach!

> *As he speaks, the theatre is suddenly filled with a choral passage from J.S. Bach's "St. Matthew Passion": "O Haupt voll Blut und Wunden" etc., sung in German by an unaccompanied male choir. Blackout.*

Scene Five

Out of the darkness the voice of MENDEL is heard, singing the "kiddush" before Sabbath-eve dinner. He sings with a sad doggedness, neither intense nor perfunctory. The lights come up to reveal a table set for dinner. MENDEL is standing at his place. His daughter, SOPHIE Mendel, and NATALYA Sedova are seated. The setting suggests poverty bordering on squalor. There is an air of tension, as of an argument which has been interrupted by the brief moment of ceremony.

MENDEL Shabbat shalom.

SOPHIE Shabbat shalom.

MENDEL *(after they have begun to eat)* Your boys should be here, Natalya Ivanovna. They should learn these things.

NATALYA They are sleeping.

MENDEL Their father should teach them.

NATALYA *(returning abruptly to the attack)* You made a promise to their father.

MENDEL I promised nothing. He asked me.

NATALYA He asked you to do one thing for him! I would do it myself if I could speak a word of English. Well, never mind that. I shall go anyway.

MENDEL Go where? You can't go anywhere, Natalya Ivanovna.

NATALYA To the telegraph office. You will direct me.

MENDEL You're not permitted to go anywhere, except to the police office. I gave my word.

NATALYA Your word! "I gave my word." What are you, aping the gentleman? "Upon my word of honour…." This is a poor interpreter? This is a poor Russian Jew, the servant of the British police?

MENDEL Natalya Ivanovna, I am a school-teacher.

NATALYA Oh, he is a school-teacher! What school do you teach in? Where are your pupils? Where are your books? What you are – you are a village scribe, with the soul of a slave.

MENDEL Why should you insult me, Natalya Ivanovna? I take you in, with your boys, into my house, my home. You see how little we have – I give you my own room, my own bed. Why should I do this?

SOPHIE You do it for money, Papa.

NATALYA *(with sudden remorse)* No, no, he does it out of kindness for a fellow Russian, out of respect for Lev Davidovich. Isn't that so?

MENDEL *(with a shrug)* We have to help each other.

NATALYA Forgive me, David Abramovich. Forgive my impatience and injustice to you.

MENDEL There is nothing to forgive, Natalya Ivanovna. You are anxious, you are upset. Forget it.

NATALYA But you must understand. Lev Davidovich absolutely requires that you send a telegraph for him, at once, to our comrades in New York. Do you understand how important that is?

MENDEL At once, at once – what is the hurry?

NATALYA The hurry? Do you know what is happening in the world? Sophie – does your father read the newspapers?

MENDEL I read the newspapers. I know what is happening. I know. What is it to do with me? Tell me. I left Russia ten years ago. Yes, I know what is happening in Russia. But it's a long way away. There was no future for us there.

NATALYA What future is there for you here?

MENDEL Here? The future is good here. People like us, we have a chance. We can make a good life here.

SOPHIE You call this a good life, Papa? What kind of a good life is this?

MENDEL So, now it's not so good. With the war. Maybe we will go to Chicago.

SOPHIE It's never been any good for us.

MENDEL We had some bad luck. We came at a bad time. Too many immigrants came, and not everybody could find work. But we have a chance here, Natalya Ivanovna. Sophie has a chance here. She's a clever girl. She could be a nurse, a teacher.

SOPHIE Papa, how can I go to a school for teachers? How can I?

MENDEL She could find a good husband with a good job. Sure, why not?

SOPHIE Do you think that's all I want? A husband with a job?

MENDEL All? Is it all she wants? Back in Russia you'd be lucky to get that! What would your mother have done in Odessa? Tell me. If she hadn't married me?

SOPHIE She'd have had a life of drudgery, and died young.

MENDEL And there is a chance here for a Jew. You don't know anything about that, Natalya Ivanovna. Maybe Lev Davidovich knows.

NATALYA There is no persecution here? No discrimination?

MENDEL Well, you know, people are people anywhere. Compared to Russia, it's nothing.

NATALYA David Abramovich, Russia has changed. There is no more religious persecution in Russia.

MENDEL Yes, of course, of course, and the stars are all blue...

NATALYA The Jews are free and equal citizens. The Jewish Pale has been abolished. There has been a revolution, David Abramovich! The revolution we have been working for. And that is why Lev Davidovich must get back to Petrograd. Do you see? And that is why you must send a telegraph for him to New York. He trusts you to do this for him.

MENDEL He hasn't any right to "trust" me. I'm not his servant. I'm not one of his "comrades." I don't know anything about politics.

NATALYA Never mind politics. He is a prisoner, when he has legal papers to go to Russia. He turns to you for help, as a fellow Russian.

MENDEL I'm not a Russian. I'm a Canadian citizen, a British subject.

NATALYA And this is what your precious free country does to foreign citizens? Throws them in prison?

MENDEL Look, there's a war on. In a war they can't be so nice about the rules. What do I know about it? Maybe they have a good reason to put him in prison.

NATALYA Of course they have a good reason! They know if he gets back to Russia he will fight against this rotten bourgeois regime and its rotten bourgeois war! And Canada keeps him in prison because Canada will do anything Britain tells her to do.

MENDEL And he wants me to help him escape?

NATALYA He's not asking you to help him to escape. He has comrades in Russia, powerful comrades who can demand that the government call for his release.

MENDEL So let them demand. I'm not stopping them. I wish them luck.

SOPHIE But they don't know where he is, Papa.

MENDEL *(after a pause)* What do you want me to tell them? The "comrades" in America. What do you want to write?

SOPHIE Papa!

NATALYA You'll send the telegraph? David Abramovich, I knew it! I knew we could count on you. But it has to be sent right away.

MENDEL All right, all right! Listen, don't push me. *(gesture of helpless impatience by NATALYA)* Get me a piece of paper.

NATALYA Can we send it tonight?

MENDEL The office is closed.

SOPHIE *(with paper)* Here, Papa.

NATALYA You can write it, Sophie. Address it to: Madame Kollontai, *New World*...

MENDEL What is that *New World*?

NATALYA Never mind, it doesn't matter.

MENDEL Doesn't matter? You ask me to go the telegraph office with this – what if they ask me? A poor Jew goes in there – I've never sent a telegraph in my life, I don't know how – and they say, "What is this *New World*?" What am I to say? "I don't know?"

SOPHIE I'll send it, Papa, if it's so difficult for you.

MENDEL You'll do nothing! If anybody sends it, I'll do it.

NATALYA *New World* is a newspaper. 177 Saint Mark's Place, Lower East Side, New York.

SOPHIE You'll go tomorrow morning? You promise, Papa?

MENDEL I've said what I will do!

> *As the lights fade, there is again the sound of Morse telegraph, and the VOICE of a telegraphist.*

VOICE Buchanan, Minister Plenipotentiary of the Government of Great Britain in Petrograd, to Foreign Office, London. Stop. With respect to detention of Bronstein, alias Trotsky, in Nova Scotia. Stop. Trotsky considered dangerous extremist, hostile to present government, suspected German agent. Stop. Minister Miliukoff requests His Majesty's Government to prolong detention as long as possible. Stop. Also to keep secret, repeat, to keep secret. Stop.

David Bolt and Paula Groves
photo by Michael Cooper

Scene Six

In the bunkhouse, TROTSKY is addressing a mass meeting of the prisoners.

TROTSKY Comrades, I thank you for your confidence! As chairman of this assembly, allow me to congratulate you on establishing the authority of the revolutionary masses in this committee of workers and prisoners. Understand that I accept the position of chairman for a strictly limited time! Pressing obligations elsewhere forbid my making a long stay in your excellent company. Comrades, we shall now proceed to construct the socialist order! I propose, as resolution number one, that this revolutionary body be named the Karl Liebknecht Commune, in recognition of the socialist struggle waged by Comrade Liebknecht, now in prison in Germany.

PLAMBECK *(interrupting suddenly from his enclosure)* Karl Liebknecht is a renegade and a traitor to the Fatherland!

TROTSKY The chair does not recognize Comrade Plambeck at this time. All those in favour? Opposed? The resolution is carried unanimously. *(At this moment a red banner with the words "Karl Liebknecht Commune" appears magically across the stage.)* Resolution Number Two: that this revolutionary body, declaring its opposition to the Imperialist war, demand immediate release and compensation from the government of Canada, as neutrals and non-combatants. All those in favour?

PLAMBECK This is treason to Germany. You will pay no more attention to these outrages. I order the non-commissioned officers to silence him immediately.

TROTSKY Comrade Plambeck, you must address all remarks to the chair. Your intervention is out of order. All those opposed? The resolution is carried. Resolution Number Three: in the revolutionary Karl Liebknecht Commune of workers and prisoners, all distinctions of rank and privilege are to be abolished. In favour?

PLAMBECK The rank and privilege of an officer derive solely from his majesty the Kaiser. You have no authority to make such a resolution.

TROTSKY Opposed? *(PLAMBECK vigorously raises his hand.)* Resolution carried. Resolution Number Four: in accordance with the principle established by Resolution Number Three, that Comrade Plambeck be immediately stripped of rank and authority, and of all the privileges and services pertaining thereto. In favour? Opposed? Carried. *(At the word "Carried," the enclosure surrounding PLAMBECK collapses, revealing that PLAMBECK has removed his uniform trousers. TROTSKY heightens PLAMBECK's discomfiture by exclaiming:)* Cover yourself, comrade! An officer never exposes his flanks! Resolution Number Five...

WHITMORE *(entering and seeing PLAMBECK's exposure)* Captain Plambeck! What on earth are you doing?

OGILVIE (*enters from a different direction*) What in the name of God is going on in here? With your permission, sir, I want a dozen men in here, with bayonets fixed.

PLAMBECK (*clicking his heels and saluting with whatever dignity he can muster*) Leutnant Vitmore, do you see what is happening here? They are making mutiny!

OGILVIE It's that Russian bugger's at the back of it! Excuse me, sir. But we'll see how he takes to the oven, eh sir?

TROTSKY (*commandingly, to WHITMORE*) Vitmore. We have internal political question. We make here demokratisch transformation of the society. The majority has choose end of privilege for officer class – German officer class.

PLAMBECK Leutnant Vitmore, this is untrue. They have made a mutiny. He talks of "demokratisch"!

TROTSKY (*to WHITMORE*) You understand this, I think? We are not any more soldiers and sailors here. We are a commune of prisoners. We make our internal order by the majority. This is the democracy, as you have in the Canada.

OGILVIE Bloody insubordination is what Colonel Morris would call it.

WHITMORE Sergeant, when I want your opinion I will ask for it.

OGILVIE Sir, with your permission, I could deal with this lot…

WHITMORE …with one hand tied behind your back. I'm sure you could.

OGILVIE Sir. (*The unintended jibe at his amputation echoes.*) Will that be all, sir?

WHITMORE Ah, yes it will. Thank you, sergeant. Dismiss.

   OGILVIE salutes and exits.

PLAMBECK This assembly is dismissed! Do you hear what I say? You will return to your quarters. These meetings are finished, forbidden. I have given an order!

TROTSKY (*to the audience*) Comrades, I declare the first plenary session of the Karl Liebknecht Commune of workers and prisoners adjourned. (*The lights change. TROTSKY sits on a bench and begins to peel potatoes.*)

WHITMORE Captain Plambeck, perhaps you should, ah, retrieve your uniform. (*PLAMBECK retires. WHITMORE approaches TROTSKY diffidently.*) Well… ah… Mr. Bronstein. (*TROTSKY looks at him.*) Mr.… ah… Trotsky.

TROTSKY Yes? You have come to spy on me?

WHITMORE No, no, indeed. I just thought…. What are you doing?

TROTSKY "He who does not work shall not eat." (*TROTSKY continues to peel potatoes.*) You wish to scale potatoes?

WHITMORE Well…

Ross Manson and Angelo Rizacos
photo by Michael Cooper

TROTSKY Sit down please. You know how to make this? Or have you servant? Your father is a rich landlord, is he not?

WHITMORE Oh dear me, no! My father is a poor clergyman.

TROTSKY What is clergyman?

WHITMORE A clergyman? Oh well, a minister, you know?

TROTSKY Your father is a minister? What minister is he? Foreign minister? Minister for Justice?

WHITMORE No, no, an Anglican minister.

TROTSKY Anglican minister?

WHITMORE As you might say, a priest.

TROTSKY *(disappointed)* A priest. The son of a priest. With no servant. And you also, do you become a priest?

WHITMORE I... I have thought about it.

TROTSKY So. The soldier priest.

WHITMORE *(after a pause)* I wish to say, Mr. Trotsky, that I sympathize with your predicament.

TROTSKY   You sympathize what?

WHITMORE   I'm sorry you're kept in prison here.

TROTSKY   I have been in prison many times.

WHITMORE   But I believe you are being held unjustly.

TROTSKY   Ah! Then you would like to let me out? That is very good.

WHITMORE   You know I couldn't do that. And anyway…

TROTSKY   I could not get on a boat. So we must wait for the official release. How long is it take for telegraph to London?

WHITMORE   *(uncomfortably)* Well, I don't know – quite a few hours, I expect. And it's Easter, of course.

TROTSKY   So tell me how long?

WHITMORE   A couple of days, perhaps. *(TROTSKY doesn't understand "couple.")* Two. Two days?

TROTSKY   Two days. And Morris, he gets nothing from New York? *(WHITMORE is silent.)* Sit down, please. *(WHITMORE sits.)* You have brothers, sisters?

WHITMORE   I have a brother, Eddie. He's over in France.

TROTSKY   You admire to him?

WHITMORE   Yes, I do.

TROTSKY   So. And you wish also to fight?

WHITMORE   More than anything.

TROTSKY   *"Dulce et decorum est pro patria mori."*

WHITMORE   Yes, I do believe that. I do believe it.

TROTSKY   To die for your country? Your Colonel Morris, he does not want that you die for your country. He wants that you kill, for *his* country. To kill for the English factory-owners, yes? What is your country that you want to die for?

WHITMORE   I don't *want* to. I only say that one should be…

TROTSKY   What is *your* country?

WHITMORE   *(perplexed)* My country? Canada.

TROTSKY   And what is Canada? *(pause)* What is Canada? You are ready to fight, ready to kill, even to die – for what?

WHITMORE   For my country! I know what that means, even if you don't. Just the same as Russia is *your* country. You're ready to fight for Russia, I suppose?

TROTSKY   No. I do not fight for Russia. Or for Germany, or for Austria, or for Turkey.

WHITMORE You're a pacifist, then?

TROTSKY I do not fight for any bourgeois imperialist state. No, I am not pacifist. You can tell Colonel Morris. I will fight, yes, when the time comes. I will fight with the revolutionary working class against the forces of the bourgeoisie – in Russia, in Germany. And you, you are fighting for your class also, that you call Canada. But the worker in the factory, in the mine, why should he fight also for you? You are to him class enemy. Why should he fight for what you call Canada?

WHITMORE Because Canada is at war! The nation is at war. Never mind upper class and lower class. We all have to pull together now. And I believe that when the war is over, we will all understand one another better, *because* we have fought side by side. *(TROTSKY snorts derisively.)* Yes, I do. I'm not just being sentimental. I think the comradeship of war will lead to a new recognition of our common humanity. I don't know what it's like in Russia, but in Canada we have thousands upon thousands of working men coming forward, eager to serve their country. They don't think about upper class and lower class. They think about Canada.

TROTSKY They are traitors of their class. They are either fool who cannot see the reality, or the government makes them go. "The common humanity" is a bourgeois lie. Yes, of course. You say "the common humanity" to make the under-class fight for you. *(pause)* What age have you?

WHITMORE I'm twenty-one.

TROTSKY Twenty-one years. When I was twenty-one years, I was in prison in Siberia.

WHITMORE What for?

TROTSKY For "revolutionary activity against government of the Tsar."

WHITMORE Were you guilty?

TROTSKY Of course! In Russia only the guilty go to prison. This is different to the Canada, eh? *(He pats WHITMORE on the knee.)* But Mr. Lloyd George will send the order, yes? In the "couple days."

WHITMORE Did you throw bombs?

TROTSKY Never. To blow the brains of police chief or the government minister is not any use for us. You see what an idea you have of the revolution! You have read Dostoevsky, and you think we are all crazy men, with the devil and the God in our brains, and the bomb in the pocket.

WHITMORE So you think it is wrong to throw bombs?

TROTSKY Wrong? What is "wrong?" It is useless.

WHITMORE But not wrong in itself?

TROTSKY Is it wrong to kill?

WHITMORE Yes, I believe so.

TROTSKY But you are soldier – as well as priest – you are not pacifist?

WHITMORE But killing *in itself* is wrong – as an act in itself.

TROTSKY There is no killing "in itself"; there is only killing of this person, in this place, now. Sometime to kill may be necessary. Other time it may be a mistake, or useless, or have bad effect.

WHITMORE *(winning a point)* So then, for you, the end justifies the means!

TROTSKY For you also! But you call as the "end" another thing. The "end" is for you the victory for English Empire, or for the Christianity, or I don't know. And for this you kill millions. For me, the end is: Abolish the exploitation of men. Abolish the exploitation of men – the using of men's work for profit, the using of nature for profit.

WHITMORE *(after a pause)* Well, I respect that. I'm in sympathy with that. Every Christian must be, I think.

TROTSKY It is no matter to have the sympathy, the subjectivity. Only important question, your objective social role. History is bringing all the time forward the end of the system of capitalist production. Soon or late, it will come. There is a struggle – the old system, the old class, against the new. In your action, in your life, you are on which side?

WHITMORE *(after a pause)* Those telegraphs you gave to Colonel Morris…

TROTSKY Yes?

WHITMORE He didn't send them. He tore them up.

TROTSKY *(standing)* So. It will take more than couple days, then.

WHITMORE I'm afraid so.

TROTSKY It is not just, I think. *(WHITMORE is silent.)* In Petrograd now, history stands on one leg. *(TROTSKY mimes this metaphor.)* Shall it step back? Or forward? For main part, it is the historical conditions which decide. But for other part, also, it is the will and action of men. And I cannot get there! Minister Miliukoff has give me a passport, but the government of England, with their puppet, the government of Canada, is sitting like an old cow in the path of human history! *(pause)* There is telegraph in Amherst?

WHITMORE Yes.

TROTSKY You cannot make telegraph to London or Petrograd.

WHITMORE No!

TROTSKY Everyone will know. *(a beat)* But you can make telegraph to New York. *(WHITMORE protests.)* Ah yes, you can! Here is what to say. I will write for you. *(He takes paper and pencil from his pocket.)* No name. You will only say L.D. "L.D. detended in Amherst…"

WHITMORE "Detained."

TROTSKY "…detained in Amherst, Nova Scotia. Tell our friends." And here is the address – I will write. Do you see? Do you see? Time. The time is so short. The door to the future is open, for one hour. If we cannot pass through the door before one hour, it will be closed perhaps for many years. Here, take it. *(giving the message)*

WHITMORE You're asking me to disobey the Colonel's explicit order.

TROTSKY Is the Colonel right to make this order?

WHITMORE I could be in terribly serious trouble. What if I am suspected?

TROTSKY You deny it. You tell the lie. *(seeing WHITMORE's discomfort)* What are the uses of truth? You do not owe truth to the injustice. You owe truth only to the masses.

WHITMORE And why should I help you? Why should I help you? I don't accept your philosophy. I don't even…

TROTSKY You believe in the justice.

WHITMORE You want to surrender to the Kaiser.

TROTSKY We want a peace with the German people.

WHITMORE But don't you want to defeat Kaiserism?

TROTSKY The Kaiser is not in the front lines. In the front lines are German workers and peasants, shooting at Russian workers and peasants.

WHITMORE But if you simply give up, after all this time, after so many lives lost, then all those lives were lost… for nothing!

TROTSKY *(sharply)* They were lost for nothing anyway! *(pause)* We do not defeat Kaiserism. The German people will defeat Kaiserism. When we make a cease-fire, and tell to the German soldiers that we have put away the Tsar, that we have no more enemy to them, they will join with us. We will give the signal for a European revolution.

WHITMORE But what if they don't? What if the Germans don't make an end of the Kaiser? What if they take advantage of Russia?

TROTSKY *(It is his worst nightmare.)* They will not! The revolution must be international. Without a revolution in Germany, the Russian revolution cannot survive. It is not to think. In one country to have the socialism, a poor backward country, it is not possible. *(WHITMORE seems unconvinced.)* It is not possible! *(pause)* You will make the telegraph? *(He holds out the paper to WHITMORE.)*

Lights to black.

Part Two: Prelude

Sounds of crashing artillery and the rattle of machine-gun fire. Lurid flashing of lights, to suggest battle. Three men, in Canadian battle dress, rush some kind of large block or box to the middle of the stage and urgently assemble a machine-gun on top of it: setting up the tripod, mounting the barrel, bringing up ammunition, loading the belt, etc. – very realistically, in the lurid half light, as though under fire. Gradually the three men compose a tableau – one man in the centre behind the gun; one on his right preparing to toss a grenade; the third on the left fixing a bayonet to a rifle, as though about to charge. Suddenly, after a particularly loud explosion and a brilliant flash, the third man claps one hand to his face, as though wounded in the eyes. The three figures freeze; the sounds of battle cease, and the lights change to a spotlight on what has become a bronze war-memorial sculpture group. A veil slips from the front of the plinth, to reveal the words: VIMY RIDGE, APRIL 9, 1917. A woman comes into the light and places a wreath against the plinth. The "Last Post" is sounded on a bugle. Two of the men climb down from the plinth, which is thereupon transformed into a cart. The third man, his hands to his eyes, crouches in the cart and is dragged off.

Scene Seven

MORRIS's office: MORRIS, WHITMORE, PLAMBECK, OGILVIE and BAXTER.

MORRIS And do I understand that you permitted all this, lieutenant? That you stood by and allowed a mutiny to be carried on before your eyes?

WHITMORE Sir, I did not judge it to be a mutiny, sir.

MORRIS And what did you "judge" it to be, lieutenant? I'm telling you, I'm not very impressed with this judgment of yours. When you see men refusing to take orders? When you see men wilfully damaging their quarters? When you see men physically attacking and humiliating their superior officer...?

WHITMORE They didn't attack Captain Plambeck, sir.

MORRIS I understand they attacked him and stripped him of his uniform. Isn't that so, Captain Plambeck? Isn't that so, sergeant?

WHITMORE They didn't take Captain Plambeck's trousers off, sir. He took them off himself. He wasn't wearing any trousers at the time.

MORRIS Do you deny that the men rebelled against the authority of their officer and menaced him? Captain Plambeck, they menaced you?

PLAMBECK I was subjected to threats...

MORRIS Exactly. You were menaced.

WHITMORE But I thought…

MORRIS What did you think?

WHITMORE Well, they're all Germans, sir. I didn't think it was any particular concern of mine.

MORRIS Lieutenant, an officer has been compelled by his own men to perform… latrine duty! An officer. Does that strike you as normal?

WHITMORE No sir.

MORRIS Does it strike you as being no concern of yours?

WHITMORE Sir, I…

MORRIS The authority of an officer over his men supersedes nationality, lieutenant. It is a principle. It is part of the very fabric of civilization. Do you see that?

WHITMORE Yes sir, but…

MORRIS Do you see that?

WHITMORE But you yourself said…

MORRIS What did I say, lieutenant?

WHITMORE Well, sir… *(He doesn't like to repeat it.)*

MORRIS *(ignoring BAXTER's warning cough)* What did I say that could possibly condone such an abuse?

WHITMORE *(blurting it out)* "Bloody Prussian jack-in-the-box, do him good to be taken down a couple of pegs…." Sir!

PLAMBECK *(after an awkward pause)* Kolonel Morris…

MORRIS Captain Plambeck?

PLAMBECK Kolonel Morris, to say my opinion, it is the Russian who makes this trouble.

MORRIS Ah! Now that doesn't surprise me at all. Eh? I suspected from the start he was the nigger in the haystack. What do you say, sergeant?

PLAMBECK Kolonel Morris will recall that I have before requested that he is removed.

OGILVIE Sir, it was my thought to put him in the dungeon, sir.

MORRIS Yes?

OGILVIE But I was overruled by Lieutenant Whitmore, sir.

PLAMBECK He is a Socialistic agitator. He is my enemy also as yours. Enemy of decency and order and religion. I need not say that he is Jewish. He has preached to the men disloyalty and pacifism.

MORRIS Pacifism?

PLAMBECK Kolonel Morris, may I request that you forbid further agitation on this subject. It makes the unrest in the prisoners.

MORRIS Absolutely Captain. You have my word.

PLAMBECK Thank you, Kolonel. *(He salutes, clicks heels, and exits.)*

MORRIS Do you hear that, Whitmore? I'm not having any more talk of pacifism in this camp. Understood?

WHITMORE Yes sir, but surely German pacifism helps us win the war?

MORRIS Only one thing helps us win this war, lieutenant, and that is getting more men into the line, and keeping them on their feet longer than the Boches can! *(pulls out envelope)* Come here. Do you know what I've got here? Your marching papers, lieutenant. Your battalion's sailing for France in a week.

OGILVIE *(to a rather stunned WHITMORE)* Congratulations, sir.

MORRIS Yes indeed! Time to go where it really counts – under fire. Join your brother. Show him what you're made of.

WHITMORE Yes sir! Thank you, sir.

> *Telephone rings. BAXTER takes the call.*

MORRIS As for this business, we'll say no more about it.

BAXTER Amherst.

WHITMORE Thank you, sir.

BAXTER One moment, please.

MORRIS Error in judgment.

BAXTER Sir, it's the *Herald*.

MORRIS It's the what?

BAXTER Editor of the *Herald*, sir. Halifax.

MORRIS What the devil does he want?

BAXTER *(to phone)* May I ask what you wish to speak to the Colonel about?

MORRIS Tell him I never talk to the press.

BAXTER Yes sir. *(to phone)* Colonel Morris… oh, you heard.

MORRIS The only people who talk to the press…

BAXTER He says it's an urgent matter, sir…

MORRIS …are politicians and divorcees.

BAXTER He says it's about Trotsky, sir. *(silence)* The Russian, sir.

MORRIS Give it to me. *(to phone)* Yes? Morris here. *(pause; then, grimly)* Yes. Read it to me. *(pause)* I have nothing to say on the subject. No, I would seriously advise you *not* to reprint it. *(pause)* Because it's a matter of national security, man! *(pause)* No, I do not know how the news reached New York, but I certainly intend to find out. Good day. *(hangs up; then, quietly, after a pause)* Well, gentlemen. It appears that our Russian friend has succeeded in reporting his whereabouts to the *New York Times*.

WHITMORE *(a beat)* Really, sir?

MORRIS Yes, lieutenant, really. Quite strange, is it not? Considering that there are strict orders to keep him incommunicado. How the blazes did he do it?

WHITMORE *(a beat)* I don't know, sir.

MORRIS No? I thought you'd been hobnobbing with him. I thought perhaps he might have confided to you just how he managed this little stunt. Resourceful chap, I'll say that for him.

WHITMORE Perhaps the, er, authorities in Halifax… made an announcement?

MORRIS Oh yes, of course, I'm sure that's the answer. Silly of me not to have thought of it. I expect Captain Makeweight telephoned the *New York Times* to give them the glad tidings. Couldn't bear to keep it to himself, I expect. *(beat)* Don't be childish, lieutenant! The word came from Trossky himself, from inside this camp.

WHITMORE Trotsky, sir.

MORRIS What?

WHITMORE His name is Trotsky, sir. You said "Trossky."

MORRIS Don't correct me, boy! They got the message from this camp, and I want to know how. I have orders from Ottawa to keep him quiet, and he manages to squawk all the way to New York! Well? *(pause)*

WHITMORE *(clears his throat)* It, er, could have come from his wife, possibly, sir.

MORRIS He's got a wife?

WHITMORE Oh yes, sir. And two children.

MORRIS Where the devil are they?

WHITMORE In Halifax, sir. In the custody of a police interpreter. Russian, sir.

MORRIS Really?

WHITMORE *(hates to say it)* Jewish, I believe.

MORRIS Indeed?

WHITMORE Just to judge by the name, sir. And the… you know…

MORRIS Appearance? Well, good God! That's it then, isn't it? Hah! *(to BAXTER)* Wind up that thing of yours, and get me Makins, Naval Control. He can haul the fellow in, and roast him over a slow fire.

WHITMORE It's only a guess.

MORRIS Nonsense. It's perfectly clear. Isn't it?

WHITMORE I suppose so.

MORRIS What kind of a damn fool thing is that, billeting the bugger's wife on one of his own tribe? Is that what they call "Naval Intelligence?" It's bloody idiocy.

OGILVIE *(coughing)* Excuse me, sir.

MORRIS Baxter, have you got Halifax yet? Well don't.

BAXTER Sir?

MORRIS I've changed my mind. You see what's going to happen, don't you? Navy's going to try and shift the blame onto us – onto me! They're not going to admit to being damn fools. They're going to point the finger right here.

OGILVIE Sir...

MORRIS God blast it! I'll be a bloody laughing-stock.

OGILVIE Colonel Morris, sir...

MORRIS Got any bright suggestions, sergeant?

OGILVIE What if we were to, er, nab the chap ourselves?

MORRIS What if what?

OGILVIE Bring him up here. Get the truth out of him. Before the Navy can get their hands on him.

MORRIS *(He thinks about it.)* Damn it, sergeant, you may have had a good idea. By God, it'll be a race to the finish, though. Lieutenant, how fast can you get to Halifax? Look up the trains, Baxter. *(He does.)* Tell him we've got some questions to ask him. Better still, tell him we need some interpreting. Don't get him rattled. Take Baxter down with you – get him off his arse. And Whitmore... don't make a hash of it!

WHITMORE No sir.

MORRIS I'm going to crucify somebody for this. Do you understand?

> *As WHITMORE and BAXTER prepare to leave, there is a brief echo of the "St. Matthew Passion": "Lass Ihn kreuzigen!" – "Let Him be crucified!"*

Scene Eight

MENDEL's house in Halifax, evening. NATALYA and SOPHIE enter from the rain, wet, excited, carrying covered baskets with some basic foodstuffs, bread etc.

SOPHIE   Shall I fetch the boys?

NATALYA   No, leave them for a while longer. Your neighbour is very good to them. I think they are learning some English. *(She calls out.)* David Abramovich! *(pause; to SOPHIE)* Where is your fool of a father? Ah, now, forgive me, I mustn't say that. He's a good man.

SOPHIE   He is a fool.

NATALYA   Sophie, Sophie, have patience with me, with him.

SOPHIE   Don't you know he follows us every time we leave the house? He is doing his duty for the officer. "He gave his word." Shall I make tea?

NATALYA   Tea? I can't stand any more tea. It makes me feverish. Give me a sleeping potion till we are on a ship, far out to sea. I'm seething, seething. So many days we're losing, so many hours. Do you know, in Russia now it's tomorrow morning already, and here we are, still trapped in yesterday. *(noticing)* My dear, my dear, you're wet to the skin. Find me a dry towel and a blanket. Get out of those clothes, you'll catch pneumonia.

SOPHIE   *(going out of the room)* Oh, what do I care? I'll catch pneumonia and die. I'm sick of this miserable hovel we live in!

NATALYA   Sophie! Don't let me hear you talk like that. Lev Davidovich says, "Defeatism is the privilege of the defeated."

SOPHIE   *(calling)* Yes, little mother.

NATALYA   Don't make a mockery of it. *(SOPHIE returns with a towel and blanket.)* People with nothing better to do than complain should be hitched to the plough, instead of horses.

SOPHIE   Is that something Lev Davidovich says?

NATALYA   It's something *I* say. Sit here. I will dry your hair. *(She does.)*

SOPHIE   What were you doing in Paris when you met Lev Davidovich?

NATALYA   Wasting my time. Studying art. I was a young "lady," with rebellious sentiments.

SOPHIE   And he?

NATALYA   He was newly come from Russia, from Siberia. He was young and brilliant and fierce. Comrade Lenin sent him to Paris. We walked everywhere, all night. I loved the city, but he hardly looked at it. When I asked him what he thought, do you know what he said? "It's like Odessa, only Odessa is better." He talked all the time – very excited, very scornful, intolerably sure of himself.

SOPHIE He sounds horrible. Has he changed?

NATALYA Oh, not much. A little more fierce, a little less excited.

SOPHIE How could you marry him? Was he very insistent? Did he sweep you off your feet?

NATALYA I didn't marry him. His wife was in Russia. We became comrades.

SOPHIE Is that all?

NATALYA All? That is everything!

SOPHIE But you're not married? What about his other wife… his real wife? Is she still in Russia?

NATALYA As far as we know she is still in Petrograd, with their two daughters.

SOPHIE But what will happen when you go back there?

NATALYA We will see her. Lev Davidovich will meet his daughters again. The older one is sixteen or seventeen now. *(renewing an attack)* You could be friends with her – if you would come back to Russia with us.

SOPHIE *(torn between attraction and despair)* Don't keep saying that, Natalya Ivanovna. How can I? You talk as if I could just step on a ship and go!

NATALYA Come with us. What is stopping you? Are you satisfied with your life here?

SOPHIE How can you ask? You see what my life is!

NATALYA Your life is nothing, because you have no purpose. In Russia now the lives of all young people are filled with purpose.

SOPHIE What about Papa?

NATALYA Are you going to wither away here for the sake of an old man who has no more faith in anything? Come back with us.

SOPHIE What could I do? I haven't any education, any training. I never went to Paris to study art.

NATALYA Political work. *(SOPHIE makes a despairing gesture.)* Yes! When we take over state power we are going to need hundreds of thousands of people – young people – to go into the towns and villages, to explain and educate and organize.

SOPHIE Natalya Ivanovna, I don't know anything about politics. Not even in Canada. Liberals, Conservatives, I don't know one from the other.

NATALYA This is not politics! This is only monkeys quarrelling in a tree. Politics is the transformation of human life. How is work to be shared? What shall be the limit of personal property? What is the task of the scientist, of the teacher?

What is the duty of the artist, of the critic? What shall be the laws of marriage? In Russia, now, everything is on the agenda. Look, do you see how I have done your hair? *(She takes off her own glasses and puts them on SOPHIE.)* Now you look like a real revolutionary. You look like Krupskaya!

SOPHIE   Who is Krupskaya?

> *SOPHIE, wearing a blanket, her hair drawn tightly back, and glasses on her nose, is peering in the mirror. At this moment, MENDEL enters from the rain.*

NATALYA   David Abramovich!

MENDEL   Such a night! It's good to be home. And where did you young ladies go to this afternoon?

SOPHIE   *(taking off NATALYA's glasses)* Why are you pretending, Papa? You know where we went.

MENDEL   How should I know?

SOPHIE   You know because you followed us. Yes you did, don't deny it. I saw you. Outside the bakery. You thought I didn't recognize you? Look, look at this! *(She pulls a false beard out of his coat pocket and puts it on him.)* What do you think you look like? Papa, you are such a fool!

MENDEL   Listen to me, young lady. I have orders. From the officer who gives us our daily bread. "Keep a close watch on Mrs. Bronstein."

SOPHIE   *(decisively)* Papa, listen to me. I have made a decision. I am going to Russia with Natalya Ivanovna. I am going to dedicate myself to the service of the revolution.

MENDEL   *(eating bread)* Eh? What's she talking about?

SOPHIE   I want to go to Russia.

MENDEL   Now listen who is calling me a fool. Do you know how hard it was to get out of Russia?

SOPHIE   You've told me.

MENDEL   Yes, I've told you. How much money, how much trouble to get passports? You can't remember it, you can't remember what life was like.

SOPHIE   When will you understand – it's all changed. It's quite different now. I want to work for the new society.

MENDEL   The new society! Natalya Ivanovna, why do you fill her head with your stories? It's all a fantasy. You haven't even seen it for yourself. Believe me, I know what is going to happen. Germany will win the war. Germany will beat Russia, and they will bring back the Tsar. Life will be worse than before. For the Jews, for everyone.

NATALYA Sophie, he doesn't know what he's talking about. The Russian people will never again accept the rule of the Tsar. There has been a revolution of the whole people.

MENDEL So what if you have a revolution of the people? So what is going to happen? Let me tell you. Nothing. All the rich will leave, all the educated people. There will be nobody to run the businesses, no doctors, no engineers, no teachers. The workers in the city are lazy and greedy. The peasants are ignorant. They want land – so you give them land. You think they will grow food for you? Only for money. And there will be no money to pay them.

NATALYA Then they will have to be educated.

MENDEL Do you have a hundred years? Fine, educate the peasants. Otherwise you will have to beat them like mules. Yes, and you will become as brutal and cruel as the Cossacks. Listen! I know about history. I am a teacher. What happened in France? A revolution. Ten years later, they have a Napoleon.

SOPHIE Natalya Ivanovna is right. You don't have any faith, Papa. I want to go back.

MENDEL Sophie, Sophie, you're a little girl. Now think a little bit. How can I go back there? I left everything. Here I've learned English. I'm not so young now. How can I go back to Russia? Natalya Sedova, explain this to her.

SOPHIE *(simply)* I'm not asking you to come with me. I'll go by myself.

MENDEL *(after a shocked pause)* You're going to leave me here alone? *(to NATALYA)* You're telling her to leave her father alone, in a foreign country? With nothing, no life?

SOPHIE You're always saying you have such a good life here.

MENDEL For you! I'm making a life for you! We'll go to America. You can get a job in an office. You'll meet a good man. How can I stay here by myself? Look at it. I'm nothing. I don't know anybody here.

NATALYA David Abramovich, you must come back too. In the new Russia there will be a great need for teachers.

MENDEL Teachers! I don't know anything anymore. What could I teach, when I can't tell my own daughter anything?

SOPHIE Oh stop all this, Papa.

MENDEL Sure, I'm not to say anything. I give my life for my child. After her mother died. But I'm not to say anything. You know my nightmare.

SOPHIE Yes, Papa, I know it.

MENDEL Natalya Ivanovna, you know the nightmare I have?

SOPHIE Papa, please!

MENDEL   I am back in Russia, it's winter, I'm walking on a long road. There's deep snow, I can't lift my feet. And I'm carrying Sophie's mother in my arms. She's sick, and I have to get to the next village…

SOPHIE   Please! Don't!

MENDEL   And then it's Sophie I'm carrying, and she's going to die, and I can't move through the snow… *(There is a knock at the door, then a pause, then another knock, more peremptory. MENDEL tenses nervously.)* Yes?

   WHITMORE enters, followed by Private BAXTER.

WHITMORE   Mr. Mendel?

MENDEL   Captain…?

WHITMORE   Lieutenant. Whitmore. *(He acknowledges NATALYA awkwardly.)* Mrs. Trotsky.

MENDEL   My daughter. Sophie. Like I told you. *(pause)* It's a poor house. Do you want…? Will you sit down? Everything is fine? *(to NATALYA)* Maybe he has good news for you.

WHITMORE   Please speak only in English! Mr. Mendel, Colonel Morris wishes you to come to Amherst with me.

MENDEL   What for?

WHITMORE   To serve as an interpreter.

MENDEL   What is this soldier here for?

WHITMORE   It's rather urgent. He wants you to come back tonight, with me.

SOPHIE   *(explaining to NATALYA)* He wants Papa to go with him.

NATALYA   To the place where they are keeping Lev Davidovich?

MENDEL   He speaks English well enough. He doesn't need me.

WHITMORE   You are ordered to come to Amherst with me.

MENDEL   Ordered?

SOPHIE   What has he done? Papa, you don't have to go anywhere. *(to WHITMORE)* You can't take him away without telling him why.

WHITMORE   *(stiffly)* Colonel Morris has been informed that there is news in New York about…

MENDEL   *(shaken)* Lev Davidovich? In New York?

WHITMORE   A telegraph was sent…

SOPHIE   Papa! *(to NATALYA)* They know in New York! They know you're here!

NATALYA   *(coming to embrace him)* David Abramovich, you are a good comrade. We will always thank you.

MENDEL *(repelling her embrace)* I never sent any telegraphs!

SOPHIE Papa!

MENDEL *(to WHITMORE)* They tried to persuade me. Right in front of you, Lev Davidovich was saying, "Send a telegraph to New York." They gave me a message to send – this one, the wife. But I never sent it.

> *There is a pause, while WHITMORE and SOPHIE consider this.*

SOPHIE *(in "Russian")* Is that true, Papa. You never sent it?

NATALYA Of course he did. How else could the comrades have heard? How else?

SOPHIE Papa, you did, didn't you? You did!

MENDEL They are going to arrest me. I could be deported.

WHITMORE *(rapping his swagger stick)* Speak in English!

SOPHIE This is our house. We can speak together in our own language.

NATALYA What is happening? Sophie, what is this about?

SOPHIE *(to WHITMORE)* What are you going to do with him?

WHITMORE I'm taking him to Amherst.

SOPHIE To prison? He is a prisoner?

WHITMORE To answer some questions…

MENDEL But I don't know anything. I didn't do anything. I've told you. Why do you want to make this trouble for me? I've got my child here…

SOPHIE Papa, don't plead with him! You will make me ashamed.

WHITMORE Get ready now, anything you're going to need.

SOPHIE When does he come back?

WHITMORE I don't know. I'm sorry. *(He leaves them alone and motions BAXTER to follow.)*

SOPHIE Be brave, Papa. You have done a good thing. I'm proud of you.

NATALYA *(to MENDEL, taking his hands)* Comrade, forgive us, if you can, for the trouble we have brought you. Don't be afraid of being deported. For a poor Russian Jew, there is nothing in Canada. Come with us. We have been away from Russia longer than you. We will return together. Believe me: in the new Russia, the comrade of Trotsky can have nothing to fear!

> *MENDEL moves away from them and is isolated in a spotlight, as the stage darkens and NATALYA and SOPHIE exit.*

Scene Nine

MORRIS is at his desk, with a tray of tea. WHITMORE and OGILVIE are in attendance. As the light changes from the preceding scene, MORRIS calls to MENDEL.

MORRIS *(to MENDEL)* You – the Jew – what's-your-name? Come in here. Sit down. Sit down there. What *is* your name?

MENDEL David Mendel, sir.

MORRIS You are an interpreter?

MENDEL For the British Navy.

MORRIS Well, Mr. Mendel, we have to have a little chat. We want you to help us clear up a little mystery.

MENDEL You wish me to make translation?

MORRIS In due course, perhaps.

MENDEL There is some difficulty?

MORRIS A cup of tea, Mr. Mendel? You do drink tea, do you?

MENDEL Thank you.

MORRIS Thank you yes? *(MORRIS pours tea, calls off.)* Baxter, make another pot would you? Milk?

MENDEL No. Thank you.

MORRIS No milk in tea?

MENDEL Do you have… sugar?

MORRIS Sugar? Baxter! Find some sugar for Mr. Mendel, will you? *(BAXTER obliges.)* Lieutenant Whitmore tells me you've been sending letters to New York. Isn't that so, lieutenant?

WHITMORE Sir… *(WHITMORE cannot reply.)*

MENDEL I have never sent letters to New York or anywhere – I told him.

MORRIS In collusion with the wife, I think you said.

WHITMORE It was only a guess…

MORRIS Now, I happen to take a rather dim view of that.

MENDEL I am never letting Natalya Sedova outside of my sight. I swear this. I never sent anything.

MORRIS Well of course you did. Why wouldn't you? One of your own people.

MENDEL Never, sir.

MORRIS It's the betrayal of a trust, you see.

MENDEL   I gave my word.

MORRIS   To Captain Makins?

MENDEL   Sir?

MORRIS   You made an undertaking to Captain Makins, when he made the foolish decision to entrust you with custody of the wife.

MENDEL   Captain Makins?

MORRIS   Don't pretend to be an idiot. You know who I'm talking about. Captain Makins of Naval Intelligence.

MENDEL   *(looking at WHITMORE, realizing there is something MORRIS doesn't know)* It was not Captain Makins, sir.

MORRIS   Well, whoever the dickens it was – you gave your word.

MENDEL   Yes sir.

MORRIS   *(change of tone)* When did you come to this country, Mr. Mendel?

MENDEL   Nineteen hundred seven.

MORRIS   And you want to stay, I expect? Stay in Canada?

MENDEL   Yes sir, I do. *(He spills his tea over MORRIS's desk.)* Oy, God! *(He attempts to wipe up the tea with his handkerchief.)* Please, I am sorry, I am sorry. *(He wrings his handkerchief into his tea-cup.)*

MORRIS   Baxter! *(BAXTER takes stock of the situation and cleans up.)* Well, then, if you want to stay, you'd better come clean. Thank you, Private Baxter. You made a mistake. You thought you could do a little favour for your… compatriot. But aiding a German spy is a serious crime! I could have you shipped back to Russia for less than that.

MENDEL   No sir.

MORRIS   No sir?

MENDEL   Sir, I am a natural Canadian. I have my papers!

MORRIS   Don't you worry about that, my friend. The Lord giveth, and the Lord can damn well take away again. I should think a troublemaker like you would find things pretty much to your taste in Russia just now – what do you say?

MENDEL   Sir, I sent nothing for the Russian.

MORRIS   *(suddenly harsh)* Don't lie to me, damn it, you little Hebe! I didn't bring you in here to string me a line of blasted twaddle! Bronstein got a message to his cronies in New York. I want an explanation, and I want it out of your mouth, or I'll tear you into little pieces and send you back to Russia in a paper bag! Have you got that?

MENDEL   *(desperate)* I send nothing for these people! They are not my people. They are fanatical, ruthless. He wanted me to. In front of him, Lev Davidovich was saying, "Send a telegraph, send a telegraph." I said to him, "It's not for me to interfere." He said, "You are Russian." I told him, "My country is Canada. I have to obey the law here. I can't help you." I don't know who sent the telegraph. I took them in only for money. The lieutenant knows…

MORRIS   What does Lieutenant Whitmore know?

WHITMORE   Sir…

MORRIS   One moment, lieutenant. Mr. Mendel, just what are you suggesting?

MENDEL   *(stubbornly)* You ask him, sir, what he knows.

MORRIS   Let me give you a piece of advice, my friend! Don't you start throwing around back-handed insinuations about any of my officers, or you'll find yourself in hotter water than any you've got into yet!

MENDEL   But I'm innocent!

WHITMORE   *(He is in anguish.)* May I speak, sir?

MORRIS   Not just now, lieutenant.

WHITMORE   Sir, I do feel I ought to say…

MORRIS   No, lieutenant.

WHITMORE   Sir, I don't think… that Mr. Mendel…

MORRIS   Well? *(He gives WHITMORE a hard stare.)*

WHITMORE   Sir… *(He is unable to speak. At last the phone rings. BAXTER takes it.)*

BAXTER   Amherst. Yes, he's right here. One moment, please.

MORRIS   *(preparing to take the telephone)* Who is it?

BAXTER   It's a call for Lieutenant Whitmore.

WHITMORE   *(startled)* For me?

BAXTER   From Antigonish, sir.

WHITMORE   It must be my father, sir.

MORRIS   Carry on, lieutenant. Tell your father I'd rather he didn't make a habit of it.

WHITMORE   *(taking the telephone)* Yes, Father? *(He is about to speak, but instead listens without expression.)*

MORRIS   Now then, Mr. Mendel, let us stop beating about the bush, and get right to the point. I don't want to hear any more shilly-shallying, and I don't want to hear about your precious Canadian citizenship. I want a confession, and I want it now. Do we understand one another?

WHITMORE (*The lights change to isolate WHITMORE, who hands the receiver to BAXTER and walks out of the office without speaking. Out of the gathering dark, MORRIS calls to him.*)

MORRIS Lieutenant Whitmore! There wasn't anything you wanted to say, before I proceed with Mr. Mendel here? (*There is no reply.*) Lieutenant Whitmore? Lieutenant Whitmore!

> *MORRIS's call to WHITMORE alternates with that of TROTSKY from the next scene.*

Scene Ten

Using his swagger stick like a blind man's cane, WHITMORE crosses toward TROTSKY, who is revealed by a change of light to be reading a newspaper.

TROTSKY Comrade Vitmore! (*There is no response.*) Comrade Vitmore! (*TROTSKY takes WHITMORE by the sleeve as he passes.*)

WHITMORE (*flinching in horror*) What? What do you want?

TROTSKY (*showing him the newspaper*) Comrade Vitmore, do you see here?

WHITMORE What?

TROTSKY My friend, you have a famous victory! You have capture a hill in France.

WHITMORE (*dully*) Yes.

TROTSKY The Canada.

WHITMORE I know.

TROTSKY Do you see? (*shows newspaper*) Here is the cartoon picture of an animal with a German soldier in the teeth. What animal do you call this?

WHITMORE A beaver.

TROTSKY A beaver. So. Soon the war will be finished, yes? The Canada has capture a hill of Vimy. The British general says "a splendid effort." You are proud for this, Vitmore? Proud for your country?

WHITMORE Yes, it's very fine.

TROTSKY And you hope also to go to France – to capture another hill with your brother. And will you stand on the hill with a German soldier in the teeth, like this? (*He mimes.*) Eh? Like the beavle?

WHITMORE Beaver. (*pause*)

TROTSKY *(avidly)* So, Vitmore...

WHITMORE What do you want?

TROTSKY The Colonel Morris – does he hear anything?

WHITMORE *(almost accusingly)* There's news of you in New York. In the papers.

TROTSKY What you say?

WHITMORE In New York. They know you're here.

TROTSKY When is this happen?

WHITMORE I don't know... two or three days ago.

TROTSKY The "couple" days? *(exultant, going to embrace WHITMORE, who shrinks away)* So, Vitmore! We are soon going. He gets the order, yes?

WHITMORE Colonel Morris wants to know how they found out.

TROTSKY Ah! *(pause)* And what you tell to him?

WHITMORE He sent me to Halifax, to arrest...

TROTSKY David Abramovich?

WHITMORE The Jew. Mendel.

TROTSKY Ah. *(pause)* You saw there my wife?

WHITMORE What?

TROTSKY In Halifax. You saw there my wife.

WHITMORE Yes. I saw her.

TROTSKY And you told to her this news?

WHITMORE I told her, yes.

TROTSKY Ah! That is very good! Now you must send to her another message...

WHITMORE Don't ask me anything more!

TROTSKY Vitmore, I ask you one more thing... *(He catches at WHITMORE's wrist.)*

WHITMORE *(pulling away)* I could be court-martialled! He's got Mendel in there – tearing him to pieces. He could be deported. What can I do? I have to get to France now. I can't jeopardize that. Don't you see? If I'm suspected.... Don't you see? The battalion is sailing next week. I have to be on that boat! I waited a year before enlisting. More than a year. *(He is talking almost to himself.)* I could have volunteered right away, but... it wasn't cowardice, certainly not. At first, you see, we all thought it would be quite short, and people said "Wait a bit, finish your schooling." And then, of course, it's harder if you haven't jumped in right away. You think, "Well, next spring for sure...." But Eddie wasn't like that. Eddie wasn't like that. Father didn't want him to go, of course. He cried. But he was proud of him, all the same. You could tell. Proud of his son. And Eddie never said, never once, that I should go too.

TROTSKY   *(after a pause)* Your brother is dead?

WHITMORE   He's blind. *(pause)* They're sending him home. I can't be here… when he gets back.

TROTSKY   *(quietly)* Your brother is blind in the war.

WHITMORE   He's only twenty-three. For fifty years – he won't ever see anything.

TROTSKY   *(after a pause)* Your brother is blind – and so you also must go?

WHITMORE   Can't you understand that?

TROTSKY   No, I do not understand that.

WHITMORE   What would you do?

TROTSKY   I? I would fight against this war which has blind my brother.

WHITMORE   I can't do that.

TROTSKY   Why you cannot? There are many who fight against the war, even in the Canada.

WHITMORE   But I can't! *(pause)* My brother has been blinded.

TROTSKY   And you have to go. To take for your brother the eyes of a German boy?

WHITMORE   No, no!

TROTSKY   No. *(pause)* To give your own, is it not? *(WHITMORE says nothing.)* Because your brother is blind, you will give your eyes. Because your brother is hungry, you will take no food. Because your brother is sick, you will… drink the bad water. Because he is a slave, you will give up your freedom.

WHITMORE   *(uncertainly)* That's what Christ said.

TROTSKY   That is what the Christ said. And in this Christian world, your brother still is every day blind, still every day hungry, every day sick, everyday in chains. You have the pity for this, you have the sympathy. *(TROTSKY's tone changes to a sharper note.)* In nineteen-hundred-twelve I saw in Servia the young boys going to war. They had shoes made of – what you call the side of the tree?

WHITMORE   Bark?

TROTSKY   And in the hat, they have little pieces of green leaf. And I feel then the terrible pity for these boys. But the pity makes me helpless, makes me weak. Shall I put the green leaf in my hat, and go with them to death? In Russia now are many thousand blind, without the arm, the leg, many hundred of thousand dead, while I am in Switzerland, in France, America. Shall I go to Russia to give my eyes for them, to give my arm? No! I go to give them my seeing, what I see with my eyes, what I strike with my arm!

WHITMORE And what about me?

TROTSKY You do not know how much you have made! Because the news is sent to New York, we have good hope now to leave. And you have made this. *(WHITMORE is leaving.)* I am sorry to your brother. You are a good boy. I am sorry to your brother.

> *Lights fade to a spot on WHITMORE, in the position in which the next scene will find him.*

Scene Eleven

Lights up on SOPHIE, who is reading from the newspaper.

SOPHIE Listen to this! "Canada's action a damnable outrage, say pro-Germans." Listen. "An international movement which, though avowedly aiming for peace, has as its object an uprising of workers in this country and in the countries of the allies, was launched today at a meeting held in this city" – that's New York – "to protest against the action of the Canadian government in detaining Leon Trotsky, a Russian revolutionist, in Halifax."

> *Light on a bespectacled MORRIS, who is reading from the same article.*

MORRIS "The meeting was announced as being under the auspices of the Russian, Jewish, Lithuanian, and German 'revolutionary socialists,' but the majority of the five hundred men and women who packed the Manhattan Lyceum were apparently of German birth or extraction."

SOPHIE "In a resolution vigorously applauded and unanimously adopted, workers the world over were told to 'use all the force in their possession to bring about the release of Trotsky, and to bring peace.'"

MORRIS & SOPHIE "In the course of the meeting, children of the Ferrer Anarchistic School sang a number of revolutionary songs, in English and German, including 'The International' and 'I Didn't Raise My Boy to Be a Soldier.'"

> *A chorus of voices breaks out into "I Didn't Raise My Boy to Be a Soldier" (Bryan/Piantadosi), until a furious MORRIS, pounding on his desk, manages to put a stop to it. Lights up on MORRIS, TROTSKY, WHITMORE, PLAMBECK, OGILVIE and BAXTER.*

MORRIS And what, I want to know, is this doing in the paper? In the Halifax blasted *Herald*! What the devil is the editor doing, printing inflammatory stuff like this? Eh? I'm not a politician or a policeman, thank God, I'm a soldier. But this is insurrection. This is anarchy! And as for you, Bronstein, you can forget about your plans to leave here. You're not going to be leaving here in a hundred years – unless it's to go down to the fortress in Halifax in leg-irons and hand-cuffs. It seems, doesn't it, as if your precious government doesn't want you back in a hurry – and I'm damned if I can say I blame them. Eh? Pretty slow in replying, aren't they, wouldn't you say?

TROTSKY Colonel Morris, you have prevent me to communicate with my government. Again I demand you send telegraph to Petrograd…

MORRIS Come now, Bronstein, how many more times? You were waltzing in here weeks ago with your telegraphs to "Mr. George" and Petrograd and heaven-knows-where…

TROTSKY And in your knowledge, Colonel Morris, they are never sent.

MORRIS Now who gave you that idea, Mr. Bronstein?

TROTSKY They are never sent.

MORRIS Who has given Mr. Bronstein that idea?

WHITMORE I… told him, sir.

MORRIS You told him sir. Yes?

WHITMORE I was not specifically ordered not to, sir.

MORRIS You were not specifically ordered not to swim the Atlantic Ocean, lieutenant.

WHITMORE Sir, I believed Mr. Trotsky was being denied a legal right, sir.

MORRIS Are you a lawyer, lieutenant?

WHITMORE No sir.

MORRIS Are you a padre? Are you?

WHITMORE No sir.

MORRIS Are you a Justice of the Peace?

WHITMORE No colonel.

MORRIS And yet you have taken it into your head to become an advocate for a German agent trying to communicate with his government, with a view to escaping from British custody – is that so? *(no reply)* And doubtless, lieutenant, your sympathy for Mr. Bronstein and all his works and pomps could have led you to the further step of directly helping him to transmit messages to foreign powers.

WHITMORE Sir, I…

MORRIS I'm telling you, if that Jew of yours hadn't confessed, I'd have a finger pointing directly at you, my boy!

WHITMORE Mr. Mendel confessed?

MORRIS You see, I don't think you have any idea of what we're dealing with here. *(becoming milder)* Gullibility, lieutenant. Do you see how easy it is for a trained agent, whose whole stock-in-trade consists in deception and guile, how easily, you see, he can… bewilder a young man, turn his head around with talk of rights and innocent civilians?

TROTSKY Do you hear, Vitmore, how he is ignorant? It is to me no interest who will win this war – Germany, Russia, England. All he can think is German agent, German spy. I was *expelled* from Germany. In Germany in nineteen fourteen I am tried in absentia. If I am find in Germany, I will be hang. As you *(MORRIS)* will wish if we are in Africa.

MORRIS Oh, we may not have to travel that far, Bronstein! *(cunningly)* Does the name "Lenine" *(rhymes with "benign")* mean anything to you?

TROTSKY *(guardedly)* What name?

MORRIS You heard me.

TROTSKY I did not hear you.

MORRIS *(He puts on glasses and reads in very British accent.)* "Vladimir Ilyich Lenine."

TROTSKY *(pronouncing correctly)* Vladimir Ilyich Lenin.

MORRIS Mean anything to you?

TROTSKY I know him, yes.

MORRIS Friend of yours?

TROTSKY Politically we are not agreed always. But we are comrades, yes.

MORRIS I see. Comrades. And where is Lenine now, would you say?

TROTSKY Comrade Lenin is in Zurich, in Schweiz, Switzerland.

MORRIS Oh really?

TROTSKY *(note of vindication)* He also was expelled from Germany.

MORRIS Comrade Lenin, my friend, is in Russia – in Petrograd. And how did he get from Switzerland to Petrograd, you well might ask? Simple. He went through Germany, on a train.

TROTSKY *(agitated)* Lenin is in Petrograd? When is he there?

MORRIS Never mind "when is he there?" The point is, the Germans, the Kaiser, helped him get there. Your friend Lenin has been shipped to Petrograd, courtesy of Kaiser Wilhelm the Second. What do you think of that, lieutenant? *(WHITMORE is silent.)* You know, I have to blame myself. Good Lord, I should have seen right away that we were dealing with a real snake-in-the-hole here. *(pouring tea)*

PLAMBECK With respect, the Kolonel will recall that I have two times…

MORRIS *(to WHITMORE)* He talked to you quite a bit, I expect, did he?

WHITMORE Yes sir, he did.

MORRIS Talked about his plans for when he gets back to Russia, did he?

WHITMORE Once or twice, sir.

MORRIS Yes, and what did he say? How does he propose to help us beat the Germans when he gets back to Petrograd? Joining the colours? Raising a regiment? Selling defence bonds?

WHITMORE Well, not exactly that, sir.

MORRIS Not exactly...?

WHITMORE Not that at all, sir. You see, he has quite a different idea about the war from ours, sir.

PLAMBECK To the men he has been urging disloyalty and mutiny!

MORRIS Thank you, Captain. And what is this different idea, lieutenant, that you obviously found so impressive?

WHITMORE Well, sir, he says that the war is a struggle between the commercial interests, and that, er, working men have no quarrel with each other, but with their employers.

MORRIS Ah ha! And does Mr. Bronstein explain to you why so many thousands of working men have flocked to the colours from the very first, begging for a chance to serve their country? Did you ask him that?

WHITMORE I did, actually, yes sir.

MORRIS Did you actually? And what did he say?

WHITMORE Well sir, they have been deceived and coerced. And many of them took the opportunity for employment.

MORRIS Sergeant Ogilvie, what is your army pay, if you'll forgive my asking?

OGILVIE Not at all, sir. One dollar and sixty-five cents a day, sir. Sergeant's pay.

MORRIS And when did you enlist?

OGILVIE November 'fourteen, sir.

MORRIS Yes. And what was your occupation in peace time, sergeant?

OGILVIE With the mining company, sir. Two-seventy a day. It'd be more than that now, sir, if I may say so.

MORRIS And you were forced to join the army, were you? Conscripted?

OGILVIE No indeed, sir, volunteer.

MORRIS Well you must have been deceived, then. There you were, a working man, with nothing to gain by fighting a war for your employers – what lies were you told at the recruiting station?

OGILVIE No lies at all, sir! Defending the Empire, sir. That was enough for me.

TROTSKY And the workers of Germany which you went to fight, what lies did they telling them? Comrade Ogilvie, come to Russia with me. I will recruit you for the Cossack Regiment. You can have a horse and a sabre and a fur hat, yes? No, you will stay here, and when the war is finish, you will go back to the mine. Only you are wounded, I am sorry, so you cannot find work. And after the war, Colonel Morris and Kapitän von Plambeck will write letters, "My dear Arthur," "My dear Heinz." And Vitmore, what will you do, after the war? Nothing. Why nothing? Because you will be dead. You will go to France to defend his empire, my poor brave boy, and you will lead your poor stupid men out from the trench, and his son *(indicating PLAMBECK)* will kill you with the machine gun, da-da-da-da-da-da-da-da-da-da! *(pause)* But you have to go. Because you are a brave boy. And because your brother is blind.

WHITMORE Yes sir.

TROTSKY *(gently)* I am not your sir, Vitmore. He is your sir.

MORRIS *(after a short pause)* What's this about your brother, Whitmore?

WHITMORE Sir?

MORRIS Your brother.

WHITMORE Yes sir. My father telephoned.

MORRIS Blind? Oh good God – my dear boy, I'm terribly sorry! Gas?

WHITMORE I don't know. Father didn't say.

MORRIS Filthy Huns! I expect it was gas. What a filthy way to fight a war!

OGILVIE May I say that I'm very sorry to hear it, sir.

WHITMORE Thank you, sergeant.

MORRIS You should have told me! You've no business to be talking to them. *(meaning TROTSKY)* You should have told me at once. I'm sorry to say that I consider it a betrayal on your part, not to have told me. What a terrible thing! *(an outburst of personal pain)* My God, they're such swine. Swine! *(pause)* Naturally I exempt a naval officer. *(to PLAMBECK, who acknowledges the point with a click of the heels)* Well, lieutenant, in a week you'll be on your way to take his place. And I trust you'll be a credit to him, and to your father, and to me.

PLAMBECK May I also congratulate you, Leutnant Vitmore? *(shakes hand)*

WHITMORE *(visibly bewildered)* Thank you, sir.

MORRIS And don't let me get the idea that Mr. Bronstein has given you any second thoughts!

WHITMORE Oh no, sir.

MORRIS Eh? All this guff about the working men having no quarrel with each other! Get over to France, and you'll find out P.D.Q. who has a quarrel with *you*! Don't forget which side you're on, lieutenant – because nobody else is going to! *(to TROTSKY)* But that's exactly the work of an agent, isn't it – to spread disloyalty and defeatism? You give yourself away, Bronstein, just as plainly as your Jew-Hun name. Insubordination, incitement to mutiny, communicating with hostile powers, fostering demoralization... you tell me you're not working for the Germans, and I tell you there isn't much more you *could* be doing for them, short of bearing arms. But then, your tribe isn't awfully partial to actual combat, I gather.

TROTSKY Morris, this is now enough, enough! You are stand in my way for too much. There is no more game. After one month Lenin is in Petrograd! If not for you, I am there before him! You will now do what I tell, and send at once telegraph... *(He is pounding on MORRIS's desk. MORRIS takes up his walking cane and beats TROTSKY's hands furiously, while calling to OGILVIE.)*

MORRIS Sergeant! Sergeant!

OGILVIE *(grabbing from the wall a rifle with fixed bayonet, and jabbing at TROTSKY with it)* Back, back now! Back! You nasty animal. Get back, stand to attenSHUN! Shut your mouth, or I'll stick you! I'll stick you! Stick it right through your beastly guts – and I'll love to do it! Just give me the chance, man!

MORRIS *(with suppressed excitement)* Thank you, sergeant. That will do.

OGILVIE Sir.

MORRIS Satisfied, lieutenant? Now let me tell you, Bronstein, nobody gives orders here except me. Yes, the Germans have sent your friend Lenine back to Petrograd, to do heaven-knows-what kind of dirty work for them, and that's why you're staying right here. Sergeant. Detention cells. Solitary confinement. Bread and water – until further notice. Take him out!

OGILVIE Sir! All right, you heard! Move! *(OGILVIE marches TROTSKY out.)*

MORRIS Thank you, Captain Plambeck, for your assistance. That will be all.

PLAMBECK Kolonel Morris. *(PLAMBECK clicks his heels and exits.)*

WHITMORE Solitary confinement, sir?

MORRIS You heard me, lieutenant.

WHITMORE In one of the ovens?

MORRIS Where else?

WHITMORE They're hardly fit for rats, sir.

MORRIS Oh, I'm sure they are! And you, lieutenant, are to have nothing more to do with him. Are you clear about that?

WHITMORE Yes sir.

OGILVIE *(returning to the office)* Prisoner in the cells, sir.

MORRIS As far as I'm concerned, he can blasted well rot in there. I will not have my authority undermined. Is that clear, Whitmore?

WHITMORE Perfectly clear, sir.

MORRIS Dismiss, lieutenant.

WHITMORE Yes sir. *(WHITMORE salutes and exits.)*

MORRIS *(with finality)* He gets out of this camp over my dead body.

> *Freeze and a change of lights. Sound of Morse telegraph, and a voiceover reading the text.*

VOICE Foreign Office, London, to Naval Control, Halifax. Stop. At request of provisional Russian government, Leon Bronstein, alias Trotsky, taken into custody April 2nd, to be released with official apology and assisted to resume journey on next available ship. Stop.

> *The lights return to normal. BAXTER, replacing the telephone, hands MORRIS the text of the telegram which has just been dictated to him, and exits. Pause, as MORRIS reads the message, then hands it to OGILVIE.*

MORRIS *(with surprising restraint)* With official apology, eh? *(pause)* And so he released unto them Barabbas. Eh, sergeant?

OGILVIE Excuse me, sir?

MORRIS Damn fools in Whitehall. Don't know what they're doing. You mark my words. *(suddenly harsh)* You mark my words! *(an ominous pause, while MORRIS drums on his desk)*

OGILVIE Well then, sir...

MORRIS Sergeant?

OGILVIE Shall I haul him out of the oven?

MORRIS When he's only half baked? *(pause)* No sergeant.

OGILVIE *(confused)* Sir?

MORRIS I said "No sergeant." *(pause)* Leave him there. Let him stew for a bit. *(pause)* Damn fools in Whitehall. *(pause)* A telegraph, Sergeant – dictation: "Foreign Office, London. Stop. Regret to inform you Bronstein-alias-Trotsky shot while trying to escape. Stop. Most unfortunate. Stop. Sorry your message arrived too late. Stop. Morris. Stop."

OGILVIE Sir.

MORRIS What do you think, sergeant?

OGILVIE Not for me to say, sir.

MORRIS Come now, sergeant, don't be so mealy-mouthed!

OGILVIE Fine by me, sir.

MORRIS But it wouldn't be cricket, eh? English fair play, and all that?

OGILVIE Wouldn't know about that, would I sir?

MORRIS Nor you would.

OGILVIE Just you say the word, sir.

MORRIS Yes. *(briskly)* Well then. *(calls out)* Kettle boiling, Private Baxter? Carry on, sergeant. "England expects this day each man to do his duty," what?

> *As the lights change, a melancholy piano plays "There's a Long, Long Trail A-winding" (Alonzo Elliott/Stoddard King).*

Scene 12

Night. Fog. A barbed wire fence drops into view, dividing the stage. SOPHIE, wrapped in a coat, hovers outside the fence. BAXTER, who has been patrolling the perimeter of the camp on guard duty, speaks to WHITMORE.

BAXTER Excuse me, Lieutenant Whitmore, sir, there's a young lady wants to speak to you.

WHITMORE To me? What does she want?

BAXTER Wouldn't say, sir. *(suggestively)* She's over there.

WHITMORE I see. Well, carry on then.

BAXTER Sir.

WHITMORE *(approaching the fence)* What is all this? What do you want?

SOPHIE You must help me.

WHITMORE I can't see you.

SOPHIE You have my father in there.

WHITMORE What are you talking about?

SOPHIE You took him away.

WHITMORE You! How did you get here? What are you doing here?

SOPHIE I came on the train.

WHITMORE I can't talk to you. You must go away.

SOPHIE Captain, please, you must listen to me.

WHITMORE I'm on duty! The guard…

SOPHIE *(simply)* It's all right. He thinks I'm your girl.

WHITMORE It's not all right!

SOPHIE Captain, please listen…

WHITMORE Not Captain… Lieutenant.

SOPHIE You have my father in there. When do you let him go?

WHITMORE I don't know. It's not up to me.

SOPHIE He didn't do anything. He is not a brave man. Natalya Ivanovna asked him to help, but he couldn't do it. I wish he did. I would have done it myself. But he didn't.

WHITMORE He confessed.

SOPHIE What?

WHITMORE He confessed to Colonel Morris.

SOPHIE No, he could not! He is innocent!

WHITMORE *(emphatically)* He confessed! Colonel Morris told me. He was helping Bronstein escape.

SOPHIE What did you do to him?

WHITMORE Nothing.

SOPHIE You did something to him. You said something.

WHITMORE He told Colonel Morris himself.

SOPHIE Did you beat him? Did you?

WHITMORE Nobody beat him! This isn't Russia.

SOPHIE You think only in Russia they beat people? What did you do to my father?

WHITMORE Nothing. Nobody did anything. He confessed.

SOPHIE He was afraid. Perhaps you would tell the colonel too… if you were afraid. But he didn't do it. I know. I asked at the telegraph office in Halifax.

WHITMORE You what?

BAXTER comes by again. They draw back.

SOPHIE I asked at the telegraph office. Nobody sent such a telegraph to New York. *(pause)* So you have to let him go.

WHITMORE I can't. He's under guard.

SOPHIE You can give the order, now, in the night.

WHITMORE No. I can't give an order to release a prisoner.

SOPHIE   You are an officer. You can go, now, to the soldiers, and tell them to let him go.

WHITMORE   I can't do that.

SOPHIE   Listen, if you let him go, I will... *(Is she propositioning him?)*

WHITMORE   What?

SOPHIE   *(She wasn't.)* I will take him away.

WHITMORE   I have to get to France...

SOPHIE   I am going to Russia with Natalya Ivanovna. I can't leave him here alone. He doesn't want to come, but there is nothing here for him now.

WHITMORE   I have to get to France...

SOPHIE   We are going to a new life...

WHITMORE   I can't!

SOPHIE   Why can't you? Why not?

WHITMORE   Because... because I have *orders*. If you disobey orders, you're court-martialled. You lose your commission; you're sent to military prison. Do you see? I'd never get to France.

SOPHIE   Is that so bad? You want to go so much?

WHITMORE   I don't want to go! I don't want to! I have to go.

SOPHIE   What is your name?

WHITMORE   Whitmore.

SOPHIE   Your other name.

WHITMORE   Philip.

SOPHIE   My name is Sophie.

WHITMORE   Yes. I know.

SOPHIE   *(taking his wrist through the wire)* Philip. If you tell him, the colonel...

WHITMORE   What?

SOPHIE   That you know my father is innocent – that you know it – even if he confessed – you know he did nothing – they will let him go.

WHITMORE   Why should he believe me?

SOPHIE   Because it is the truth.

    BAXTER comes by again. Seeing WHITMORE, he stops and comes to attention.

BAXTER   Sir?

WHITMORE *(faintly)* Carry on, Baxter.

BAXTER Yes sir. *(He marches on.)*

WHITMORE *(his mind made up)* Tomorrow...

SOPHIE Yes?

WHITMORE In the morning, today... I will speak to the Colonel.

SOPHIE You will tell him?

WHITMORE I will speak to him.

SOPHIE You promise you will do this?

WHITMORE In the morning.

SOPHIE *(releasing his wrist, and slipping her grasp instead to his hand)* Philip, you are a good man.

>As WHITMORE is about to speak, there is a heavy metallic clang and OGILVIE's voice sounds harshly out of the darkness.

OGILVIE All right, let's be having you! Come on out of there – move! *(OGILVIE drives TROTSKY into the light. TROTSKY is blinking and dishevelled, cleaning his pince-nez.)*

WHITMORE *(urgently motioning SOPHIE into the shadows)* Get back! Get away from here!

OGILVIE Get a move on, damn you!

WHITMORE *(shrilly)* What's going on there?

OGILVIE Who goes there?

WHITMORE Sergeant Ogilvie?

OGILVIE Lieutenant Whitmore... sir.

TROTSKY Vitmore – you have seen this? This oven?

WHITMORE Where are you taking him?

TROTSKY You admire to this?

OGILVIE Colonel's orders, sir.

WHITMORE Where sergeant?

OGILVIE Excuse me, sir, colonel's orders.

TROTSKY In Siberia never have I known this!

WHITMORE Sergeant, I am asking you a question.

OGILVIE *(insolently)* And I am telling you... sir... colonel's orders. Will you let me pass?

WHITMORE Tell me where you are taking the prisoner!

TROTSKY Vitmore, what is this?

WHITMORE He's taking you away.

TROTSKY Back to the bunkhouse, yes?

WHITMORE *(rising panic)* No, I don't think so. Sergeant, what are your orders?

OGILVIE Will you let me pass, sir?

WHITMORE *(unholstering his revolver)* Let him go, sergeant!

OGILVIE *(quietly)* Don't do that, sir.

WHITMORE Don't argue with me!

OGILVIE Colonel Morris wouldn't like it.

WHITMORE Sergeant, I'm ordering you…

TROTSKY *(commandingly)* Vitmore!

OGILVIE What are you ordering… sir? And don't point that thing at me.

WHITMORE I'm ordering you…

TROTSKY Listen me, Vitmore…

WHITMORE *(bitterly)* Oh I've listened to you, Bronstein!

OGILVIE Just get out of my way, boy. You've caused enough bloody trouble already.

WHITMORE How dare you, sergeant? How dare you? Stay back! Stay back!

TROTSKY *(a warning)* Vitmore!

WHITMORE *(to both of them)* Stay back, both of you! Stay back!

> WHITMORE *is holding the gun with both hands, retreating in front of the advancing* OGILVIE. SOPHIE, *from the darkness, lets out a piercing scream.* MORRIS *suddenly emerges from the shadows behind* WHITMORE, *overpowers him, and takes his revolver.*

MORRIS What is going on here, lieutenant? *(WHITMORE is speechless.)* Sergeant?

OGILVIE Lieutenant Whitmore, sir, was, ah, questioning your orders, sir.

MORRIS Indeed? It's becoming quite a habit.

WHITMORE *(recovering his voice)* I demanded to know where he was taking the prisoner.

MORRIS *(a beat)* To the station, lieutenant. It had been my intention to get our friend here away on the night train, to avoid any wretched bally-hoo among the prisoners. *(Train whistle.* MORRIS *checks watch.)* You have managed to thwart that plan. *(to* TROTSKY*)* Mr.… Trotsky. I can't imagine why any responsible authority would want you anywhere but behind bars – but it appears that your misguided government wants you back in Russia. I am sure they will have ample reason to regret it, but as far as I'm concerned it's good riddance.

TROTSKY *(not fully comprehending)* What is he say to me?

MORRIS You will be taken to Halifax, to await the next ship bound for Norway. Your wife has already been notified. I have been instructed to offer you an official apology for detaining you here, but that, I'm afraid, is something I cannot bring myself to do.

TROTSKY Colonel Morris, I must tell you that, for my first business in the Constituent Assembly in Petrograd, I shall question to Minister Miliukoff about this outrageous treatment of Russian citizens by Anglo-Canadian police…

MORRIS It is my pious hope, Mr. Trotsky, that you never set foot in the Constituent Assembly. *(pause)* You will spend the night in the guard-house, and leave in the morning. Sergeant!

MORRIS and OGILVIE freeze.

TROTSKY *(to audience)* Comrades, in perhaps two weeks I shall be in Petrograd, in the country of the revolution. My comrades, I take you with me. There is need of you there. The revolution has many enemies. There will be no easy victories. But history is on our side. The first action of a Revolutionary Socialist government in Russia will be to offer to the people of Germany and Austria-Hungary an end to the war which has butchered our men, starved and widowed our women, and beggared our nations. Across the boundaries of Europe, when this war is ended, we shall reach out hands of friendship in the common fight against the crumbling bastions of capitalism. The revolution we shall make together will lead men and women out of the prison of servitude, the prison of poverty, the prison of ignorance, the prison of disease, into the freedom of their full humanity. This shall be the last generation of enmity between peoples, of war between nations, the first generation of the true brotherhood of man. In the twentieth century, all mankind shall at last inherit the earth! *Auf Wiedersehen! (to WHITMORE)* Vitmore, my friend, priest-son, it will be more simple in France.

TROTSKY turns once more to the audience. He is joined on stage by NATALYA, and together they climb a ship's gang-plank into the wings, turning to wave at the top before they disappear. "The Internationale," sung in German, bursts suddenly through the theatre.

SOPHIE *(a cry)* And what about me?

"The Internationale" ends abruptly. There is silence. WHITMORE is at centre stage. MORRIS and OGILVIE unfreeze and turn towards him.

WHITMORE Colonel Morris?

MORRIS Lieutenant?

WHITMORE It's about Mr. Mendel, sir.

MORRIS *(pause)* He confessed, lieutenant.

WHITMORE I know, but…

MORRIS He *confessed*.

WHITMORE Yes sir, but…

MORRIS One culprit is quite enough, don't you think?

> *WHITMORE is silent. BAXTER, who has been prowling around the back of the stage, behind the map of Europe that has formed a back-drop, now approaches MORRIS.*

BAXTER Excuse me, sir…

MORRIS What is it?

> *Without a word, BAXTER pulls aside the backdrop, which tumbles down to reveal the body of David MENDEL hanging from a beam. At a nod from MORRIS, OGILVIE goes to cut MENDEL's body down, allowing SOPHIE to take it in her arms. WHITMORE continues to face forward. After a few moments, BAXTER begins to hand to WHITMORE: a steel helmet, which he puts on; a rifle, which he shoulders; a gas mask, and various other accessories of combat dress.*

> *As WHITMORE stands inertly, the tune "Mademoiselle from Armentieres" (traditional) becomes audible, played on a concertina, and gathers in volume and tempo to become a march, accompanied by a whistling chorus. WHITMORE gradually straightens his shoulders, comes to attention, makes a sharp left-turn and, with eyes-right toward the audience, marches off the stage.*

> *End.*

PUBLIC LIES

Public Lies was first produced by the Tarragon Theatre in Toronto, in November 1993, with the following company:

JOHN GRIERSON	Layne Coleman
JANE BARNES	Dixie Seatle
MACKENZIE KING and others	Graham Harley
BERNIE SLATER and others	John Jarvis
MICHAEL SCHNEIDER and others	Andrew Akman
TANYA ROSSIDES and others	Elizabeth Marmur
Direction	Richard Greenblatt
Set and Lighting Design	Glenn Davidson
Costume and Props Design	Teresa Przybylski
Stage Management	Laura Astwood

The play had earlier been workshopped by the CanStage company.

John Grierson in the 1930s. A cartoon by Max Anderson from *World Film News*

CHARACTERS (with suggested doublings)

JOHN GRIERSON, born 1898, short, dapper, aggressive Scot.
JANE BARNES, born 1921.
BERNIE SLATER, born 1920 / Presenter of Academy Award / Voice of Counsel to Gouzenko Inquiry / Member of Parliament.
PRIME MINISTER MACKENZIE KING, born 1874 / Igor Gouzenko (defector from the Soviet Embassy in Ottawa) / Jack McPhail (a Cape Breton miner).
MICHAEL SCHNEIDER, born 1948 / Todd Parker (itinerant NFB projectionist) / Production Assistant / Dr. Joseph Goebbels.
TANYA ROSSIDES, born 1950 / Presenter of Academy Award / Voice of Freda Linton (Assistant to Film Commissioner Grierson) / Young woman with a lens (Ruby Grierson).

SETTINGS

One part of the stage represents Grierson's 1970 apartment in the rather tacky Crescent Hotel in Montreal. Impersonal hotel furniture – couch, table, chairs, and a little kitchen area with a pass-through counter and a couple of barstools. The rest of the acting area serves as a variety of 1940s locations, including: the office of the Prime Minister, Mackenzie King; Grierson's office in the National Film Board in Ottawa; an editing room; a mine and a local tavern in Glace Bay, Nova Scotia; and in the opening scene, a union hall, also in Nova Scotia, in which a program of films is about to be presented.

PLAYWRIGHT'S NOTE

The original idea for the use of film and video footage was that, while characters are watching film or television on a number of occasions during the play, the audience would never actually be able to see any of it – only to hear the soundtrack, loud and clear. The light of a projector would be playing, ideally through cigarette smoke as in old-time cinemas, on a screen angled away from the auditorium. Likewise a TV screen would be glowing, out of direct sight. But only the words and accompanying music would reach the audience. The rationale for this is that looking at film footage seems to jolt an audience out of its engagement with the action on the stage in a way that hearing recorded sound does not. Moreover, the soundtrack was by far the preponderant element in NFB movies of this era anyway.

In the Tarragon production it was agreed to show a number of actual film clips, transferred onto video, on the grounds that "in a play about filmmaking, you've got to show some film." If the play were ever to be remounted, I would advise that the notion of using only sound be seriously considered. While a tape of the suggested clips from NFB movies may be available from The Tarragon Theatre in Toronto, permission to use them must always be freshly obtained from the NFB.

PUBLIC LIES

Scene One

In a union hall in Glace Bay, Nova Scotia, an itinerant projectionist, TODD Parker, is setting up to present a program of films from the National Film Board. The year is 1942.

TODD Well, isn't this a good looking audience! I was saying to Mr. Campbell, I was saying as we were coming along, I'd be glad enough of a dozen souls on a night like this. I was in a union hall over by Stellarton the other week, and nobody showed up at all! Well, there'd been a bit of a mix-up about the dates, eh? So there I was, lugging in all my gear, well I know it's not "Gone with the Wind" we've got here, but I'd thought they'd be pretty excited to see a few Canadian movies! It's not every day that folks get a chance to see five different movies, and one of them in Technicolour, yes sir! One of them in Technicolour. That's it, come on in, plenty of room down front. *(A MINER [Jack McPHAIL], identifiable by his helmet and lamp, has come clumping into the hall, greeting people he recognizes, and asking what's going on.)* Just don't trip over those wires, eh?

MINER *(loudly)* You the fella was here last month, then?

TODD What?

MINER Last fella we had in here with fillums wasn't you?

TODD No, that was Jack Cavendish.

MINER What happened to him, then?

TODD He's gone for the Navy.

MINER Is that so?

TODD *(to the rest of the audience)* And, folks, the good news is, this show's coming to you for the best price there is, absolutely free, courtesy of the government in Ottawa. *(humorously)* Now then, now then, let's have no rude remarks! Maybe I didn't vote for 'em either. I'm not saying I did, I'm not saying I didn't. It's a secret ballot – though as the lady said, it can't be all that secret, seeing as so many people know about it!

MINER They payin' you to do this?

TODD What's that?

MINER To come here to Glace Bay with these here fillums of yours…

TODD I should hope so! Eh? Now, as I was saying, if you're willing, I'll be coming out from Halifax every month, with a brand new show…

MINER What they want to send us these fillums for anyway?

TODD Eh?

MINER What's the big idea? Sending these fillums.

TODD Well, it's information, like. To put you in the picture, you might say. What they call the document'ry.

MINER And what might that be, then?

TODD Well, it's your true-life films, not your made-up films, you know what I mean?

MINER Like them newsreels, is it?

TODD That's about the size of it, I guess you could say, only more educational. And made right here in Canada. Isn't that something? Canadian movies. About us all pulling together, and tightening our belts, and what the government's doing for us, you know?

MINER What the government's doing for me? That's a pretty short fillum, eh, Mrs. Ogilvie?

TODD *(unsettled)* Well, and how the war's going, eh? That's the big thing. You can read in your *Herald*, or you can listen in on your wireless, and sure they'll tell you all about the Blitz, and the tanks in Africa, and our boys on the corvettes going out of Halifax…. But with these movies, you can see for yourself, with your own eyes, yessiree, like you was right there, over in England, with the bombers coming over, and the ack-ack guns blazing away…. I'm telling you, this is the real thing! And now, if you're good and ready, somebody get the lights there, and here we go!

> *A short opening excerpt of the film "Churchill's Island" is projected – or can be heard – with its rousing celebration of gallant little England.*

Scene Two

> *Abruptly the theatre is filled with spotlights, fanfares, and applause. It is Academy Awards night, 26 February 1942, Hollywood. A man and a woman meet at a microphone. The man hands the woman an envelope, which she opens with a flourish.*

MAN The Academy of Motion Picture Arts and Sciences introduces, for the first time, an Oscar in the category of Documentary Film. And the winner for 1942 is…

WOMAN "Churchill's Island" by the National Film Board of Canada!

> *More applause. GRIERSON, in a tuxedo, bounds up on stage to receive his Oscar.*

GRIERSON Members of the Academy. I am accepting this fetish object with entirely justifiable pride, not on my own account – for if I had any hand in the making of this film at all, it was only in prodding and chivying those who actually laboured on it with their hands and their brains – but on behalf of hundreds of people – men and women, mostly young – up there in Canada by the Ottawa River, where the ice is still a month from breaking up – hundreds of people at the National Film Board, beavering away I may say at an exciting, demanding, unglamorous but entirely honourable vocation of banging out the films that help to win this war! So I thank the Academy with pride for them. But behind my hundreds in Ottawa there are thousands more – gentlemen in England now abed, gentlemen in this country, gentlemen in Russia – and gentlewomen too – the pioneers and trailblazers and adventurers in the documentary thing that we started back in the twenties, and that you are honouring here tonight.

> *At about this point GRIERSON ceases to address the Hollywood audience, and is instead giving an account of his own speech to the people involved in the next scene. These are: Prime Minister Mackenzie KING, seated at a desk, with JANE Barnes at his side, notebook in hand, as his secretary; BERNIE, a young NFB staffer, operating a 35mm movie camera with a boom microphone; and a production ASSISTANT (male), to whom GRIERSON hands his tuxedo as he becomes part of the scene, still carrying the Oscar.*

We believe, I said to them, we documentary people, that the true vocation of film is to bring to the people not fantasy but reality, not the fiction but the fact. *(lighting the first of many cigarettes)* Hollywood, I said, has different gods, and it offers them a different worship. Our task, the task of the documentary, is to find and to fashion the images that will *inspire* the populace with noble visions, and rouse them to strenuous.... Action!

ASSISTANT *(operating the slate)* "Stand On Guard," shot fifty-three, take one!

KING My fellow Canadians. We are living in a time of unprecented, of unprecedenteted...

BERNIE Cut!

KING I'm sorry. I'm a little unfamiliar with all this.... Wireless, you know, is a more congenial...

GRIERSON That's all right, Prime Minister. Take it nice and easy now. *(He motions to the ASSISTANT to wipe KING's brow.)*

KING The lights and everything...

GRIERSON It's quite disconcerting at first.

KING   Shall we try it again?

BERNIE   *(to the ASSISTANT)* Here, take hold of this. *(A measuring tape is stretched from KING's nose to the camera.)*

JANE   Careful what you're doing there!

KING   I've been wanting to mention, Mr. Grierson, that I hear very good reports of the work of the National Film Board. Excellent reports.

GRIERSON   We try to earn our keep, sir.

BERNIE   What've you got?

ASSISTANT   Ten feet.

KING   The labourers are worthy of their hire.

GRIERSON   I believe so, sir,

BERNIE   Ten feet exactly?

ASSISTANT   Ten feet three inches.

GRIERSON   I've told them until they're tired of hearing it, they're public servants first, filmmakers second, and *(to BERNIE)* artists never.

BERNIE   Good enough. Just angle that light a bit for me, will you?

KING   Treasury won't pay for fripperies, Mr. Grierson.

GRIERSON   Treasury won't be asked to. I've said to them, "The king's shilling must not be abused."

KING   I beg your pardon?

JANE   It's an allusion to the press gang, sir. Taking the king's shilling.

BERNIE   That's lovely.

KING   Yes. I see. Very good. The king's shilling.

GRIERSON   The king's millions, we should say.

BERNIE   All set? *(KING clears his throat.)* Roll sound.

ASSISTANT   "Stand On Guard," shot fifty-three, take two.

KING   My fellow Canadians. We are living in a time of unprecedented turmoil and conflict never before in human history. I'm sorry. Never before in human history...

BERNIE   Cut!

KING   Oh dear.

GRIERSON   Dinna fash y'sel, P.M. Clark Gable has the same trouble.

KING   It's hard to see the text as clearly as one could wish, when the er...

Layne Coleman, Andrew Akman, Graham Harley, Dixie Seatle and John Jarvis
photo © Lydia Pawelak

JANE   Might I suggest...?

KING   Yes, yes, anything you think...

JANE   If the Prime Minister could be a little more elevated...

KING   I'm trying to speak very naturally, Miss Barnes, as it were across the kitchen table.

JANE   Sitting a little higher, I meant.

GRIERSON   How does that seem to you, sir?

KING   Oh. Yes. Well it might be easier, that's true. *(He stretches himself to a more erect position, shuffles with his text, glasses, etc. The phone rings.)* It feels rather awkward, however... *(JANE, who has taken the phone and answered in fluent French, passes it to KING.)* What? No, no, he'll have to wait. *(to phone, importantly)* I'm with Grierson. We're making a movie!

JANE   Perhaps a couple of volumes of Hansard...

GRIERSON   ...might have a suitably elevating effect.

JANE Exactly.

GRIERSON *(to the ASSISTANT)* See what you can find. *(The ASSISTANT goes, returning in a few moments with two large books.)*

BERNIE *(to JANE)* Are you busy tonight?

JANE Not necessarily.

KING *(consulting a watch on a chain)* Miss Barnes!

JANE Sir?

KING The cabinet meeting at three. I'm just wondering. This may take a little longer than I had anticipated.

JANE I took the liberty of rescheduling for three-thirty.

KING Oh did you? Very prescient of you.

GRIERSON What's your name, lassie?

JANE Jane Barnes.

GRIERSON You must be indispensable.

JANE I am.

BERNIE *(to JANE)* So what do you say?

JANE What have you got in mind?

KING This film we are engaged upon – it will be widely distributed, I dare say?

GRIERSON Right across the country! A rousing picture of a nation girding herself for total war.

KING It will be shown in Quebec?

GRIERSON In what we call a "versioned" print, sir.

KING Ah. *(a beat)* Mr. Grierson, I think you know that the matter of conscription could well precipitate a national crisis?

GRIERSON So I understand, sir.

KING Recruiting is down to little over five thousand a month. Totally inadequate for our commitments.

JANE *(JANE and the ASSISTANT have been lifting KING up to the table, like a child at dinner.)* How's that, sir?

KING That's much better. It's more... er...

GRIERSON Commanding.

KING Well, I don't know that I'd...

GRIERSON *(to BERNIE)* When you're ready.

BERNIE *(to JANE)* Want to go to a movie?

JANE Maybe. Depends what's on.

KING *(pursuing the point)* On the question of conscription, I suppose a film like this could do a lot to...

GRIERSON Indeed it could, sir!

KING ...to stimulate and reinforce...

GRIERSON To stir the patriotic passion, sir. I guarantee it.

KING ...especially if it were possible to convey that recruiting is in fact proceeding rather more, ah, vigorously than, ah...

GRIERSON What do you have in mind, sir?

BERNIE Casablanca.

KING We must convey to our Quebec brethren that English Canada has been pulling its weight. More than pulling its weight, in fact.

GRIERSON I see.

KING So if a figure like, ah, ten thousand could be implied...

BERNIE Here we go. This time, can you make a point of looking steadily into the camera, sir?

KING What?

BERNIE It's kind of unsettling if your eyes are jiggling every which way.

KING I'll certainly try.

GRIERSON *(sternly)* I'm always telling them, "Public lies must not be told."

BERNIE *(urgently, to JANE)* The Rex, seven o'clock.

KING Mr. Grierson, I was very far from suggesting...

GRIERSON Rest assured, sir, that a most constructive picture will be painted...

BERNIE *(to KING)* All set? Roll sound.

JANE I'll buy the popcorn.

ASSISTANT "Stand On Guard," shot fifty-three, take three.

KING My fellow Canadians. We are living in a time of unprecedented turmoil and conflict. Never before in human history has the destiny of mankind seemed to hang so pelorously, so pelorous, so perilously...

BERNIE Cut!

KING Oh dear. I do apologize...

GRIERSON Not at all, not at all. We've got all day.

KING But I don't like, you know, to be wasting your film, and all these people's time…

BERNIE That's okay, Prime Minister, you're paying for it!

KING Perhaps if we took it one sentence at a time, and you could join them up somehow? You do that with film, don't you? A little sleight of hand, as it were?

GRIERSON Oh, there's all manner of ways of creating an illusion…

JANE *(intervening)* But I think it would be very much more effective if the Prime Minister were to rise to the occasion and deliver the speech straight off!

KING Well, I agree, Miss Barnes, but…

GRIERSON One moment, sir! *(to JANE)* Go on.

JANE *(to KING)* What I would suggest is that I stand just here *(beside the camera)*, and that you speak directly to me. Command my attention, sir. Convince me. Captivate me!

KING Well, I…

JANE I'll stand right here. Is that okay?

GRIERSON Jane Barnes, you're wasted here, do you know that?

JANE Are you ready, sir?

KING Yes, I believe so.

GRIERSON Give up all you have and follow me!

BERNIE Here we go. All set?

GRIERSON Report to the production pool nine o'clock Monday morning.

BERNIE Roll sound.

GRIERSON I'll give you a three-month contract.

ASSISTANT "Stand On Guard," shot fifty-three, take four!

JANE *(to KING)* Convince me!

> *If film clips are being used, the image of the actor playing KING suddenly appears, pre-recorded or by live video-feed, on a large screen, dramatic and commanding; otherwise his voice fills the theatre. N.B. This is not an actual excerpt from a film.*

KING My fellow Canadians. We are living in a time of unprecedented turmoil and conflict. Never before in human history has the destiny of mankind seemed to hang so perilously in the balance. Nation is massed against nation on a scale hitherto unknown in the dreadful annals of war. For the second time in a generation, the Dominion of Canada has taken her stand at the side of the mother country, in the face of a common adversary. Canadian men and women have come forward in ever-growing numbers, to volunteer their enthusiastic service in all the branches of our armed forces. On land, at sea, and in the air, Canadians are at the forefront of those armies now massing everywhere to drive Hitler and his Nazi hordes from their ill-gotten conquests. They are ready and they are eager to enter the fray, and before too long I believe I shall be able to report to you a bold and independent undertaking by Canadian units, that will enhance the standing of this country's fighting forces among the nations of the anti-fascist alliance. The way ahead is long and steep. The end of the struggle is not yet in sight. But with God's help, and with your courage and determination, at the end of the day we shall be triumphant.

Scene Three

Police sirens. Spotlight on the solitary figure of a man apparently tied to a chair, visible in the flickering light of a black and white TV. Suddenly loud and clear, the recorded voice of Pierre TRUDEAU, announcing the imposition of the War Measures Act.

TRUDEAU   ...If a democratic society is to continue to exist, it must be able to root out the cancer of an armed revolutionary movement that is bent on destroying the very basis of our freedom. For that reason, the government, following an analysis of the facts, including the requests of the government of Quebec and of the city of Montreal for urgent action, decided to proclaim the War Measures Act. It did so at four a.m. this morning, in order to permit the full weight of government to be brought quickly to bear on all those persons advocating or practicing violence as a means of achieving political ends. At the moment, the FLQ is holding hostage two men in the Montreal area, the one a British diplomat, the other a Quebec cabinet minister. They are threatened with murder.

The figure in the chair gets up and switches off the TV. It is GRIERSON, alone in his room in the Crescent Hotel, Montreal. He is 72 years old, wears glasses, has some occasional difficulty breathing, and is obviously waging war with the onset of old age. He presses his chest, feeling for pain. A police siren is heard, passing in the street. GRIERSON parts the curtains and looks out over the city.

GRIERSON   Can you hear those sirens, James Cross? They're calling for you. Are you still there? *(pause)* A man under sentence of death. *(He presses his chest again.)* Well, we're all that, aren't we? *(a beat)* Don't give way to despair, man. *(a beat)* "For who can bear to think himself forgotten?"

Faintly, the melody of "Oh My Darling, Clementine" (Percy Montrose) is heard, played on a harmonica. A YOUNG WOMAN appears, in a jacket suggestive of the 1930s, a cap perched at a jaunty angle, and smoking a cigarette. With her fingers she makes the rectangular frame of a lens, through which she inspects GRIERSON mockingly. GRIERSON stretches out his hand to her, in vain.

Scene Four

1942. The National Film Board. BERNIE, perched on a stool, is screening silent film footage on a Moviola – an archaic editing machine. Silhouetted behind a frosted glass window, in an outer office, is FREDA Linton, GRIERSON's secretary, who will take calls and speak through an office intercom. As the scene begins, GRIERSON enters through a door, accompanied by a loud fragment of Lorne Greene's narration from the film "Churchill's Island," audible from another screening room.

NARRATION "But today, the shipyards of North America sound their answer in the clang of hammers. New ships to release British merchantmen for service in the Atlantic.... And along Canada's coasts and rivers, the corvettes take to the water, to help Britain's hard-pressed destroyers keep that vital supply line open. Already the tide of battle may be turning. Already the wide Atlantic is becoming a graveyard for the raiders themselves..."

BERNIE *(without turning round)* Somebody shut that door! Can't hear yourself think around here. *(realizing that it's GRIERSON)* Oh, good! You're just in time. Look at that shot! Now wait... wait.... Dissolve. There! Look at that!

GRIERSON *(closing the door)* I'm looking.

BERNIE Took us half a day to get that.

GRIERSON No wonder you're over budget!

BERNIE Now watch the bird hovering there, see? See? Then it's going to dive... wait... there it goes! Straight for the fish.

GRIERSON Very pretty!

BERNIE And we dissolve... there... to the anxious watchers on the deck, faces tense, every nerve strained, scanning the horizons...

With another burst of sound from the nearby screening room, JANE Barnes enters hastily.

NARRATION Among the sand dunes move the troops, troops in steel helmets and battle dress, and armed with tommy guns that can cut a man in half at two hundred yards..."

JANE Hallo Bernie. I've got the other reel.

GRIERSON & BERNIE Shut that bloody door!

JANE Excuse me, sir.

GRIERSON Grierson.

JANE Sir?

GRIERSON The name's Grierson.

JANE Yes. Well. Sorry, Mr. Grierson...

GRIERSON Not Mr. Grierson.

JANE No?

GRIERSON Just "Grierson."

JANE I see.

GRIERSON Say it.

JANE *(imitating his strong Scottish accent)* "Grierson."

GRIERSON *(He notices the impertinence.)* That's right. Now sit, Jane Barnes. Look and learn. *(They watch the little screen of the Moviola.)* For God's sake, what's that blithering bird doing there again?

JANE Isn't it a bit out of focus, Bernie?

BERNIE It's coming, it's coming. It's what we call a rack-focus shot. There... see?

JANE Oh, *trés chic!*

GRIERSON Sheer self-indulgence.

BERNIE Damn it, Grierson, just because it's documentary, doesn't mean it has to be ugly. This is art!

GRIERSON Art be buggered. Where's the *punch*? You're not in this for your own blue eyes.

In the outer office the phone rings. FREDA picks it up.

JANE Mind where you're putting your cigarette! Isn't this stuff flammable?

FREDA *(on the intercom)* Call from the minister's office.

GRIERSON *(to intercom)* Put it through. *(to JANE)* Flammable? I wish to God it was! *(to phone)* Grierson. I see. Of course it's a lot of money! *(to BERNIE)* Art is the by-product of a job done properly. *(to phone)* No, I'm listening. Now you tell the minister that the rousing of a nation's heart and will is worth every penny, and if he's not prepared to spend it, we might as well pack up and go home. And tell him the P.M. understands that, even if he doesn't. *(hangs up)*

JANE *(commenting on the film)* Now that's beautiful, isn't it?

GRIERSON Oh, I don't deny that. But we've got a war to sell. Do you think Dr. Goebbels is sitting over there in Berlin making nature study films?

BERNIE You're deliberately missing the point. I'm trying to establish a subtle mood here. Watching and waiting.

GRIERSON Spare me your moods, laddie! I've promised the P.M. an action movie, "Canada Strikes Back."

BERNIE You're watching it!

Phone rings again in the outer office.

John Jarvis, Layne Coleman and Dixie Seatle
photo © Lydia Pawelak

GRIERSON I'm watching the sea and ships and birds and anxious watchers scanning the bloody horizon – beautifully done, I grant you – but I'm not seeing a movie.

FREDA It's Miss Barton, sir.

GRIERSON There's nothing happening! *(to phone)* Judith, my dear, can you cook? Because the Department of Agriculture has a surplus of apples, and they want a little film on how to cook 'em. No more than fifteen minutes, non-theatrical. Colour. Do me a little treatment, there's a love. *(He hangs up and addresses his office intercom.)* Freda? I don't want any more calls just now.

FREDA Right you are, sir.

GRIERSON *(carrying right on)* What Slater is giving us here is a lot of very elegant, very lovingly captured, foreplay.

JANE Bernie!

GRIERSON It's very artful, as foreplay should rightly be. But it creates tension without releasing it. The spectator out there in Eyebrow, Saskatchewan, not to mention Mr. Mackenzie King, wants more for his dollar.

JANE He wants a climax.

GRIERSON He does. Set-up and pay-off. Documentary film has a job to do. The luxuries of the aesthetic approach to cinema – we don't have time for them. Do you see that, Slater? Do you grasp it?

BERNIE You want something more vigorous. More aggressive.

GRIERSON Exactly. Your picture is beautiful – but it's languid. Look at your editing – dissolve, dissolve! Take a lesson from the Russians, from Eisenstein. Dialectical cutting, the *collision* of images. A versus B equals C. Bang, bang, bang! And in a sequence about anti-submarine patrols, I want submarines.

BERNIE German submarines?

GRIERSON For preference, yes. You tell me they're out there. Find one. Sink it. *(preparing to lead them into his office)* All right now, time for a wee dram!

BERNIE Heck, they don't just pop up on command, you know.

GRIERSON Then fake it. Get one of ours and paint swastikas on it!

JANE Isn't that cheating?

GRIERSON *(grimly)* It's in a good cause. *(to the intercom)* Freda?

FREDA Yes, sir?

GRIERSON Call the P.M. for me, will you? *(to BERNIE)* Do you see it? The crippled submarine is already awash. The ocean swell foams over its deck. The conning tower sinks from sight. *(adopting the famous Lorne Greene voice)* "And so, inexorably, the menace of Hitler's prowling predators, the modern monsters of the deep, is beaten back once more…." Wide shot of convoy steaming on, martial music builds to climax, fade to black, end of sequence. *(intercom buzz)* Come on, laddie; you've got to take that talent of yours and give it a kick in the arse!

FREDA Your call to the P.M. has gone through.

GRIERSON *(to phone)* Prime Minister, very good of you to take the call. Well, here's the point. I want the loan of a submarine for a couple of days. That's right, sir. May I say that I have your authority? *(to BERNIE)* You've got one.

BERNIE Holy Jeez!

GRIERSON *(to BERNIE)* Don't mention it. *(to phone, motioning for silence)* Come again? Oh really, sir? I'm sorry to hear it. No indeed! Right you are, sir. *(hangs up)* Well, children, the P.M. tells me he has lost one of his secretaries. Rather a flighty girl, he says. He's afraid she may have absconded with the cameraman. You wouldn't do a thing like that, would you Jane?

JANE   Oh, I might.

GRIERSON   Don't. That's an order. You're here to learn and work. *(The phone rings once more. GRIERSON claps his hands.)* All right, that's it for tonight; home for your beauty sleep. Slater, show this young woman the ropes, will you? But keep your grubby paws off her. I'll have no fornicating in this Film Board. *(harshly)* And remember, I personally want to see that submarine sinking with all hands!

BERNIE   *(on his way out)* Leave it to me! You're going to love it!

GRIERSON   Oh, Jane, just hang on a minute, will you? *(She stays, questioningly.)*

FREDA   Mr. Grierson, sir…

GRIERSON   I said no more calls.

FREDA   It's Mrs. Grierson, sir.

GRIERSON   Well, that's different, put her through. *(to JANE)* Why don't you just pull the door to? *(Taking the phone, he gets out a bottle of scotch – Black & White – and motions JANE to pour a shot for each of them, also to light a couple of cigarettes. As she sits on the corner of his desk, he casually puts a hand on the back of her neck.)* Margaret, my dear. No, not at all, any time, any time. Och aye, I'm still at it. Production meetings – the usual thing. Well, a couple of hours yet, I'm afraid. The Film Board never sleeps, you know. That's right. Get you to your rest. À tout à l'heure, my love. *(He hangs up, addresses intercom.)* Freda, you can call it a day.

FREDA   Thank you, sir. *(She switches off the light in her office.)*

JANE   *(detaching herself from GRIERSON's hand)* Is this "the usual thing?"

>   *GRIERSON proceeds to turn the dial of a short-wave radio on his desk, trying to get a fix on a station. Suddenly, out of the gabble of voices and crackle of static, a German voice emerges loud and clear – actually a bit of a GOEBBELS speech from "Triumph of the Will."*

GRIERSON   *(ignoring her question)* There! Do you hear that? Berlin. That's him.

JANE   That's Hitler?

GRIERSON   Dr. Joseph Goebbels. *Reichsminister für Aufklärung und Propaganda.* That's what we're up against.

JANE   A bit late for a production meeting, isn't it?

GRIERSON   Oh, the Film Board never sleeps, you know. *(a beat)* So. Miss Barnes. What have they found for you to do?

JANE   Well, nothing at all, so far. I mean, apart from running errands, and watching Bernie.

GRIERSON And what did they say to you in Personnel?

JANE Production Assistant.

GRIERSON Aye, well, that's where most people start out.

JANE I was just hoping for something a bit less… menial.

GRIERSON Let me have a look at your hands. The lassies mostly go in for editing, or negative cutting.

JANE Of course. Like sewing and embroidery. Delicate work.

GRIERSON And to what more exalted position do you aspire?

JANE I want to make films.

GRIERSON As a director? And what experience do you have?

JANE I've seen a lot of films.

GRIERSON "Casablanca."

JANE Among others.

GRIERSON And that constitutes a grounding in the craft, does it?

JANE Well, I can't see there's all that much to it, actually.

GRIERSON Can ye not?

JANE It's only you men that make such a mystery out of it. You load the camera, point it, focus it, and shoot.

GRIERSON Aye, but what do you point it *at* Jane?

JANE Whatever tells the real story, Grierson.

GRIERSON *(a beat)* You're not just a pretty face, are you!

JANE That's not what you hired me for, is it?

GRIERSON Now don't get lippy with me, my girl, or I'll put you across my knee and smack your bottom for you.

JANE I believe you would!

GRIERSON And I believe you'd like it.

JANE *(a beat; uncomfortably)* It's quite late… I think perhaps I ought to be…

GRIERSON Running off to your chaste couch, like a good girl?

JANE Leaving you to your production meeting. *(awkward moment)* I do think perhaps I should, don't you?

GRIERSON *(a beat)* Get you gone, then.

> *A beat. JANE goes out abruptly, leaving GRIERSON to pour himself another scotch. He turns once more to the radio and listens intently. There*

is a change of light and the figure of Dr. Joseph GOEBBELS appears in the office and addresses GRIERSON.

GOEBBELS You are deceiving your people, my friend. Painting the swastika on a submarine – shame on you!

GRIERSON There's no essential deception involved.

GOEBBELS German U-boats are slaughtering your Atlantic convoys! Every month we are sinking dozens of your ships.

GRIERSON *(fiercely)* I do know that, Joseph!

GOEBBELS You think the people are stupid?

GRIERSON Disposed to believe, let us say.

GOEBBELS And you would take advantage of their credulity?

GRIERSON It's not a matter of taking advantage.

GOEBBELS You do not have to justify yourself to me, my friend. I have been in this game longer than you – and I *know* the people are stupid. The *Führer* himself has said, "When you address the masses, you must remember that they can memorize only the simplest idea, repeated until even the stupidest can grasp it. The primitive masses will never fall victim to a small lie…"

GRIERSON "…since they themselves are always lying in small matters…"

GOEBBELS "…but they will certainly fall victim to a great lie." We are in the same game, my friend, and you know it.

GRIERSON Don't you whisper to me that there's no difference between us.

GOEBBELS Leading the people to believe what it is necessary for them to believe. *Ja?*

GRIERSON It's not the same.

GOEBBELS No?

GRIERSON You seek to enslave them in their ignorance.

GOEBBELS Do we really want them to be free?

GRIERSON I am giving them hope! I am on the side of the angels.

GOEBBELS …and that makes all the difference? *(GRIERSON is silent.)* There are no angels, Herr Grierson.

GRIERSON *(Butting out his cigarette and switching off the radio. GOEBBELS is disappearing.)* There are angels and there are devils, *Herr Reichsminister*, and the angels are going to prevail! *(quietly)* The angels are going to prevail.

Stage lights to black. A spotlight picks out the figure of the YOUNG WOMAN from the earlier scene, setting out to cross the stage, as if on a balance beam. She has a travelling bag in one hand, and a parasol in

>   *the other, like a circus performer. There is a muted roll of drums, as at a circus. GRIERSON, like a ringmaster, encourages the young woman commandingly through a megaphone.*

(almost whispering at first) Come! Come on! That's the spirit! You can do it. Come to me now! You're going to make it. Don't look down! Just keep going. *(etc.)*

>   *When the YOUNG WOMAN is about two-thirds of the way along the beam, there is heard suddenly the urgent hideous whooping of a ship's emergency klaxon. The drum roll increases in intensity. She hesitates, stops, fearfully.*

Don't look down! Come to me! Come on! You're nearly there! *(a great cry)* NO!

>   *Suddenly BERNIE appears, on the deck of a ship heaving in the ocean swell, a camera precariously balanced on a tripod. He is yelling directions through a megaphone into the teeth of the wind. He wears a hat like GRIERSON's.*

BERNIE Is everybody set? Okay, roll camera! Let go depth charges! Go! Go! We haven't got much film left. Only two hundred feet. It'll have to do! Come on, it's our last chance! Where's that explosion? We can't hold it much longer! Okay, go submarine! *(orgasmically)* Jesus, there she goes! Jesus! Jeeeeeeesus! I did it! I did it, Grierson, you bastard, I did it! *(There is a dreadful, low, reverberating boom. The light goes out, the drum roll and the klaxon cease. In the silence that follows, a flute plays the melody of "Oh My Darling, Clementine.")*

Scene Five

>   *Police sirens, as before. GRIERSON is back in his 1970 apartment. Bottles, a couple of glasses, and some bowls of nuts are set out. The phone rings, and he answers it.*

GRIERSON Grierson. *(pause)* Och, aye, so I have heard! Congratulations! *(There is a knock at the door. GRIERSON calls without looking.)* Come in, you're early, get yourself a drink! *(to phone)* I had nothing to do with it. They didn't ask me. Eh? Oh, you flatter me. *(JANE has entered. Nearly thirty years older, but unmistakable, she actually looks a bit like GRIERSON used to do, with a rather mannish trench coat and hat.)* No, not tonight. I'll be having some students here, my Saturday night crowd. *(pause)* If martial law doesn't keep them away, that is.

JANE *(mimicking his accent, as of old)* "Grierson?"

GRIERSON *(looking over his glasses and recognizing her)* Angels and ministers of grace defend us! *(to phone)* What? Eh, well now, on second thoughts, do if you like! Come right over. They'll be tickled pink to meet the Big Cheese. Whenever you like. À toute à l'heure! *(hangs up; pause)* And is it Jane Barnes?

JANE Do you mind?

GRIERSON   How could I mind?

JANE   Well, I just thought...

GRIERSON   *(taking her hands)* I'm very glad.

JANE   I'm just passing through. On my way to India, actually.

GRIERSON   You certainly picked a dramatic time to arrive.

JANE   Can you believe this is happening? In Canada?

GRIERSON   But you passed through the barricades unscathed? How did you...?

JANE   They told me at the Board you were here.

GRIERSON   As you see. Grierson's second coming.

JANE   *(a beat)* You're looking good.

GRIERSON   All things considered. *(pause)* Well. Is this a social call, or...?

JANE   Or what?

GRIERSON   Or do you want something?

JANE   *(lightly)* Oh, I may want to pick some bones with you.

GRIERSON   *(also lightly)* Mine or yours? Well. Take off your coat. Have a drink. Scotch still to your liking?

JANE   *(looking around)* You're having a party?

GRIERSON   Students. My "seminar." Let me have a look at you. Age hath not apparently withered you. And as for your infinite variety, I can't imagine it growing stale. *(as JANE offers to pour him a drink)* I'm off it.

JANE   You're not!

GRIERSON   Off it altogether and completely. Doctor's orders. My brother, actually. Gave me an ultimatum. It nearly killed me.

JANE   The booze?

GRIERSON   No, giving it up. The ciggies too. *(a beat)* Scarcely a pleasure left to call my own. And what have you been doing with yourself?

JANE   I've been living in Vancouver.

GRIERSON   Pleasure enough in itself, I'm told.

JANE   Making documentary films. What else did Grierson's girls ever do?

GRIERSON   Oh, all manner of things. Marry, have babies...

JANE   *(taking a gulp of scotch)* Tried that.

GRIERSON   You ran off with young Tarzan, as I recall. Spiteful wench.

JANE   Didn't last, of course.

GRIERSON I knew it wouldn't.

JANE You should have told me.

GRIERSON Would you have listened?

JANE You had a TV program or something? Back in Scotland?

GRIERSON I've knocked around. Preaching and teaching all nations. If you happen to think you've got hold of a bit of the truth, then it's your God-given duty to hammer it into as many other heads as your situation gives you access to.

JANE Sounds like the Grierson we knew and loved!

GRIERSON Did we?

JANE *(ignoring the question)* And they finally brought you back to Canada?

GRIERSON Well, not exactly. Different "they."

JANE It was shameful, what was done to you. Russian spy indeed!

GRIERSON Nobody quite said that.

JANE Nobody "quite said" anything. Not a voice raised in your defence.

GRIERSON Oh, voices were raised. Good, hesitant Canadian voices. *(a beat)* It changed my plans rather.

JANE It destroyed you, that's what it did!

GRIERSON *(needled)* I wouldn't say that. I'm still here.

JANE *(a beat)* I would have given them such a blast, they'd never have known what was hitting them. You know that, don't you?

GRIERSON Jane, I believe you would. Help yourself, by the way. Nobody waits to be asked around here.

JANE But I was in London by then.

GRIERSON With young Tarzan.

JANE *(pouring herself another scotch)* Among others.

GRIERSON The Prime Minister always said you were a flighty one.

JANE I did think about contacting you a number of times, but…

GRIERSON Aye. *(a beat)* And you're on your way to India, did you say? What for?

JANE It's a UNESCO project…

GRIERSON I did a stint with them myself.

JANE …training local medics to use eight millimetre cameras.

GRIERSON *(quoting himself)* "Eight millimetre films for eight millimetre minds."

JANE Don't start! It's to help people in the villages use film as an educational tool.

GRIERSON *(skeptically)* Sounds very worthy, I'm sure.

JANE Yes, it is. *(a beat)* Want to come?

GRIERSON To India? What would I do there?

JANE What are you doing here?

GRIERSON Have ye no heard? I am a "professor." Old "Doc" Grierson. I harangue the young. And what is more remarkable, they listen to me. At three-score-and-ten, I think I have found my vocation. Word has got round that I am a "groove," and also a "gas," and now I have an audience scarcely less than Jesus for the Sermon on the Mount, hanging on my every preachment. In these anarchic times, they hunger for authority.

> *As he speaks, a young woman, TANYA Rossides, silently prepares a lectern, adjusting the height of a microphone, providing a jug of water and a glass, and setting a little vase of flowers. She also prepares to tape GRIERSON's lecture, and at an appropriate moment, whispers a brief sound cue into her own mike.*

They're a sweet, ingenuous bunch, for the most part. They know of nothing prior to 1955. They smoke "pot," and seem to sleep with each other all the time – sometimes, I gather, in multiples of three and four. They cannot, or at all events will not, read. They desire to make movies, and to exercise their artistic freedom. To paraphrase the late lamented Hermann Goering, when I hear the words "artistic freedom," I reach for my gun! *(He moves to the lectern.)* Believe me, the much-ballyhooed freedom of the artist is earned, not given. "Poetic licence." It's a good idea. No-one should be allowed to practice poetry without one. In any civilized country, people need a licence to drive a car. In Great Britain you need a licence to own a dog! But on this great continent, any idiot can use a movie camera, or have a baby, without so much as a with-your-leave or a by-your-leave. Now that's where I'd be issuing licences! And not every Jack and Jill would get one either. For babies, perhaps. Put a baby in indulgent hands, and you can only ruin one mind at a time. Besides which, babies have a way of getting their own back! But a movie camera is a gift of God, and should only be entrusted to his priests, sworn to poverty, chastity, and, yes, obedience! The filmmaker, above all the documentary filmmaker – and that's the only member of the species worth his salt – is first and foremost a teacher. If he's not a teacher, he's nothing. He or she, I make no distinction. And you don't hear a lot of bleating, thank God, about the "freedom of the teacher." "Men have no rights, only duties" – so said my compatriot Carlyle, and I would apply that to teachers five times over. *(TANYA takes a flash photograph of GRIERSON, catching him for a moment in a prophet-like pose.)*

> *Wearing a leather NFB jacket and a Che Guevara beret, MICHAEL Schneider bursts into the lecture hall, full of excitement. He and*

GRIERSON will contend for mastery in front of the class of students, while TANYA records and takes pictures.

MICHAEL Grierson! Have you seen what's going on out there?

GRIERSON *(looking over his glasses)* Mr. Schneider, if you plan to continue attending these lectures, would you do us all the courtesy of arriving on time?

MICHAEL Grierson, it's happening! It's happening, man. Right down there, it's the real thing – the fucking army, they're all over the streets.

GRIERSON Spare us the expletives, if you please!

MICHAEL There's a guy with a machine gun, right outside this building!

GRIERSON It's not a machine gun, it's an M-16 automatic rifle.

MICHAEL What's he doing there?

GRIERSON Sit down and be quiet, young man. You're disrupting my class.

MICHAEL Grierson, there's an armoured car at the corner of Sherbrooke and Guy. What's it doing there?

GRIERSON You know quite well what it's doing; it's protecting me. Protecting you too.

MICHAEL It's not protecting me, that's for sure!

GRIERSON Then it's protecting me from you. Now, will you...

MICHAEL It's an army of occupation. We've been invaded, man! Like Czechoslovakia. Moscow sending in the tanks. Trudeau's declared war on Quebec!

GRIERSON Would you care to examine that analogy, young man?

MICHAEL Don't keep giving me that "young man" shit. "Old man." You don't know what's going on here. You're old. And you're English.

GRIERSON *(with mock outrage)* How dare you!

MICHAEL Scottish. Same difference.

GRIERSON *(He's enjoying the whole process.)* We'll deal with that one later!

MICHAEL You don't know what's happening. How can you?

GRIERSON I've got a television. I can see what's happening.

MICHAEL You can't see anything on television.

GRIERSON I can see that a terrorist group is attempting to blackmail the government, by means of kidnapping and intimidation.

MICHAEL It's the action of a revolutionary vanguard.

GRIERSON A few isolated hooligans do not constitute a revolution – except in the overheated brains of bourgeois romantics with nothing better to think about.

MICHAEL Then why is the army out there in the streets? Why the War Measures Act? That's a counter-revolution!

GRIERSON It's a police action. A reinforcement of the civil power.

MICHAEL Trudeau himself says it's an apprehended insurrection. He's scared, man. They're scared.

GRIERSON Insurrection, nothing.

MICHAEL You mean he's lying?

GRIERSON I mean that we're in absolutely no position to judge.

MICHAEL Right! No-one's in a position to judge. No-one knows anything. We only know what they tell us. And they lie to us all the time!

GRIERSON "They" lie to us?

MICHAEL The gang who control things. The bosses, the politicians, the bankers, the newspaper owners, the sell-out managers of American branch-plants…

GRIERSON Good God, man, you've lost all your critical faculties. You're simply parrotting the FLQ manifesto.

MICHAEL You saw that?

GRIERSON A shameful capitulation. Putting that inflammatory nonsense on the air!

MICHAEL It was fantastic, man! Millions of people saw that. Everyone in Quebec. And they knew it was *true!* People aren't stupid. The TV, the newspapers, it's all bullshit, all the crap about democracy and free choice and freedom of speech, and we just eat it up, and go on buying things and think that's freedom…. But when someone comes along and tells the truth, that the whole system is controlled by the big corporations who manage *everything*, including the TV and the newspapers, then people wake up and say *That's right! (pause)* And they saw it on TV. I mean, that is fantastic.

GRIERSON And you think that justifies kidnapping…?

MICHAEL Yes!

GRIERSON …and the threat of murder?

MICHAEL Yes! If that's what you have to do. There's no freedom of speech until there's freedom to be heard. Access, right?

GRIERSON So any maniac with a gun can go into a TV studio and force the producer to put his rabble-rousing clap-trap on the air – or he'll blow his head off?

MICHAEL   As long as the means of communication are controlled by the capitalist establishment.

GRIERSON   Oh, Michael! And the same goes for the Fascists? Well? The Neo-Nazis? The White Supremacists?

MICHAEL   It's not the same.

GRIERSON   Of course it's the same! Will I hear you cheering when some little thug gets onto national TV and tells us that the world is run by a Jewish conspiracy and we should send them all to the gas chambers?

MICHAEL   It's not…

GRIERSON   And when millions of people hear this message and suddenly say to themselves *That's right!* Because they will, you know. They did already. And we fought them. When the monster of cynicism raises its head, you don't debate with it, you fight it.

MICHAEL   Oh sure, it was so simple, back then. The Nazi monster. But where is it now?

GRIERSON   It's holding a gun to the heads of two innocent men. And to your head, and my head.

MICHAEL   No! The monster is out there on the streets, with guns and tanks. To defend their precious "free society," they send in the army. "Apprehended insurrection"? Do you buy that? Look out the window. Can you see an insurrection? All you can *see* is armed soldiers and tanks. So if you want to find out what's really happening, you have to look at the TV. Only *that* little window doesn't open on the real world at all. There's only images, flickering lights. You know that, Grierson. You practically invented it, back in the war. It's what they hired you for. People across this country saw what you showed them. "Canada Carries On," Lorne Greene, "the mighty struggle of free peoples everywhere…"

GRIERSON   *(finally angry, overlapping MICHAEL)* Young man, I will not have you saying to me that what we were doing in the war, in this country, for this country, is now to be construed in the eyes of bistro radicals, too young to know anything about it, as some kind of a crime!

> On the screen, or on the audio track, an excerpt from "Corvette Port Arthur" – the sinking of a German submarine.

Scene Six

GRIERSON is meeting with a distraught Mackenzie KING.

KING   A disaster, Mr. Grierson. Dieppe. Dieppe! An unmitigated disaster.

GRIERSON   It was a bold undertaking, sir.

KING I have sent hundreds of Canadian boys to be slaughtered. Possibly thousands. As many more taken prisoner.

GRIERSON The fortunes of war, Prime Minister, the fortunes of war.

KING Do not attempt to make light of it!

GRIERSON I am very far from making light of it, sir.

KING And I shall be held personally responsible, do you see?

GRIERSON You did not give the order, sir.

KING I concurred in it. I was consulted and I concurred. What am I to tell the Canadian public? A monumental folly.

GRIERSON It might be wiser not to tell them that for a start.

KING I was led on. Churchill himself was most persuasive.

GRIERSON I'm sure he was!

KING An all-Canadian effort, he said. Such a tonic for recruiting!

GRIERSON If I may say so, sir…

KING Politically disastrous, of course. No positive construction to be put on it. When the whole story of this gets out…

GRIERSON Perhaps a greater good dictates that it should not.

KING Ah. A greater good. *(a beat)* The newspapers can, of course, be depended upon.

GRIERSON The stories so far say only that a raid took place. *(reading headlines from newspapers on the desk)* "Dieppe Raid a Second Front Dress Rehearsal." "Canada Rolls Drums of Death for Hitler."

KING *(back in the distraught mode)* Such a tragic waste of life. One can only feel it as a test of some kind.

GRIERSON We must take it in our stride.

KING *(peevishly)* I must say, Grierson, that I was looking to you to retrieve something from this debacle!

GRIERSON Prime Minister?

KING I have always defended the Film Board's budget – against considerable opposition, I might add.

GRIERSON May I remind you, sir, that our entire film crew were killed.

KING I stand admonished. *(a beat)* Everything lost, then?

GRIERSON I'm afraid so.

KING No photographic record. *(a beat)* We have to give the public some account. Silence would be all too eloquent.

GRIERSON *(reluctantly)* We do have a film nearly ready for release.

KING A film?

GRIERSON Arising from a suggestion of your own. "Canada Strikes Back."

KING What a painful irony!

GRIERSON Canadian troops in action in various theatres of the war.

KING It will, of course, have to be withheld.

GRIERSON It gives a rather forceful picture of Canada's contribution, in a general way. There are actual scenes of an amphibious landing.

KING Ah.

GRIERSON Filmed on manoeuvres, naturally.

KING *(despondently)* Yes, yes, I see. Quite useless, of course.

GRIERSON But which might conceivably…

KING Go on.

GRIERSON Which might be presented in such a way…

KING …as to convey the impression… it is possible to do that with film, is it not?

GRIERSON It is possible.

KING To convey a positive impression, without actually drawing attention to the, ah, specifics of the case. *(pause)* I see. *(pause)* The truth will come out eventually, of course. *(There is a lighting change. Lights fade on KING, GRIERSON crosses to JANE and BERNIE, still in 1942.)*

GRIERSON *(aggressively)* What are you going to do? Are you going to tell the mothers and fathers of thousands of boys that a stupid, bloody mistake was made, a futile cock-up for the sake of a public relations stunt?

BERNIE *(blankly)* So…?

GRIERSON So you're going to take that film of yours and recut it.

BERNIE What with?

GRIERSON I want you to construct a commando raid.

BERNIE We haven't any footage.

GRIERSON Improvise, Slater, improvise! You've got footage of troops embarking, you've got assault craft, troops wading ashore, charging up a beach…

BERNIE Jesus Christ, you're not asking me to recreate Dieppe? Our guys were killed, for God's sake!

GRIERSON You know how it's done. Cut it together with naval bombardment, air support by fighter planes, lay in a whole lot of smoke and banging, and you've got a raid.

JANE Excuse me, but isn't there another small problem here? *(They look at her.)* All the boys who died. We don't mention them? We say it didn't happen?

GRIERSON You say nothing. There was a raid. The public knows that much already. The film will show a raid. Canadian troops in an aggressive action. The public will make certain desirable inferences.

> *There is suddenly an excerpt from the 1943 film, "Letter from Overseas," implying that the Dieppe raid has been a successful undertaking.*

SOUNDTRACK *(after a few moments of hectic battle-sounds and martial music)* "…And when we sailed away, we left the littered beaches to remind the Germans that we had punched one hole in Hitler's fortress, and that it wouldn't be the last!"

> *The scene shifts to GRIERSON's office. Silence.*

JANE *(shocked)* But that's sheer bloody propaganda!

GRIERSON It's not sheer bloody propaganda, my girl, it's genuine, unabashed, wholehearted, bloody propaganda! What are these timid, shrinking little sensibilities that cower before the word "propaganda," as if it were a communicable disease? "Propaganda." From the Latin, "things to be propagated." As in "the Propagation of the Faith." We are propagating a Faith, and so is everybody in this whole bloody organization. Or if they aren't, they shouldn't be here. Grierson's first commandment: "No-one without a Faith should be allowed to propagate." *(pause)* We are not reflecting reality, we are creating reality. "Art is not a mirror but a hammer." Who said that? *(no reply)* Trotsky. If you say with sufficient authority that something is true, it becomes true.

JANE *(bitterly)* As Joseph Goebbels knows better than anyone.

GRIERSON Exactly. Do you think you can shoot me down by firing Joseph Goebbels out of your little pop-gun? German propaganda is brilliant, masterful, and if we can't match it, we're done for. *(JANE is walking out.)* Jane! Come back here, damn it!

JANE *(turning on him)* It's such a shoddy deception. And for what? To save Mr. King's bloody bacon. Is that all we're here for?

GRIERSON It's a question of national morale. There's no room here for private scrupulosities.

JANE *(wildly)* What about integrity? What about telling the truth?

GRIERSON *(This is his creed. He demands their belief.)* Now listen to me! It's a necessary job – you do it and get it over with. And if you have to hold your nose a bit, well, so be it. But then, if you want a film worth making, give me one!

Give me something to dramatize the values that we're fighting for. Can you do that? Can you bring alive the idea of democracy, the idea of equality, the dignity of labour.... What do you say, Jane? What do you say, Slater?

JANE All right, then... labour, work, the home front... what about that?

GRIERSON The drama of the working man....

BERNIE A drama, with a story? Dialogue?

GRIERSON If you can find the voices, let's hear them. The steelworkers, the train men...

JANE The dockers...

GRIERSON Miners.... Now there's a film for you! Coal. The men in the mines. "Blood and toil and tears and sweat." You want truth? Show me the truth of that! All grit and no glamour. The drama of the Fact.

BERNIE (*enthusiastically*) Now you're talking! When do we start?

GRIERSON Finish the job you're doing, then go at it. Give me something sensational – the grime on the faces, the straining muscles, the ordinary heroism of work. Do you see it? "We are but warriors for the working day."

BERNIE It's gotta be! Trotsky?

JANE (*despite herself*) Shakespeare. *Henry the Fifth.*

BERNIE Right! I was going to say Shakespeare.

GRIERSON And there's your title: "Workers are Warriors." What do you say, Slater?

BERNIE Theatrical release, say fifteen minutes?

GRIERSON Shoot for a twenty.

BERNIE All original footage?

GRIERSON Plus compilation. Go wherever you need to go. Go to Alberta, go to Cape Breton. Shoot five thousand feet. Intercut footage from Britain. Better still, from Russia. Get it from the embassy. (*to intercom*) Freda, love, are you there?

FREDA (*becoming visible in silhouette behind her frosted glass*) Here, sir.

GRIERSON Give a call tomorrow to Colonel Zabotin at the Soviet embassy. Tell him Grierson is wanting that little deal we talked about.

FREDA Just that?

GRIERSON He'll know what it means. (*to JANE and BERNIE*) Our Bolshevik friends owe me a couple of favours.

BERNIE Could I have Jane on this?

GRIERSON Have you shown her the ropes? *(to JANE)* Can you tell the front end of a camera from the arse end?

BERNIE *(ardently)* She's pretty damn good.

GRIERSON *(an arm round her shoulder)* Are you, Jane? Are you pretty damn good?

JANE I think I am, yes.

BERNIE Put her on as assistant director!

GRIERSON You think she can handle that, do you Slater?

BERNIE I'd say so. Sure she can!

GRIERSON Fine. I'll take your word for it.

BERNIE Great!

GRIERSON *(to JANE)* Jane. You're the director.

JANE Seriously?

GRIERSON Why not? You can take Slater here as the cameraman, if you like.

BERNIE This is a joke, right? You're joking.

JANE *(teasing)* Is he any good?

BERNIE Damn it, Grierson, you can't do that!

GRIERSON Oh yes I can. *(phone rings)*

BERNIE *(He is really mad.)* I have a right to that film. I have two years experience. How much does she have? None at all. *(to JANE)* No offence, but it's true!

GRIERSON *(to BERNIE)* So she'll be relying on you to help her! *(to intercom)* Who is it?

FREDA It's Mrs. Grierson, sir.

GRIERSON Ask her to hold a minute, would you? *(to JANE)* Do you think you can do it? Speak now, or forever hold your peace.

JANE Yes, I can do it.

GRIERSON Good girl! Take the ball and run with it.

BERNIE This really stinks, you know that? *(He is leaving.)*

GRIERSON Stop sulking, Slater, and see that she does a professional job. I expect you to teach her everything I know. *(BERNIE has gone. JANE is about to follow.)* Oh, Jane! *(JANE looks at him questioningly.)* Why don't you just, ah, pull the door to? *(As on the previous occasion, he gets out a bottle of scotch. Without having to be told, JANE pours a shot for each of them, and lights two cigarettes. He takes the glass of scotch from JANE and addresses the phone.)* Margaret, my dear. No, not at all, we're just wrapping up. The young people are going home to their beds. *(to the intercom)* Freda, love, you can pack it in for today. *(to phone)* Oh, in an hour or two. The usual thing. A bunch of paperwork. Is it midnight? *(He looks at his watch.)* No, don't wait up. À toute à l'heure, my love. *(He hangs up, raises his glass to JANE.)* Well, here's to your first Oscar!

JANE   Thank you.

GRIERSON   *(finding some big band jazz on the radio – "One O'Clock Jump", by Count Basie, Benny Goodman Orchestra)* I'm giving you a big chance, girl.

JANE   You won't be sorry.

GRIERSON   Don't let me down, now. I'll be looking for something exceptional.

JANE   You'll get it, I promise you. *(She sits in his desk chair.)*

GRIERSON   I must say you're pretty cocky, for one so young. *(JANE says nothing.)* How old *are* you?

JANE   What has that got to do with anything? How old are you?

GRIERSON   More than twice your age.

JANE   So what?

GRIERSON   So what, indeed!

JANE   Does that bother you?

GRIERSON   And don't you be taking any nonsense from young Slater!

JANE   What kind of nonsense do you mean?

GRIERSON   He's obviously daft about you.

JANE   Obviously.

GRIERSON   Can't keep his eyes off you… dishiest thing he's ever seen.

JANE   *(inspecting the Oscar on GRIERSON's desk)* All adoration gratefully accepted.

GRIERSON   Oh Jane, he's still wet behind the ears!

JANE   He's a nice boy.

GRIERSON   Oh, they're all nice boys. You want better than that.

JANE   Really? What do I want? *(pause)* What do I want? *(Standing behind her, he puts his hands on her shoulders.)* Is this what I want?

GRIERSON   Is it not? *(There is a slow number playing on the radio. He draws her to her feet, and into a slow dance with him. She is as tall as he is, and thoughtfully removes her shoes.)*

JANE   Is this part of the deal?

GRIERSON   That's a low blow!

JANE   Is it?

GRIERSON Do you think I'd stoop to that?

JANE How would I know?

GRIERSON I don't do this every day, you know.

JANE Not what I've heard, actually.

GRIERSON Then you've heard wrong! *(a beat)* You're a very captivating young woman, Jane Barnes.

JANE You're not such a bad old buffer yourself, Grierson.

GRIERSON Not so much of the "old buffer," if you please.

JANE You're more than twice my age, so I've heard.

GRIERSON All the better to keep you in line.

JANE *(a beat)* And you're a married man.

GRIERSON Does that constitute an impediment, Miss Barnes?

JANE Does it for you, Mr. Grierson?

GRIERSON "Let me not to the marriage of true minds admit impediment."

JANE I don't think it's "minds" we're talking about here.

GRIERSON You know, I've not encountered anyone quite like you.

JANE Does that frighten you?

> At this moment, BERNIE marches in.

Oh! Bernie!

BERNIE *(He is breathless. This is a speech he has been rehearsing.)* Look, I just want to say, er, that I've thought things over, and of course Jane should direct the film, and, er, I'd be only too glad to help in whatever way I can. *(a beat)* Oh. Excuse me. Am I interrupting something?

JANE Oh no!

GRIERSON Not at all, not at all. We're just wrapping up. Well, Jane…

JANE I'll get you a treatment by Monday.

GRIERSON Yes. Good. That would be… good.

BERNIE *(to JANE)* Do you want a lift, by the way?

JANE What?

BERNIE I can give you a ride home, if you like.

JANE Oh, no, that's okay, really…

BERNIE It's no problem. It's not even out of my way.

JANE I'd really quite like the walk, actually.

BERNIE It's pouring rain out there!

JANE Oh. Is it?

BERNIE Let me give you a ride.

GRIERSON Why don't you, Jane? It's late, it's raining…

JANE *(looking at GRIERSON)* What about you? Bernie, could we…?

BERNIE Oh… ah… sure!

GRIERSON *(wryly)* I appreciate your offer, Slater.

> *GRIERSON, BERNIE and JANE leave, closing the door behind them. A dim red light illuminates FREDA in her office. She picks up the phone.*

FREDA *(conspiratorially)* Red Wing? It's Blackbird. Blackbird! You can't have forgotten – it was your idea! Listen. I don't know what I'm supposed to be doing here. I'm not getting anywhere. I mean, there isn't anywhere to get. I think he's sympathetic, in a general way you know, but that's not the same as…. Well, he quotes Trotsky. Well, exactly! *(pause)* Sure. I handle all his calls! He talks to everybody, from the Prime Minister to the Russian embassy. Yes, the Russian embassy – don't they tell you anything? And another thing – he tries it on with some of the girls. Me? Oh, he thinks I'm part of the furniture. Listen, give me another couple of months. If I'm still drawing a blank, I'll try for a transfer to somewhere more useful. It's weird, though, you know? He's hard to figure out. *(FREDA hangs up; light out in her office.)*

Scene Seven

> *The scene might open with an excerpt from the "Just watch me" interview with Pierre Trudeau, October 1970. GRIERSON and JANE are back in the 1970 set. GRIERSON is at the stove.*

JANE Tell me something, Grierson: did Margaret know about your "production meetings?" *(He is silent.)* Where is she?

GRIERSON She's in England. She's not well.

JANE And you never had children.

GRIERSON No.

JANE Why not?

GRIERSON None of your business.

JANE You know, when you sent me off to make that mining film, I didn't know the first damn thing about movies.

GRIERSON Any fool can point a camera.

JANE Oh thanks a lot!

GRIERSON   You said so yourself.

JANE   So what else?

GRIERSON   Oh, you were bright, you were brave… *(a beat)* You were truthful.

JANE   What else?

GRIERSON   Isn't that enough?

JANE   What did you want from me?

GRIERSON   *(after a silence)* You were a special one, you know.

JANE   Yes, well, it was a long time ago.

GRIERSON   Doesn't seem so to me.

JANE   You're getting sentimental in your old age.

GRIERSON   I should never have let you go.

JANE   Not quite how I remember it, actually. *(She empties her glass.)*

GRIERSON   It's a cruel trick to play on a man, old age. "A tattered coat upon a stick."

JANE   Oh cut it out, Grierson. *(She gets another drink.)*

GRIERSON   I've got cancer.

JANE   What? *(He taps his chest.)* Oh shit. Is it… I mean… you know for sure?

GRIERSON   I know.

JANE   You've had tests?

GRIERSON   Inconclusive. A couple of "shadows."

JANE   Then you don't know.

GRIERSON   I know. "The valley of the shadow of death." *(He turns to the stove.)*

JANE   Come to India, Grierson. I'm leaving at the beginning of December. *(A pause. She joins GRIERSON at the stove.)* Seriously, why don't you? You can still tell the front end of a camera from the arse end, can you?

GRIERSON   Och, you don't need me.

JANE   It's what *you* need I'm thinking about.

> *At this moment, TANYA arrives. She comes in very familiarly, bringing two long loaves of bread, and a bag with her still camera and her portable tape recorder. She does not at first see JANE.*

TANYA   Hi, Grierson! Sorry I'm a bit late.

GRIERSON   I was afraid you had jilted me.

TANYA   Thrown you over for an older man?

GRIERSON Something o' that.

TANYA Don't be silly. Here, take these. *(She thrusts the two loaves of bread at GRIERSON. Clutching the loaves, he looks like Moses with the tablets. TANYA whips out her camera and takes a picture.)*

GRIERSON You're making a scarecrow out of me.

TANYA Wait! *(She takes another picture.)*

GRIERSON *(With feigned surliness. He dotes on her.)* What's all this for anyway?

TANYA You said we could do our projects in any medium.

GRIERSON I never said you could use me as a guinea pig!

TANYA *(taking another picture)* Portrait of the artist as an old tyrant.

GRIERSON And you propose to paste these snaps of yours all over the wall, and write underneath, "Here you may see the monster?"

TANYA I told you, Grierson. It's a film.

GRIERSON A motion picture without any motion?

TANYA *(getting out her tape recorder)* Oh come on! Use your imagination!

GRIERSON And you can put that thing away!

TANYA This is my soundtrack.

GRIERSON And I'm supposed to "grade" this raggle-taggle thing?

TANYA Why not?

GRIERSON It'll be as much as I can do to sit through it.

TANYA It's going to capture your essence!

GRIERSON Spare me! So what am I going to see, besides a lot of pictures of myself?

TANYA *(vaguely)* Oh, you'll see.

GRIERSON Have you thought this thing out or haven't you? Nobody ever got a penny out of me without a treatment.

TANYA I'm not asking you to pay for it!

JANE *(coming into the room from the kitchen)* Don't take his money! I'm warning you!

TANYA Oh, I'm sorry, I didn't realize…

GRIERSON Jane Barnes… Tanya Rossides. Tanya, as you can hear, is the bane of my existence!

JANE Really?

TANYA *(offering to take over the cooking)* Let me do this for you.

JANE *(ironically)* You always did like a hand-maiden.

GRIERSON Certainly not. "He who does not work shall not eat." Who said that?

TANYA & JANE *(together)* Trotsky?

GRIERSON Trotsky indeed! Saint Paul! Second Epistle to the Thessalonians. Did you not know I was once a lay preacher?

JANE What do you mean, "once"?

GRIERSON Och, a shrewd thrust, lassie! *(to TANYA)* Now, this is the one you should be interviewing. She can tell you all you need to know.

JANE Oh I can, can I?

GRIERSON Do you young people know about Jane Barnes? Jane is a veritable pioneer of Canadian cinema.

JANE God! Makes me sound about a hundred.

TANYA Far out!

GRIERSON *(translating for JANE)* A tribalism meaning, "How interesting!"

JANE I *have* heard it, Grierson.

GRIERSON Of course you have. You've been living in Vancouver. *(to TANYA)* I sent Jane off to... where was it? Nova Scotia?

JANE You know bloody well where it was!

GRIERSON Spring of 1943.

JANE It was February, you bastard. Thirty-six hours on the train, with the heater on the fritz.

GRIERSON Made a man of you, Jane.

JANE Day and a half before the camera was warm enough to run!

GRIERSON And we're talking 35 millimetre here. None of your dinky-toy portable stuff.

> *MICHAEL knocks at the door and enters. He has a portable Arriflex camera on his shoulder, plus a battery belt and a Nagra tape-recorder slung around him. He is wearing an NFB jacket. He is very agitated, but under control.*

MICHAEL I'm sorry about yesterday...

GRIERSON So you should be. Take off that gear and have something to eat.

MICHAEL That's okay, thanks. *Salut*, Tanya! *(MICHAEL and TANYA embrace.)*

GRIERSON You're wasting to a shadow. I'm going to call your mother, tell her to feed you properly.

MICHAEL Grierson, I don't want anything to eat!

GRIERSON Have a drink, then. Jane, give the boy a scotch. Do you know about Jane Barnes?

JANE I'm a pioneer of Canadian cinema. How do you take it?

MICHAEL Straight, thanks. *(He puts down his gear.)*

JANE A man after my own heart.

TANYA *(indicating the film equipment)* What's up?

MICHAEL *(challengingly)* I'm going out to document what's happening.

GRIERSON "Document?"

At about this point, TANYA discreetly begins to tape the conversation.

MICHAEL Hundreds of people are being arrested, Grierson. Thousands, probably.

GRIERSON Suspected terrorists.

MICHAEL Thousands of them? Do you seriously believe that?

GRIERSON Until it's proven otherwise.

MICHAEL Nothing's going to be "proven." We're living in a police state, man! They're rounding up anyone they don't like. They can throw you in jail, break into your place, seize anything they want…. People are being dragged away in the night, strip-searched, roughed-up…. And nobody knows what's happening! There's a ban on reporting.

GRIERSON Which you intend to ignore.

MICHAEL I have to get evidence! Some kind of documenting of state terror.

GRIERSON And what do you propose to do with this "evidence" – if you get any?

MICHAEL Expose the government's lies.

GRIERSON Your Prime Minister has called for your trust that what he is doing is necessary. Do you not feel obliged to believe him?

MICHAEL Oh sure! Sure! Martial Law. News blackout. Trust Trudeau. I mean, it couldn't be better if he'd planned it himself.

TANYA So what are you going to do?

MICHAEL I've got a camera. I've got a budget. I'm supposed to be doing interviews for this thing "Separate Ways" – you know? – "what young Quebecers think about independence." Shit, I'll show them what young Quebecers think!

TANYA But I mean, what are you going to shoot?

MICHAEL Testimony from the families of political prisoners. Witnesses of police violence. Whatever I can get.

GRIERSON You'll be playing into the hands of the terrorists, you know that. Giving the means of propaganda to the enemies of the state.

MICHAEL To the enemies of the dominant class.

GRIERSON Of which you are a member. Michael, you will be used! You'll become a dupe, an accomplice in the propagation of an ideology.

JANE What do you call working for the Film Board?

GRIERSON *(drily)* There *is* a difference.

MICHAEL Don't tell me. The NFB is my independent, arm's length, publicly-funded dispenser of truth and beauty...

GRIERSON It's the best thing you've got! Don't abuse it.

MICHAEL And my documenting of police repression – will they let me go ahead with it?

GRIERSON Soliciting anti-government propaganda.

MICHAEL The government has all the propaganda it needs. I'm putting myself at the disposal of those who are being silenced.

JANE *(meaningfully)* Giving them a voice, Grierson.

GRIERSON So what do you want from me? My blessing?

MICHAEL *(a beat)* Yes. I want your blessing.

GRIERSON Well, you're not getting it. *(He turns to the window.)*

MICHAEL *(preparing to gather up his equipment)* I can't believe this. I can't believe that I am hearing Grierson – *Grierson* – becoming an advocate for a police state. I thought he was supposed to be, I don't know, like, some kind of a real leftie. Wasn't he?

> *There is a sudden change of light, momentarily isolating GRIERSON who turns in alarm as an amplified VOICE addresses him.*

VOICE Mr. Grierson, would you mind telling the Commission whether you yourself are a Communist, or Communistically inclined?

GRIERSON I would be delighted to answer. I have been a public servant now for eighteen years. That is as much as to say that I am affiliated to no political party or doctrine.

VOICE That is, officially. What would you say about subscribing to any of their views? Would you say that your inclinations were of the leftist variety?

GRIERSON *(a proud claim)* I have been a civil servant.

> *The lights revert to normal. With a loud knock at the door, a 50-year-old BERNIE Slater breezes in, confident, expansive, smartly dressed, bearing champagne. GRIERSON is not immediately visible.*

BERNIE *(to TANYA, JANE and MICHAEL)* Excuse me, am I in the right place?

JANE Who can say?

BERNIE I'm looking for John Grierson.

JANE *(turning to face him)* Aren't we all, honey!

BERNIE *(incredulous)* Jane?

JANE Got it in one, Bernie!

BERNIE Holy shit! Is that you?

JANE Gracious as ever!

BERNIE What the hell are you doing here?

JANE It's a free country.

BERNIE Is it? I got frisked on the way here!

JANE Did they find anything interesting?

BERNIE *(looking around)* Jeez, what sort of a dump is this? *(He sees MICHAEL in his NFB gear.)* Do I know you? No, don't run away.

JANE It's a minimum security hotel.

BERNIE And, what, are you just visiting? I mean, you're not…?

JANE I'm just visiting, Bernie. *(realizing)* Oh! So you're the Big Cheese!

BERNIE Didn't you see the press release? Head of English production.

JANE Sidney Newman's new man. My goodness! Well, congratulations. Virtue rewarded, I'm sure.

GRIERSON *(turning from the window)* "He polished up the handle so carefully, that now he is the leader of the Queen's Navy."

MICHAEL *(aghast)* That's Mr. Slater?

GRIERSON Your new boss. The chap whose arse you'll have to kiss from now on.

BERNIE *(greeting GRIERSON)* Okay, Doc! Good to see you! You're looking great, isn't he?

GRIERSON Only my students call me "Doc." Are you prepared to sign up?

BERNIE Oh, I think I'm a bit beyond that.

GRIERSON Never too old to learn. *(indicating MICHAEL)* I've got some of your apprentices in these seminars of mine.

BERNIE *(an arm round MICHAEL's shoulder)* Well, do me a favour and keep reminding them they're living in the real world, not in some kind of sheltered workshop.

GRIERSON The real world, is it?

BERNIE Folks at the Board have been pampered far too long. Sucking on the public teat. I tell you, if they're not prepared to get off their fannies and come up with something people actually want to see, well, thank you, but it's time to move on!

JANE The all-new, tough-talking Bernie Slater!

BERNIE Look, I've spent the last seven years in L.A., and down there, let me tell you, they cannot believe the kind of cosy billet we've created – with taxpayers' money, no less! And what do we get? If it's not elitist navel-gazing, it's the kind of naïve political shit that got us in the mess we're in right now. The inmates have been taking over the asylum, for God's sake.

GRIERSON And you've been appointed to restore sanity, have you?

BERNIE I've been appointed to see that what we do with public money reflects popular demand.

GRIERSON Bread and circuses.

BERNIE I'm talking about stories, fictions, something for the imagination, for the spirit. Seriously, we've got to give Joe Public what he wants, or we're dead.

GRIERSON Your mandate is to give Joe Public what he *needs*.

BERNIE There speaks the true John Grierson. He'll never change – and who would want him to?

GRIERSON Leave entertaining to the entertainers. Your vocation is for the documentary.

BERNIE Your Calvinist insistence on documentary has blighted our imaginations! Thanks to you, Canada still *dreams* in black and white!

GRIERSON Canada doesn't need to be pandered to by the National Film Board.

BERNIE *(a beat)* Look, we're not at war anymore.

GRIERSON You and I?

BERNIE The world is not at war. Do you grant that?

GRIERSON I'm not at all sure that I do. But go on.

BERNIE Society isn't a school, it isn't bible camp! It's a place where adults make their own choices.

GRIERSON Society *is* a school. A democratic society has to be educated constantly. If you go whoring after audiences, Bernie Slater, you betray your very *raison d'être*.

BERNIE *(patronizingly)* Look, John, I apologize. I didn't come here to fight with you. I'm here to thank you, and to celebrate.

GRIERSON Why don't you open your champagne? *(to TANYA)* There are more glasses in the kitchen. You may have to wash them. *(to BERNIE)* What are you thanking me for?

BERNIE *(to MICHAEL)* This man taught me everything I know about film-making.

GRIERSON The responsibilities we get saddled with!

BERNIE He also taught me a respect for its purposes.

GRIERSON He never got this Joe Public business from me!

BERNIE But there isn't a captive audience anymore. We're not the lone projector, beaming in the wilderness. Sure, back in '43, in Armpit, Saskatchewan, the poor buggers would watch anything. "Canada Carries On," "Seven Ways to Bake an Apple." Nowadays, my friend, if you don't show them a good time, there's others that will. Now who said *that*? *(He pops the champagne.)* T.S. Eliot, that's who.

JANE Bernie's been reading!

GRIERSON Or his girlfriends have.

TANYA *(bringing tumblers)* These are all I could find.

GRIERSON They'll have to do. Champagne's such a pansy drink, anyway. *(as BERNIE offers to pour)* Not for me. Give it to your wife.

BERNIE / JANE She's not my wife. / I'm not his wife.

GRIERSON You know who I'm referring to, I dare say.

BERNIE *(amiably, pouring champagne)* You know, I never could decide if I was more of a fool to marry her or to leave her.

JANE Can't help you there, Bernie.

TANYA *(getting him one)* Do you want a mineral water, Grierson?

BERNIE *(pouring MICHAEL a glass of champagne)* And what are you spending the public's money on, young man? Is it something I'd feel good about?

MICHAEL What? Oh! I've been getting material for "Separate Ways" – the thing about kids and separatism, what they think of it…

BERNIE Oh yes? Well, I'm sorry to be the bearer of bad news, but that little hot potato has been dropped rather hastily.

MICHAEL What? Since when?

BERNIE Since about five hours ago, my friend. Definitely not a good idea right now!

JANE And, by the way, I kicked you out.

BERNIE I was on the point of leaving.

JANE   Too bad – you weren't quick enough.

BERNIE   And how's the lovely Sarah?

JANE   Sarah has a ten-month-old baby. You're a grandfather, Bernie.

BERNIE   I know that, thank you. I'm asking how she is.

JANE   You could try phoning.

GRIERSON   Enough of this love talk. You're embarrassing the children. Here. *(raising his glass of tonic water)* To Bernie, who is now Le Grand Fromage de Disneyland. Congratulations, Slater. I mean it.

> *Clinking of glasses. There is another wail of police sirens from the street. MICHAEL goes to the TV.*

Now if it's something entertaining you want, you should pay attention to young Tanya here.

TANYA   Oh Grierson, really!

GRIERSON   She's got an entertaining little film for you, isn't that right?

BERNIE   *(not very interested)* Oh yes?

GRIERSON   About me, if you please! The wit and wisdom of old Doc Grierson.

TANYA   Well, it's nothing, really.

GRIERSON   A subjectivist collage.

TANYA   Please! You're making it sound really dumb.

GRIERSON   Not at all. I just want to know what's going to be on the screen.

TANYA   *(They are looking at her expectantly.)* Well… all kinds of things… I'm still collecting them. Images, ideas, pictures from books, Napoleon and John the Baptist, and animals and birds…

GRIERSON   Birds?

TANYA   I have this terrific picture of a fierce old owl…

GRIERSON   I see.

TANYA   And a hawk hovering in mid air, waiting to pounce…

GRIERSON   And anxious watchers scanning the horizon…

TANYA   What?

GRIERSON   Nothing. Go on.

TANYA   I mean, the point is, how *do* you convey the reality of a person?

GRIERSON   How indeed!

TANYA   All we have is snippets and glimpses and what we imagine, so it's all very subjective anyway, and my Grierson isn't going to be the same as another person's Grierson, but I'm trying to capture different aspects and moods, with the visual images sort of complementing the soundtrack. I'm editing together a kind of scrapbook of things you've said – questions and pronouncements and just, you know, snatches of talk…

GRIERSON   "Grierson for Beginners."

TANYA   Yeah. And the images are kind of like thrown off by the words – associations, impressions that occurred to me…

GRIERSON   Reducing me to a McLuhanesque, metaphorical mush.

TANYA   *(a beat)* No, I don't think so. I think it will have a kind of truth.

JANE   You should be flattered, Grierson.

GRIERSON   We'll see about that. And how's it going to end? With a bang or a whimper?

TANYA   Well, I have an idea for that. I've got this one picture of you that I really like, where you're staring straight into the camera, and I'm saving it for the last. We've had all these images, all black and white, some of them quite short and abrupt, some of them dissolving into one another…

GRIERSON   Dissolves are expensive.

TANYA   *(matter of factly)* Not if you do them right in the camera. *(GRIERSON is impressed)* I mean, you have to plan everything really carefully, because it's actually one continuous take. One four hundred foot roll. It's all I could afford. And the soundtrack is all these fragments, overlapping and repeating, and quite, you know, bombarding.… But then, gradually, the sound level begins to fade, getting more distant, like a voice in a dream, as though all the talk is kind of beside the point.… And finally there's just this one picture of you, staring out at the viewer, in total silence. Slow fade. Finish.

GRIERSON   *(as though he's been watching the film on a screen)* And you're editing that right in the camera?

TANYA   Yep.

GRIERSON   Maybe Mr. Slater will buy it from you.

BERNIE   Oh, well now, you see, the Board doesn't…

MICHAEL, who has been looking at the television, suddenly interrupts.

MICHAEL   They've found Pierre Laporte.

BERNIE   What? Let me have a look.

MICHAEL   The police. They've found Laporte.

JANE   You're kidding! Where?

MICHAEL   Somewhere out near the airport.

GRIERSON Well, God be thanked for that!

TANYA Is he all right?

MICHAEL He was in the trunk of a car.

BERNIE What?

TANYA Oh my God!

MICHAEL Strangled.

BERNIE Holy shit!

TANYA Oh my God!

GRIERSON *(after a pause)* God rest his soul.

> *They all stare silently at the TV, as a French announcer is heard to sign off at the conclusion of a news bulletin - an excerpt from the film "Action: The October Crisis of 1970." The sirens wail unrelentingly in the streets below.*

Part Two: Scene Eight

Isolated in a spotlight, the hooded figure of Igor Gouzenko appears. An amplified VOICE of Counsel to the Gouzenko Inquiry addresses him. The other actors are sitting casually in the GRIERSON apartment set.

VOICE   Mr. Gouzenko! *(The figure responds.)* Mr. Gouzenko, the Inquiry now asks you to take up Exhibit 37. Do you have it? It is a cryptic memorandum. I will read it. "National Research Council. Report on the organization and work. Freda to the Professor, through Grierson." Is that right? *(The figure nods.)* "Grierson." I understand that to be a reference to John Grierson, until recently the Commissioner of the National Film Board – is that correct? *(The figure nods.)* Your honour, we shall be calling Mr. Grierson himself to testify in due course.

A cell phone begins to ring. TANYA moves hastily to answer it. For this short scene, she is quite a bit older, bespectacled, and much more businesslike than her 1970 self. She carries a ring binder marked "Public Lies."

TANYA   Shit! *(The Gouzenko figure appears confused; the other actors look out into the auditorium expectantly.)* I'm sorry, could we just hold it? No, no, that was fine. *(to phone, impatiently)* Tanya Rossides. Oh, Mike! I thought you were coming down. *(to Gouzenko)* Just relax for two minutes, okay? *(to phone)* We're in the middle of a run-through. So what do you think? *(She indicates to the other actors that she's not talking to them.)* Now? You're just reading it now? Christ, you've had it for three weeks! Okay, okay, so tell me. *(pause)* You personally are unhappy, or the programming committee is unhappy? *(pause)* Well, you're the producer. You can talk them round. That's what producers are for. Oh Michael, don't be embarrassed. It doesn't make you look like a jerk. Well, you were! Slater was going to fire you, remember? It's what I loved about you, actually. Look, we'll change the name. *(The MICHAEL actor has come forward, asking in dumbshow if it's the "real Michael" she's talking to. She nods "yes.")* Oh, you'll like him. He's really cute! *(MICHAEL acknowledges the compliment.)* Of *course* it's just my version of things. What else could it be? Listen, it's a dramatization. That doesn't mean it isn't true. "Documentary: the creative treatment of actuality." Who said that? Right! *(pause)* What are you afraid of? A horde of crazed NFB veterans dragging you in front of a Senate committee? *(pause)* Oh, well... *(considering)* To get him right, I suppose. To do him justice. To get him out of our system, maybe. *(signalling to the actors to be ready)* Look, do me a favour. Just finish reading it, and we'll talk, okay? We're going on. À toute à l'heure! *(She terminates the call. To the actors, clapping her hands.)* Okay, positions for the top of scene nine, where we left off. Lights, please. Let's go!

On the screen – or over the sound-system – an excerpt from "Action: The October Crisis of 1970", in which a young woman journalist tells, in

French, with voiceover translation, how she witnessed the discovery of Laporte's body.

Scene Nine

GRIERSON has resumed his position at the end of Part One, staring at the TV set in his Montreal hotel room. His first line calls the others back together and initiates the new scene. JANE, BERNIE, TANYA and MICHAEL reassemble at the TV, champagne glasses in hand. Police sirens are heard from the street.

GRIERSON   Well. I trust this will put the ki-bosh on that plan of yours.

MICHAEL   Why should it?

BERNIE   What plan is this?

MICHAEL   *(a beat; defiantly)* I'm going out to document police repression.

BERNIE   Like hell you are!

GRIERSON   A man is dead, Michael.

MICHAEL   *(He begins to gather his equipment.)* I'm still going.

BERNIE   Those bastards!

MICHAEL   It's a war. People get killed.

TANYA   Oh Michael!

BERNIE   Hostages?

MICHAEL   It doesn't make any difference. The death of a single individual.

GRIERSON   It's the only kind of death there is.

MICHAEL   The execution of a class enemy.

BERNIE   That is the most disgusting thing I've ever heard. He was at the mercy of these bastards, and they murdered him.

MICHAEL   *(a beat)* Well, suppose they didn't do it?

BERNIE   What's that supposed to mean?

MICHAEL   I mean suppose the FLQ didn't kill Laporte.

TANYA   They've found his body!

JANE   *(She is drinking quite a bit.)* "Habeas corpus." Whatever that means.

MICHAEL   I'm not saying he isn't dead. I'm asking who killed him.

BERNIE   What kind of a stupid question is that? We know who killed him.

MICHAEL   Do we? How do we know?

BERNIE   There's a note from the Chenier cell right on the body. It's right on the damn TV, for Christ's sake!

MICHAEL   So it is! It's on the TV! Dolly in, camera one. Trunk lid opening. Move in for a close-up. Body in trunk. Get a light on the note. Can we all see what it says? "We killed him, signed, the FLQ."

BERNIE   And as far as I'm concerned, it's game over for them. Nothing but a bunch of thugs.

MICHAEL   Right! Game over. They've lost it. Trudeau's got it all back. Nothing but a bunch of thugs.

TANYA   What are you saying?

JANE   And get me another drink while you're on your feet.

MICHAEL   We all know the cops have infiltrated the FLQ. Suppose it was a plant, you know, like an agent provocateur, set them up to kill him, pushed them into it.

BERNIE   Don't give me some ridiculous conspiracy theory…

MICHAEL   It's not ridiculous. A live hostage gives you some power. Once he's dead, you're finished. Look at it. Laporte is dead, the FLQ are thugs, and we, your friendly neighbourhood army in the streets, we are the good guys, and anything we do from now on is okay. Things are going to get really bad now!

BERNIE   You're saying that the Canadian government, or the RCMP, or I don't know who, had a Quebec cabinet minister strangled and dumped in a car, for the sake of a propaganda coup? Is that what's in your warped little mind?

MICHAEL   How do we know?

BERNIE   Because it's preposterous and absurd.

TANYA   Is it?

BERNIE   *(flatly)* This is not the sort of country where things like that happen. Period.

JANE   Bullshit. We know how it's done.

MICHAEL   *(appealing to GRIERSON)* How do we know what sort of country this is?

JANE   Michael's right. I mean, maybe he's right, maybe he isn't. The point is, we don't know. We don't know anything for sure. Anything they say can be a lie. And we know how it's done, don't we?

MICHAEL   *(gathering his equipment)* I'm leaving.

BERNIE   Put that stuff down. You're not going anywhere. Grierson, for God's sake, talk some sense into him.

MICHAEL   I have to get footage right now, tonight. I have to be a witness.

BERNIE Look, I'm sorry, but you don't have any authorization.

JANE You could give it to him, Bernie.

BERNIE Oh sure! And you'd go along and shoot it with him, I suppose?

JANE What do you say, Michael? I'm a pioneer of Canadian cinema.

BERNIE I told you, I've cancelled that show you were working on. As of now, you've got no project.

MICHAEL Are you going to stop me?

BERNIE You better believe it! The fuckin' terrorists strangle a guy, the cops are going crazy trying to find the other hostage, and you think you're going out to investigate police brutality...?

MICHAEL To get evidence, talk to witnesses...

BERNIE Running around with "NFB" written all over you – a federal agency – trying to discredit the RCMP? Stirring up shit on the night of the murder? Are you nuts?

MICHAEL What if I just go ahead and shoot?

BERNIE Not with my equipment.

JANE "Mine, my equipment, my authorization!"

BERNIE Jane, stay out of this, why don't you?

MICHAEL I've already got the gear. And a lot of raw stock.

BERNIE Okay. *(making as if to pick up the phone)* You'll be arrested and charged with theft.

MICHAEL *(a beat)* I see.

> There is an expectant pause. MICHAEL begins to shoulder his equipment. Like a soldier going off to the front, he rather melodramatically embraces TANYA, and heads out the door.

TANYA Mike! Be careful!

BERNIE *(realizing)* Where the fuck do you think you're going? Jesus Christ, I'll have the cops on *my* ass next, if they pick him up like that! Michael!

> BERNIE lurches out after MICHAEL. GRIERSON, JANE and TANYA are left alone.

JANE Like father, like son! Thank God I quit when I did!

GRIERSON I fired you.

JANE I resigned.

GRIERSON I fired you. Thirty years ago.

JANE Twenty-six years ago. And you didn't fire me. I resigned.

GRIERSON I was going to fire you. You were a pain in the arse.

JANE I was a threat to you.

GRIERSON You flatter yourself, Jane Barnes!

JANE You couldn't stand being contradicted – particularly by a woman.

GRIERSON I couldn't abide self-indulgence.

JANE There was always only one opinion – yours.

GRIERSON I couldn't abide self-indulgence and vanity and disorder.

JANE One opinion, one judgment, one point of view.

GRIERSON There were lots of opinions, as I recall. Most of them foolish and vain.

JANE Says who? Says the infallible Grierson?

GRIERSON They were self-evidently wrong.

JANE Not to me.

GRIERSON Self evidently to anyone with sufficient detachment and breadth of view to see beyond the little light of their own egotism.

JANE Egotism! You have the gall to speak to me of egotism? They don't make egos like yours anymore. You came over here and strutted around like a tin-pot dictator, demanding this and yelling for that, giving out orders, tearing our work to shreds – work we'd put our hearts into for you…

GRIERSON And you took it…

JANE …from a bloody Scotchman! *(She is about to storm out.)*

GRIERSON You all took it.

JANE I didn't take it! *(She leaves and slams the door.)*

GRIERSON *(calling after her)* You took it because I was right! There's only one right way to do a job. There's all manner of wrong ways, and no end of people ready to claim that their little light is the only light there is… *(Lights are turned on for the next scene. On the screen, if there is one, an excerpt from "Coal Face Canada.")*

Scene Ten

Glace Bay, Nova Scotia, 1943. JANE and BERNIE are shooting silent footage for the film "Workers are Warriors." A coal miner, Jack McPHAIL, equipped with helmet and lamp, pick, drill, etc, performs a series of mining routines for the camera, which is operated by BERNIE. The camera itself sends out a rectangle of light, framing the subject as though on a movie screen. JANE is directing.)

BERNIE   Camera.

JANE   *(with the slate)* "Workers Are Warriors", shot fourteen, take one. *(McPHAIL obliges.)* Okay, cut.

McPHAIL   That okay? That what you want?

JANE   That's fine. Okay Bernie?

BERNIE   Give me one more. Really swing that pick! Make it look like the real thing!

JANE   This *is* the real thing, Bernie. *(pause)* Okay, one more.

BERNIE   Right! Okay, rolling.

JANE   "Workers are Warriors", shot fourteen, take two. *(McPHAIL performs again.)* Okay, cut.

McPHAIL   So what's all this for anyway, this fillum?

BERNIE   Propaganda, my friend. "The epic of the toiling masses."

JANE   Okay, Bernie?

McPHAIL   Makin' this for the coal owners, then?

BERNIE   This, my friend, is the National Film Board. Government. Going to make you into a movie star.

McPHAIL   That the same outfit we had come in here showin' fillums? Fella from Halifax, coupla three times last fall. Pictures of the war an' all that.

JANE   That's us.

BERNIE   Did you see the one, "Canada Strikes Back?"

JANE   I want a close up now, okay, checking your sticks of dynamite. Bernie?

McPHAIL   That the one with the submarines, and the boys attacking that place in France?

BERNIE   I made that.

McPHAIL   You made it?

BERNIE   It's my film. I directed it.

McPHAIL   Yeah? Then you tell me something. That there German submarine. How come he didn't just go ahead and sink you fellas while you was takin' his picture? Eh? You tell me that.

JANE   Good question! You tell him, Bernie. *(to McPHAIL)* Okay, look at this stick of dynamite and make like you're reading the label. Don't look at the camera.

BERNIE   Ready, rolling.

JANE   "Warriors," shot fifteen, take one. *(action)* Don't move your head. Okay, cut.

McPHAIL   And another thing. How come you're not in the forces anyway? Young fella like you.

JANE   *(to the audience)* Okay, everybody, listen please! I want a general shot of everyone, looking very natural. Don't look at the camera. Pretend we're not here. Look over here at Mr. McPhail.

McPHAIL   Jack.

JANE   Look over here at Jack. Pretend he's making a speech. Can you do that?

McPHAIL   Shouldn't be too difficult.

JANE   Bernie? Are we ready?

BERNIE   Rolling.

JANE   *(as the camera and lights are turned on the audience)* Okay! "Workers Are Warriors", shot sixteen, take one. *(as BERNIE pans the camera over the audience)* Okay, that's great, just hold that, keep looking at Jack, there we go. Great! That's fine. Thank you very much.

BERNIE   *(pretending to intone a commentary in the Lorne Greene voice)* "And in the mining camps, as in the factories and foundries, assembly shops and lumber mills across the land, the families of Canada's heroic working men gather in their community halls to share in the camaraderie of all-out effort. Never before, as Churchill himself said, has so much been asked of a free people, and never before has so much been freely given."

> *The scene shifts to a tavern. A couple of round tables. JANE, BERNIE and McPHAIL are drinking beer.*

McPHAIL   So this here fillum is your idea? Makin' this big deal outta coal minin'?

BERNIE   *(wearing his GRIERSON hat)* Not my idea.

McPHAIL   Hers, then? This your idea?

BERNIE   Comes from the big boss back in Ottawa.

McPHAIL   An' it wouldn't have nothin' to do with the fact we just had a big strike out here? Strikes in coal right across the country. Wage freeze for the duration of the war, eh? And the coal owners is makin' millions. Sellin' the low-grade shit to the Navy, who don't know any better, and sellin' the good stuff to their friends in the munitions industry. You don't think? I'm tellin' you, you come down here and you make a nice little fillum to take back to your boss in Ottawa, showin' what a good job the boys in the mines is doing…

JANE   Wait a minute!

McPHAIL   And the government's payin' for it!

JANE *(to McPHAIL)* Listen, would you go on camera with this?

BERNIE Whoa back!

JANE Would you, Jack? To say just what you've been saying? The wage freeze, and selling low-grade coal to the Navy?

McPHAIL *(suddenly alarmed and conspiratorial)* Couldn't do it.

JANE Why not? Come on, Jack – it's just a matter of talking to the camera, the way you talk to us. You're a natural.

McPHAIL Any miner did that, be fired as soon the fillum came out. Blacklisted. Kicked out of company housing.

BERNIE This is not a good idea.

JANE *(ignoring BERNIE)* Couldn't you? If you don't want this to be a soft soap for the owners?

McPHAIL Sorry, lady. Couldn't do it. More 'n my life's worth, eh?

BERNIE Leave the guy alone. He's telling you he can't do it.

JANE But it's such a fantastic chance. I mean, I know what you're saying, but we have to get this on film. *(a beat)* We'll do it in silhouette. Nobody'll see your face.

McPHAIL They'd still know who it was.

JANE We'll disguise your voice. It's possible to do that, isn't it, Bernie?

BERNIE Oh sure. Filter out the highs and lows.

McPHAIL Why don't you just say it yourself?

JANE It's got to be the real person, giving his own testimony. Don't you see how effective that would be?

McPHAIL *(considering)* When would you want to do this?

JANE Have to be tonight.

McPHAIL Where?

JANE Up to you. Wherever you say.

McPHAIL District 26 Union Hall. Eight o'clock. Don't go shoutin' it around town. *(He empties his glass and leaves.)*

JANE *(pounding her hands on the table and letting out a whoop)* Zowee!

BERNIE I'm telling you, this is not a good idea.

JANE This is a bloody terrific idea!

BERNIE Grierson won't like it.

JANE He'll love it. "Art should be a hammer." This one's going to smash a few windows, boy! All this bullshit about "the camaraderie of all-out effort."

BERNIE That's all Grierson wants, believe me.

JANE Well it's not all Grierson's getting. Not from this babe! How much film have we got left?

BERNIE About 1200 feet.

JANE That's okay, that's enough. We can lug the sound gear round to the Union Hall.

BERNIE Wasting footage. He'll never go for it.

JANE Listen, Bernie, honey, it's my fillum, comprendo? You, Bernie, the cameraman; me, Jane, the director.

BERNIE I'm telling you, it's not what Grierson wants.

JANE Dinna fash y'sel, laddie! I'll be the judge of what Grierson wants.

BERNIE Are you screwing him?

JANE Don't be so relentlessly common, Bernie.

BERNIE Is that why you won't sleep with me?

JANE You stick to your business, and I'll stick to mine.

BERNIE I see.

JANE No, you don't see!

BERNIE Really?

JANE Just shoot this scene for me. That's all I ask. Okay? (*BERNIE shrugs his compliance. JANE kisses him.*)

Scene Eleven

Lights up on GRIERSON and TANYA in the 1970 location. GRIERSON, who is obviously restless and troubled, has been watching the preceding scene. TANYA is sitting at his feet, and he strokes her hair lightly.

GRIERSON (*awkwardly*) Something I've not told you…

TANYA What's that?

GRIERSON You bring to mind very strongly sometimes…

TANYA (*unobtrusively switching on her tape recorder*) Who?

GRIERSON A certain person.

TANYA Someone you loved?

GRIERSON (*brusquely*) Aye.

TANYA   And is she…?

GRIERSON   Dead.

TANYA   Oh.

GRIERSON   *(after a pause)* I've been thinking about that film of yours.

TANYA   "Raggle-taggle thing," you called it.

GRIERSON   I've been thinking about it.

TANYA   "Metaphorical mush," you said.

GRIERSON   I was wondering if I might give you a piece of advice.

TANYA   Sure. Chuck the whole thing, right? It's kind of stupid really.

GRIERSON   About the soundtrack. Instead of going for total silence at the end, you might try using a very low level of continuous sound – something rhythmic, like the sound of the sea. Waves breaking gently on a beach. "The eternal note of sadness." I'll tell you why. It's a very practical reason. Something I've learned. You almost never get complete silence when you're showing a film. You can hear all sorts of extraneous noises, the projector running, that sort of thing. So you actually get a more powerful *sense* of silence by keeping up just a minimal level of sound. *(pause)* Do you see what I mean?

TANYA   Yes. I do!

GRIERSON   I hope you don't mind my intruding a suggestion.

TANYA   No!

GRIERSON   It's kindly meant.

TANYA   *(embracing him)* Oh, Grierson. I wish there was a way I could give you something back.

GRIERSON   You do a great deal for me.

TANYA   Oh, that's nothing…!

GRIERSON   More than you can imagine.

TANYA   But surely…

GRIERSON   Just… be who you are.

TANYA   There must be something!

GRIERSON   *(after a pause)* Perhaps you could…

TANYA   Tell me.

GRIERSON   Perhaps you could let me look…

TANYA   *(not yet understanding)* What?

GRIERSON   …at your breasts.

TANYA Oh. *(Longish pause. She takes a deep breath.)* All right. *(With her back to the audience, she opens her blouse.)*

GRIERSON *(after a while)* You're very lovely.

TANYA Thank you.

GRIERSON *(another pause)* Would you… lie down with me?

TANYA Oh God. *(a beat)* No, Grierson, I'm sorry. *(She turns away and buttons her blouse.)* Shit.

GRIERSON It's young Schneider, isn't it?

TANYA That's not it.

GRIERSON Stupid of me.

TANYA No, really!

GRIERSON I'm sorry. Forgive me.

TANYA Grierson!

GRIERSON "I am a foolish, fond old man."

TANYA Please listen…

GRIERSON You'll despise me, I suppose. Well, I don't blame you.

TANYA I don't despise you! It's just… I don't know…

GRIERSON I'm old enough to be your grandfather.

TANYA *(half angry, half laughing)* Well it's true, damn it, you are! *(a beat)* I'm sorry, I'd better go.

GRIERSON Please don't.

TANYA I have to.

GRIERSON *(wryly)* It's not fair, is it?

TANYA No, it's not fair.

GRIERSON Are you still my friend?

TANYA I'm your friend.

GRIERSON You won't… tell anyone about this?

TANYA *(challengingly)* Why not? *(In the silence between them, TANYA switches off the tape recorder.)* No, I won't tell anyone.

GRIERSON *(after a pause)* I'm thinking of going to India, you know.

TANYA With Jane?

GRIERSON If she'll have me.

TANYA She's pretty mad at you.

GRIERSON Unfinished business.

TANYA Was she your mistress? *(He does not reply.)* Were you in love with her?

GRIERSON *(ambiguously)* Before you were born.

TANYA What happened?

GRIERSON We had a… a falling out.

TANYA Yes?

GRIERSON She… opposed me.

TANYA Was that wrong?

GRIERSON She defied me.

Scene Twelve

A silhouette of McPHAIL, in miner's overalls, wearing a helmet with a lamp, against a screen. His voice is amplified.

McPHAIL *(clearing his throat)* Brothers – an' sisters – this here fillum you're watchin' is showin' you a mighty fine picture of the work of miners here in Nova Scotia. An' I'm as proud as anyone to see that. I've got no quarrel with that. But the record's got to be set straight on a couple of things, if the truth's gonna be told, an' you're not gonna be fobbed off with a bunch of fairy tales. First off, whichever way you look at it, while more men is working steady at a six-day week, on account of the war, it's still one helluva lousy job at a helluva lousy wage, an' don't let anyone tell you otherwise! *(a beat)* There's a war on, an' we're supposed to all pull together, an' they say a strike is like treason. But what I'm sayin' is, just 'cause there's a war on, we're not gonna get suckered into no wage cuts or no quota adjustments. 'Cause if we're diggin' more coal, then they're sure as hell *sellin'* more coal, an' I don't hear of no price cuts or no profit adjustments! They talk about strikes in the mines is sabotage and stabbin' the boys in the back that's fightin' overseas. Well I'm askin' you, what do you call sellin' the Navy number three coal at top price, an' tellin' them it's number one, and that stuff's no good for ships 'cause it's all dust, an' if that's not sabotage, then tell me what is!

> *GRIERSON intervenes at about this point, and his exchange with JANE and BERNIE overlaps the end of McPHAIL's speech. It becomes clear that the scene has shifted from shooting the film to screening the resultant footage.*

An' another thing, I don't know how it is up your way, but down here, the RCMP, if they don't like some particular union man, or if the bosses tip them off, they can jus' arrest him under the War Measures, an' if he's not got his naturalization, then watch out, 'cause they can put him in the camps along with the Germans, an' no questions asked! An' another thing…

GRIERSON *(entering the 1940s scene)* What the hell is this? What is this stuff? Did you shoot this stuff? Slater?

BERNIE Don't look at me.

JANE What's wrong with it?

GRIERSON Has anyone else seen it?

JANE No.

GRIERSON Turn that thing off! *(BERNIE obliges. McPHAIL's voice abruptly ceases, but his image remains visible on the screen. Pause.)* Soapbox oratory.

JANE I thought you'd be pleased.

GRIERSON It's raw material. It's not even half-baked. It's junk; it's unusable.

JANE Why?

GRIERSON Films are not made like that.

JANE Not by you, perhaps...

GRIERSON Not by this Film Board.

JANE But it gives a voice...

GRIERSON ...to a single individual. Why him? Why not someone else? Why not anyone who happened to come along? The purpose of documentary is to give the spectator what he cannot get for himself...

JANE Which is what?

GRIERSON The complete picture, in proper perspective. The view from above.

JANE Telling people what to think.

GRIERSON People see the world as they are taught to see it. If you don't teach them how to see it your way, someone else will.

JANE Let them see it for themselves!

GRIERSON The whole doctrine of a spineless liberal agnosticism!

BERNIE Agnostic? How did God get into this?

JANE & GRIERSON Shut up, Bernie.

GRIERSON "Agnostos." Greek word, "Unknowing." Let each make up his own mind.

JANE Yes, why not?

GRIERSON In this country?

JANE My country – not yours!

GRIERSON In this country of yours. Eleven million individual judgments, at the mercy of every headline – do we trust them to produce, from the muddle of their mental strife, the jewel of collective wisdom?

JANE It's called democracy.

GRIERSON By default. The endless hubbub of competing opinions.

JANE Why not?

GRIERSON Because we can do better than that! We can educate. We can lead men to the promised land, which they will never find for themselves.

JANE That's the whole trouble with you, Grierson – you look at everything as if, I don't know, "the view from above," knowing what's best for everyone, as if you're God almighty, peering down into an aquarium, while the rest of us…

GRIERSON *(striking the table, fiercely)* Don't say that to me!

JANE What?

GRIERSON Don't you dare say that to me! *(He leaves abruptly, crossing to the area previously identified as his office. As before, the silhouette of FREDA is visible through the frosted glass.)*

JANE *(as she and BERNIE unload the projector)* Thanks for leaping so eloquently to my defence, Bernie old comrade.

BERNIE Now you know how it feels.

JANE Shit!

BERNIE Look, for what it's worth, I think you did a helluva of a job. Just be a good girl and let it drop.

JANE Goddammit, I will not be a good girl.

JANE marches into GRIERSON's office with the can of film.

(exercising great control) This film tells a truth, Grierson.

GRIERSON It makes an assertion.

JANE A truth.

GRIERSON An unsubstantiated polemical assertion. You were assigned to get footage highlighting the contribution of coal miners to the total effort of war…

JANE *(trying to interrupt)* Yes, and why miners? That's pretty interesting in itself…

GRIERSON *(refusing to be interrupted)* You were not assigned, or given funding, to put on the screen the clichéd ranting of some local agitator.

JANE What he says is true. And anyway, this is my film, and I will not have it tampered with.

GRIERSON It is not your film, young lady.

JANE   Mine. I scripted it, I directed it, I edited it – with these hands.

GRIERSON   Did you pay for it? Did you buy the raw stock? Did you rent the camera, pay for the processing? Did you hire the crew?

JANE   This is just rhetorical bullying.

GRIERSON   Say it, did you?

JANE   You know perfectly well.

GRIERSON   Did you?

JANE   No!

GRIERSON   Then it's not your film. That film belongs to the government of Canada, that paid all the bills, and generously paid you to make it.

JANE   I was assigned to that film. I had a budget. I submitted a treatment. You approved it…

GRIERSON   I didn't approve that!

JANE   Nobody gets to take a pee around here without your approval.

GRIERSON   And nobody's going to produce any shit either.

JANE   Oh terribly funny, terribly clever.

GRIERSON   Jane, my girl…

JANE   And don't start "my girling" me, Grierson! It's a bit late for that. The point is, I'm not going to recut that sequence.

GRIERSON   *(apparently backing down)* Fine. I shan't insist on it. *(to the intercom)* Freda!

FREDA   Yes sir?

JANE   *(thinking she has won)* Really?

GRIERSON   Certainly not. *(to the intercom)* Prepare a couple of lab requisitions, will you? *(to JANE)* Slater will do it.

JANE   *(quietly)* You bastard.

GRIERSON   This may be a free and egalitarian collective of cinema artisans, Miss Barnes, but I will not be called a bastard in my own office.

JANE   *(after a pause)* What has *happened* to you, Grierson?

GRIERSON   Nothing has "happened" to me…

JANE   Some bloody radical you are!

GRIERSON   I was marching with the Ayrshire pitmen when you were still in nappies! But we operate under certain constraints. Do you not understand that? "The king's shilling must not be abused."

JANE You've said that before.

GRIERSON It refers, my dear young lady…

JANE I *know* what it refers to, and I'm not your dear young lady, not any more. But it seems to me that another of Grierson's little sayings goes something like, "Public lies must not be told." Right?

GRIERSON And no public lie will be told in this case. No-one is going to deny that the coal owners may have made unconscionable profits at the Navy's expense…

JANE Systematically cheated them! Robbed them blind!

GRIERSON …or that the miners of Nova Scotia are being exploited by the capitalist bosses. Of course they are! But a film cannot say that. Not now. Not here.

JANE Not to say it is to tell a lie.

GRIERSON To say it in that form – to let that film out of here – would be to scuttle my entire organization.

JANE And you'd rather ditch what's left of your integrity, than lose your precious little empire.

GRIERSON Oh, the easy purity of the very young! Your virginal soul pulls back its skirts from the mud of compromise.

JANE There's nothing virginal about my soul, Grierson.

GRIERSON *(crushingly)* Of many virginities, Jane Barnes, the one you are alluding to is among the least. *(a beat)* If you could see beyond your stubborn vanity, you would understand that only certain moves are possible at certain stages of the game. As a public servant, I stand just one inch to the left of the party in power. One inch! That's the space in which I am free to operate.

JANE Hardly seems worth it, if you ask me.

GRIERSON Of course it's worth it. You take that one little inch, that precious little God-given free space, and you make it as wide as possible.

JANE And that guy we filmed out in Glace Bay – he's just… wiped?

GRIERSON The film will speak for him, clearly and articulately.

JANE One of your craven hacks is going to churn out another string of platitudes about happy workers all pulling together…

GRIERSON No, you infuriating bloody woman! *I know what I'm doing!* One of my writers is going to say – much more effectively than this fellow – that things which have been *bad* and *wrong* are going to be made better. "That as this war…"

Here GRIERSON switches into the Lorne Greene voice, which is gradually taken over by an amplified, pre-recorded version, in BERNIE's voice, with accompanying martial music, as GRIERSON collapses into a fit of silent coughing.

BERNIE'S VOICE   "...as the People's War reaches its titanic climax, working men and women everywhere affirm their determination that victory will usher in an era of true brotherhood and co-operation. An era in which greed and private profit will be subordinated to an ideal of the common good. An era heralded in Russia where the heroic miners of the Donets labour willingly for the triumph of the Workers' State. An era in which the Canadian working man will never again be vulnerable to the old evils of economic insecurity and the incursion of arbitrary power. An era of freedom and prosperity for all mankind!"

JANE   *(calling after GRIERSON as he crosses to the next scene)* Oh, much more effective! That's just a load of liberal bullshit! For Christ's sake, Grierson, you've completely gutted it!

Scene Thirteen

GRIERSON has been waiting to see Mackenzie KING, who now enters busily.

KING   Mr. Grierson.

GRIERSON   Mr. Prime Minister.

KING   Very good of you to come over to see me.

GRIERSON   Not at all, sir.

KING   *(vaguely indicating a small tray of bottles)* Would you care to…?

GRIERSON   *(surprised)* Really?

KING   Christmas, Mr. Grierson.

GRIERSON   Well. Thank you sir. Don't mind if I do. *(He pours himself a large scotch.)* Yourself?

KING   No, no, no, thank you. I never indulge.

GRIERSON   Wise man.

KING   I know you're very busy over there.

GRIERSON   Oh, I keep them hopping all right. Cracking the whip.

KING   Exactly so. I often feel something like that myself.

GRIERSON   I can imagine.

KING   But if it helps Canadians to take a larger view…

GRIERSON   …of themselves and of the world around them…

KING   …a wider vision…

GRIERSON   …of Canada's relation to the major powers.

KING   Of Canada's relation to the major powers. Now there you've hit it, Mr. Grierson. It's a matter of guiding the popular imagination – fostering, I might say, certain, ah, desirable attitudes, habits of, ah…

GRIERSON   Habits of judgment. We are engaged in a war, Mr. Prime Minister, not just between nations, in a struggle for territory, but a war for the minds of men.

KING   Mr. Grierson, I could not have put it better myself.

GRIERSON   Thank you, sir.

KING   Which brings me to the point. A film of yours – "Workers At War" – has been brought to my attention…

GRIERSON   "Workers Are Warriors…"

KING   Just so.

GRIERSON   It's one of the "Canada Carries On" series.

KING   I understand that it highlights the contribution of the working man…

GRIERSON   …to the all-out effort of the fighting democracies.

KING   The fighting democracies?

GRIERSON   That's right, sir. England, America, Canada…

KING   *(a beat)* Russia.

GRIERSON   Not forgetting China…

KING   You sent photographers all the way to Russia?

GRIERSON   Oh no indeed, sir. As you know, these films are mainly compilations. *Some* original material, also stock footage, stuff supplied by the Allies…

KING   Ah. So the film as we see it…?

GRIERSON   It's an editing job.

KING   And the commentary?

GRIERSON   We write it ourselves. Record it right here.

KING   *You* write it?

GRIERSON   Members of my staff. It's like an editorial, an essay.

KING   Yes. *(a beat)* Well, it won't do, you see.

GRIERSON   Prime Minister?

KING   It won't do. It's quite unsatisfactory.

GRIERSON   How so, sir?

KING A question is going to be asked in the House.

> *A MEMBER OF PARLIAMENT rises in the audience to address a question to the Speaker of the House.*

MEMBER OF PARLIAMENT Mr. Speaker, there is a growing suspicion in some quarters that the National Film Board of Canada is becoming an advocate for a type of socialist and foreign philosophy. Heretofore it was merely an instrument to promote the interests of the Liberal government, which was objectionable enough, Mr. Speaker! My question today, however, to the minister responsible, is whether he is aware that we now have a national instrument of government that is obviously dedicated to fostering the cause of Soviet Russia! To be specific, there is a film entitled *(consults papers)* "Workers Are Warriors," that unmistakably favours and promotes the Communistic way of life! *(pounding of desks)*

KING *(after a pause)* Would you deny that the tone of this film is sympathetic to the Communistic philosophy?

GRIERSON It gives a picture of current industrial developments.

KING But how does it present those "developments?" In what kind of light?

GRIERSON In a neutral light, Mr. Prime Minister; an objective light.

KING *(quoting, from a note in front of him)* "…An era heralded in Russia where the heroic miners of the Donets labour willingly for the triumph of the Workers' State." Would you call that an "objective" commentary?

GRIERSON It's a commentary entirely warranted by the context, sir. The visual at this point is a shot of Russian miners preparing to…

KING "…An era in which greed and private profit will be subordinated to an ideal of the common good." Is that a "neutral" remark?

GRIERSON Sir, I think you'll recall…

KING I'm afraid I have not had the pleasure of viewing the film myself, Mr. Grierson. I am obliged to rely upon reports supplied to me by members of my staff.

GRIERSON *(pouring himself another scotch)* Well, sir, if I might suggest, the members of your staff whose job it is to look for subversive intentions in the productions of the National Film Board had better take a short course in the art of appropriately interpreting a motion picture film!

KING But you do not deny, Mr. Grierson, that the words I have quoted are actually spoken in the film?

GRIERSON Mr. Prime Minister, I would be only too happy to supply you with a transcript of the commentary…

KING And the pictures you refer to, of the, ah, Russian coal miners…

GRIERSON The pictures speak for themselves. It's footage supplied to us by the Russian Embassy.

KING Propaganda, Mr. Grierson, propaganda!

GRIERSON A picture of coal miners going about their work is not propaganda, Mr. Prime Minister, it is a simple visual statement of fact.

KING Mr. Grierson, I have to put it to you that this is not at all the kind of thing for which the National Film Board was created. I have heard reports that call into question the, ah, dependability of some persons at the Board…

GRIERSON Dependability, sir?

KING Their political dependability, their moral probity…

GRIERSON May I ask where these insinuations come from?

KING I am not at liberty to say.

GRIERSON I see.

KING Now do understand, I am not specifically impugning your own loyalty…

GRIERSON Thank you, sir.

KING …though it has been brought to my attention that you have accepted the post of chairman of the Canadian-Soviet Friendship Council…

GRIERSON Chairman of the Film Committee of the Council, sir. It's an honorary position.

KING Ah! But in the case of this film, "The Workers' Army…"

GRIERSON "Workers Are Warriors…"

KING …prudence dictates that the, ah, questionable, sequences be removed. It is possible to do that with film, is it not? To, ah, fix things up?

GRIERSON It is possible.

KING Then I can depend on you to see that it is done?

GRIERSON With respect, sir, it seems to me to be an unwarranted intrusion…

KING The privilege of paying the piper, Mr. Grierson.

GRIERSON *(truculently)* And if I were to say that the integrity of the film would be violated by such an excision…?

KING Of course, of course. Naturally I would defer to your judgment in such matters. *(a beat)* Then the film as a whole would have to be suppressed.

GRIERSON I see.

KING The choice is yours, Mr. Grierson. And now, if you will excuse me…. Thank you for coming to see me.

Mackenzie KING leaves. GRIERSON remains, moving over to the NFB area of the stage, where he pours himself another drink. FREDA is in her usual place.

FREDA *(over the intercom)* Mr. Grierson, sir?

GRIERSON Who is it?

FREDA It's Freda, sir.

GRIERSON Oh, well, call Mrs. Grierson for me, will you? *(to himself, lighting yet another cigarette)* Oh, he's a cautious one, that Willie King.

FREDA *(after a few seconds)* She's not there, sir.

GRIERSON What?

FREDA Mrs. Grierson's not there.

GRIERSON *(to himself)* Save me from the bloody politicians!

FREDA I beg your pardon, sir?

GRIERSON *(to intercom)* Not there? *(to himself)* What's she doing?

FREDA Mr. Grierson, sir…

GRIERSON I should have seen this coming.

FREDA You won't forget to put in a word about my transfer?

GRIERSON Transfer? What are you talking about?

FREDA To the NRC, the Research Council.

GRIERSON What do you want to go there for?

FREDA Well, sir, it's…

GRIERSON "The thanes fly from me."

FREDA Excuse me?

GRIERSON Never mind.

FREDA I don't mean to press you, sir, but…

GRIERSON What is it you want, girl?

FREDA Well, the position calls for a four, and I'm only a three.

GRIERSON And what has this to do with me?

FREDA Well, I wondered if you could, you know, put in a word…. You said you might, and I thought…

GRIERSON *(impatiently)* Freda, love, draft me a memo saying whatever you want me to say, and give it to me to sign, all right? Over and out!

FREDA Thank you, sir.

GRIERSON *(to himself)* It's the beginning of the end, you realize that?

JANE *(entering)* Well?

GRIERSON Eh?

JANE Are you going to stand up to him?

GRIERSON I'm a civil servant.

JANE Is that "civil" or "servile?"

GRIERSON "I have done the state some service, and they know it."

JANE *Othello.*

GRIERSON Clever girl.

JANE You're not answering.

GRIERSON I don't have to answer to you.

JANE You think you can dodge and dodge and not answer to anyone, don't you?

GRIERSON *(to the intercom)* Freda! Are you still there?

JANE The artful dodger.

FREDA Yes, sir?

GRIERSON Put a call through to the Prime Minister, will you?

JANE But he's more of an artful dodger than you are, Grierson.

FREDA At this time, sir?

JANE *(as if to witnesses)* I said to him, "You're going to scrap the film, aren't you?"

GRIERSON *(to the intercom)* Get a move on!

JANE I said to him, "I'm just about sick of all this political shit!"

GRIERSON You did, didn't you!

JANE I said, "You scrap that film and I am finished. Finished with this crummy outfit, and finished with you."

GRIERSON Jane, you don't understand…

JANE I said, "You can make your own damn films from now on."

GRIERSON And what did "he" say?

JANE He said…

GRIERSON Yes?

JANE He said, "There's plenty more where you came from."

GRIERSON So he did.

JANE "Plenty more fish in the sea."

GRIERSON Yes.

JANE But not like me. You know that. *(loudly)* Come on in, Bernie! Don't be shy. It's only Grierson. *(BERNIE enters sheepishly.)* Bernie and I are lovers, Grierson. Isn't that right, Bernie? *(BERNIE is dumfounded.)* I thought you ought to know.

GRIERSON No. I won't allow it!

JANE Nothing you can do about it.

GRIERSON You're being childish and pathetic.

JANE Nobody pathetic around here except you. You're getting old, Grierson. An old drunk. *(pause)* You're going to scrap the film altogether, aren't you? So much for your precious little inch! *(pause)* Shall I just "pull the door to" then? *(JANE leaves with BERNIE.)*

GRIERSON Why don't you do that? *(The door slams.)* Jane. Jane! Come back here, damn it!

FREDA Mr. Grierson…? Your call to the Prime Minister…

GRIERSON Yes. Put me through.

FREDA I'm sorry, sir, but I'm afraid Mr. King cannot be reached just now.

> *Suddenly the theatre is filled with the sounds of a victory celebration – bells, sirens, car horns, cheering – and a drunken singing of Vera Lynn's "We'll Meet Again" (Ross Parker/Hughie Charles, Vera Lynn version). As the sounds fade, the hooded figure of Gouzenko re-appears, and responds to questions.*

VOICE OF GOUZENKO INQUIRY COUNSEL *(He is reading from notes.)* "Freda to the Professor through Grierson." Is that right? *(The figure nods.)* And "Freda" was a secretary to Mr. Grierson? *(The figure nods.)* But "Freda" was also a Soviet agent, correct? *(The figure nods.)* It was part of the strategy at that time to position "Freda" at the National Research Council? *(The figure nods.)* And to use the influence of Grierson to secure this move? *(The figure nods.)* Was Grierson also an agent? *(The figure shakes its head.)* Grierson was *not* an agent at that time? *(The figure shakes its head.)* But he was a person that could be counted on for help in this connection? *(The figure nods.)* Was any consideration given at that time to recruiting Grierson as an agent? *(The figure nods.)* Consideration *was* given to recruiting Grierson? *(The figure nods.)* Thank you. You are being most helpful.

VOICES IN CHORUS *(bringing the song to an end)* "…but I know we'll meet again some sunny day!"

Scene Fourteen

The end of the previous scene has left GRIERSON back in his 1970 hotel room, brooding impassively. A distant police siren is heard. After a pause, MICHAEL comes into the room. He has a bloody bandage round his forehead, and a broken camera in his hand. BERNIE follows, still badgering him.

BERNIE For Christ's sake, Michael, I warned you!

MICHAEL Those bastards! Fascist bastards!

BERNIE What in hell did you expect? *(He gets ice from the fridge for MICHAEL's wound.)* Here. Sit down. Now listen to what I'm trying to tell you. When this thing is over, when the heat's off, I'm ready to entertain a proposal for a serious film that documents this whole business, okay? You listening? Something that goes into the history, puts it in perspective... that's just fine, I've no problem with that, and if you're prepared to be part of a team, there's no reason you shouldn't be involved in it. But this thing right now, there's no way... I couldn't be a party to it.

MICHAEL I'm not asking you to...

BERNIE *(getting himself a drink)* The Board has a mandate, do you see that?

MICHAEL Not to become stooges...

BERNIE ...a public trust.

MICHAEL ...to present the truth!

BERNIE We're accountable. This is public money, don't forget.

MICHAEL Right! The people's money.

BERNIE "The king's shilling" – you know what that means? The films we make have got to reflect a social consensus...

MICHAEL What the hell does that mean?

BERNIE We have to be seen to be objective. The space we operate in has definite limits.

MICHAEL It's such a fucking cop-out!

BERNIE For Christ's sake, if we're seen to take a political stance, my ass will be on the line!

MICHAEL Best place for it.

BERNIE *(a beat)* Let's put it another way, shall we? If you shoot one foot of film right now without my authorization, you are gone, you are finished, you are out of the NFB, you can kiss it goodbye, because there's no way you're getting back in.

GRIERSON *(suddenly intervening decisively)* No!

BERNIE What?

GRIERSON I cannot listen to any more of this.

BERNIE But Grierson…

GRIERSON Not with my liquor in your hand.

BERNIE Look, all I'm saying is…

GRIERSON *I know what you're saying!* God forgive me, I know all too well what you're saying. *(Pause. They look at him.)* Thirty-five years ago a… young woman… was making a movie for me. This was in Britain, now, in the thirties, the dirty thirties. This young woman was going to change the world. Well, we were all going to change the world, but she was the best of us, the real radical. She wanted to make a film about the city slums, the east end, the docks. It shocked her to the soul to see the conditions people were living in – worse than animals. If she could make a film to show the filth, the squalor of their lives, shine a searchlight on all that! And I got the money for it. A public utility, don't ask me how, was beguiled into putting up the cash. This is your big chance, I said to her. Play your cards right. Oh, I knew just how it had to be done!

> *During GRIERSON's speech the YOUNG WOMAN from earlier scenes of the play – doubling with TANYA – has appeared, accompanied by the melody of "My Darling, Clementine," perhaps whistling it herself. There is something roguish about her, her cap at an angle, and a cigarette in her hand. As he moves out of the 1970 set to outline the proposed film to her, GRIERSON is younger than we have ever seen him.*

The clash of opposites, the old and the new. Do you see it? *(He makes the classic "framing" gesture with his fingers.)* The wretched hovels, the sullen faces shrinking back as your camera peers in the windows. Then, smash, the wrecker's ball, and smash, again. The ring of the carpenter's hammer, the chink of the bricklayer's trowel, "as the promise of a decent dwelling rises at last from the rubble of a century of squalor and neglect…"

YOUNG WOMAN John!

GRIERSON Aye?

YOUNG WOMAN *(Scottish accent)* D'ye never listen to yourself, John? Just for a minute?

GRIERSON *(lighting a cigarette)* Never. I'm too busy talking.

YOUNG WOMAN Well, that's honest enough. But I think you should, once in a while.

GRIERSON What would I hear, then?

YOUNG WOMAN You'd hear an awful clever young man, who thinks he knows everything.

She puts her cap on his head.

GRIERSON   Are ye going to tell me that I don't?

YOUNG WOMAN   *(linking arms)* Och, it's not that ye don't know everything. I'm sure ye do. But ye know it all from the outside. Through your lens. *(She mocks GRIERSON's "framing" action.)* Peering in. Ye look at everything as though it's in a goldfish bowl, and you're the only one on the outside.

GRIERSON   *(considering)* Yes. I think I do. What's wrong with that?

YOUNG WOMAN   Oh, it's fine for you, John. But it's awful hard on the fish sometimes.

GRIERSON   It's my nature, girl. I can't change the way I am.

YOUNG WOMAN   I don't ask ye to. But it won't do for me at all. When I go into the slums to make that film, I'm not going to peer into the windows, I'm going to knock on the door. And if they'll let me in, I'll say to them, "This film's for you. Show me where to point this camera of mine. And as for what it's like to live here," I'll say, "I can't tell anything about that. But *you* can. And people will listen. All those people out there in the audience, do you see them? You take this microphone," I'll say, "and you look them square in the eye, and you let them know just what it's like to live in a slum. Give the bastards a real earful!" *(She is isolated in a spotlight.)*

GRIERSON   *(He is back in 1970.)* She was a Grierson too. My sister, Ruby. Early in the war, I told her to come over and join me. She was making a film on the children being evacuated to Canada. I told her to come along with them, to make the film from both ends. *(pause)* The ship was torpedoed by a German submarine. *(pause)* There were two-hundred and forty-eight survivors. I had summoned her to her death. *(The light fades on the YOUNG WOMAN. The melody of "My Darling, Clementine" is echoed and dies away. GRIERSON addresses BERNIE gruffly.)* Let him shoot his film, Slater. With my blessing, for what it's worth. *(to MICHAEL)* Give the bastards a real earful!

This is an emotional moment. MICHAEL and BERNIE are silenced. It feels like the end of the play. But JANE, entering the scene, punctures the mood with an ironic slow handclap.

JANE   *(She too is moved.)* Very good. But it's not enough. You don't get into heaven that easily!

GRIERSON   What?

JANE   Playing to the gallery. Grierson's deathbed repentance.

BERNIE   Don't you ever stop?

JANE   Not yet, sweetheart. If he wants a full pardon, he's got to work for it.

GRIERSON   What is it now, Jane Barnes?

Elizabeth Marmur and Layne Coleman
photo © Lydia Pawelak

JANE You're coming to India.

GRIERSON Oh, I am, am I?

JANE You are. You're going to do something useful in your old age.

GRIERSON What about my students?

JANE Oh, your students! You'll only be gone a month. I'm sure they'll manage.

GRIERSON And what am I to do when I get there?

JANE I told you. We're training young people.

GRIERSON Och, they'll have no time for an old codger like me.

JANE Nonsense, they'll be tickled pink to meet the Big Cheese. *(JANE and GRIERSON are making their way to a row of three of airplane seats. They make themselves comfortable, JANE helping GRIERSON to settle a pillow and fasten his seat belt.)* But you're coming to *help* – remember? You're coming to offer some humble assistance to people who want to make their own films for their own purposes. You're not going to shout at anyone, or order anyone around, or tell anyone that they've got to do things your way.

GRIERSON Come on now, woman – I can't change my nature!

JANE Work on it! *(pause)* Did I really say those things?

GRIERSON Which things?

JANE Calling you an old drunk. That wasn't very nice, was it!

GRIERSON I did call you back, you know.

JANE *(a beat)* I know. I heard you. Well, better late than never. *(She empties her glass.)* Listen, try and get a bit of sleep. We'll be in Bombay sooner than you think. *(She switches off her overhead light.)* Goodnight, Grierson.

GRIERSON Goodnight, girl.

He keeps his overhead light on, and begins to play with an eight millimetre camera. TANYA goes over and sits in the vacant airplane seat beside him. She takes his hand.

(reproachfully) You said you wouldn't tell anyone!

As the lights fade, the sound of waves breaking on a beach can be heard, and, if a screen is being used, a photograph of the real GRIERSON appears, staring inscrutably out at the spectator.

End.

John Grierson
photo: Grierson Archive, University of Stirling, Scotland, UK

BORDERLINE

Lucky Ejim and Niki Landau
photo by Megan Paquette

Borderline was first produced in the Toronto Summerworks Festival, in August 2004, with the following company:

PATRICE UMBIWIMANA	Lucky Ejim
NICKI OLSEN	Niki Landau
CAPTAIN LARRY BREEN	Marvin Hinz
MAJOR JOEL KANYEMERA	Ayodele Adewumi
Direction	Mark Cassidy
Lighting Design	Liz Asselstine
Set Design	Robert Fothergill
Sound Design	Peter Cassidy
Movement Coach	Simon Fon
Stage Management	Jessie Shearer

A somewhat revised version was subsequently produced by CBC Radio in Toronto, for broadcast in June 2005, with the following company:

PATRICE UMBIWIMANA	Lucky Ejim
NICKI OLSEN	Wendy Crewson
CAPTAIN LARRY BREEN	John Cleland
MAJOR JOEL KANYEMERA	Bayo Akinfemi
Director and Producer	Damiano Pietropaolo
Associate Producer	Colleen Woods
Recording Engineer	Wayne Richards
Sound Effects	Anton Szabo
Script Editor	Dave Carley
Casting	Linda Grearson

CHARACTERS

VERONICA (NICKI) OLSEN, Canadian aid worker, 42.
CAPTAIN LARRY BREEN, Canadian peacekeeper, 40.
PATRICE UMBIWIMANA, Rwandan-Hutu, 29.
MAJOR JOEL KANYEMERA, Rwandan-Tutsi, 35.

SETTING

A refugee camp on the borders of Rwanda and Tanzania.

TIME

July 1994.

NOTE

Permission to use the suggested extracts from McGarrigle Sisters songs must always be freshly obtained by anyone re-mounting the play

BORDERLINE

Scene One

The scene is NICKI's tent: table, folding chairs, cot, hanging Coleman lamp, little cupboard, large clunky cell phone. Late equatorial dusk, red sky darkening to black behind the tent – we are looking westward. There is no electricity; illumination will come from the hanging Coleman lamp.

Enter NICKI wearily; shirt, jeans, boots, headband, wearing glasses; she is dusty, tired, dishevelled. She lights the lamp, effectively obliterating the last vestiges of the sunset. She pulls off the headband, leans on the table, shaking with exhaustion and strain.

NICKI *(after a long pause)* Oh my God, I can't stand this much longer. *(pause)* Okay, I can, I can stand it. If they can stand it, so can I. I guess.

With a new access of energy she wipes her face with a wet wipe and towel, looks in a small mirror, sits at the table, tries to get some reception on a small battery-powered radio/tape player, mainly static. She puts a cassette into the player, looks at her watch, presses record button, begins to speak.

Okay it's what? *(checking her watch)* It's July the ninth. *(long pause)* July the ninth. It's very hot. Again. And… I'm still here. And they're still coming. And we're still coping. Just. Um…. That's it. Over and out. Fascinating listening this is going to be.

She stops the tape, closes her eyes for a long moment, removes the cassette, puts in another one, presses play; music: the McGarrigle Sisters singing "Complainte pour Ste. Catherine" (Philippe Tatartcheff/Anna McGarrigle/Les editions Macbec SOCAN/Bossy Publishing SOCAN). She puts on a pair of earphones and plugs them into the cassette player; the music is suddenly amplified, emphasizing her subjectivity. She removes her glasses, puts her head down on her folded arms; long pause; she is virtually asleep.

Enter Captain Larry BREEN, in the uniform of a UN soldier, blue beret etc. He stands behind her for a while, then puts his hands familiarly on her shoulders.

BREEN *(simply)* Hi. Nicki?

NICKI *(Startled into wakefulness, she covers his hands in an ambiguous gesture – clasping them or arresting their progress?)* What? Oh, Larry! *(She removes the earphones; the volume of the music diminishes.)*

BREEN   I startled you.

NICKI   No, it's okay. *(She shifts his hands slightly.)* There.

BREEN   What?

NICKI   Just… there. *(He kneads the muscles of her shoulders.)* Yes. Like that. That's good. *(pause)* What time is it? *(checks watch)* I guess I wasn't…. So, what are you…?

BREEN   I just came by to see if you're okay… if you, like, need anything.

NICKI   Ah. *(puts glasses on again)* And do I?

BREEN   Well, I think you do, but of course I'm biased.

NICKI   You are, aren't you!

BREEN   Here, I got you this. *(a chocolate bar)*

NICKI   Oh my God, comfort food! Where did you get it?

BREEN   Friends in low places.

NICKI   The Canadian army, boy! "There's no life like it."

BREEN   Do I get a thank you?

NICKI   Thank you. *(She kisses one of the hands still on her shoulders.)*

BREEN   So, how are you?

NICKI   I'm okay. Well I'm not, but I am, if you know what I mean.

BREEN   Just when you figure it can't get any worse, it does.

NICKI   It's just… Jesus, I've never seen anything like this. They just keep on coming. We can't feed them, we can't house them, there's virtually no clean water, they're dying by the hundreds. They stare at us like ghosts.

BREEN   Ghouls, more like. They're dead inside, these people.

NICKI   Jesus God! Sometimes it feels so utterly futile.

BREEN   *(bluntly)* So why do you do it? Why bother?

NICKI   How can we not? We can't do *nothing*. Once it's happening, and we know about it…

BREEN   We managed to do nothing during the massacres! Now you guys rush in to save the killers.

NICKI   Whatever they've done, they're victims now.

BREEN   Oh yeah? A lot of these people are ex-Interahamwe. They're still armed, some of them.

NICKI   Oh come on! Women and children. Terrified, hungry, sick. Babies dying…

BREEN   Why do *you* do it?

NICKI I'm on the list. I've got training. I've had experience. Call comes, I go.

BREEN You could say no.

NICKI I could.

BREEN You don't have to be the one every time.

NICKI I know that. And I've said no in the past.

BREEN Saving your soul. Relieving your First World liberal guilt.

NICKI Well, what if it is? We've got a lot of guilt to relieve!

BREEN Speak for yourself!

NICKI And I do love Africa. It's my *place*, you know? It's also my "field," my "academic area."

BREEN And the university doesn't mind you just taking off?

NICKI Shit no, they think it's great! Lots of brownie points. Picture in the President's *Gazette*. Anyway, it's out of term time.

BREEN Me, I hate it. Hate Africa, hate this job. We're ordered here, we do it. Order comes to leave, I'm first on the plane. Can't get out fast enough.

NICKI I don't believe that.

BREEN It's a job. A shitty awful job. I don't get any moral satisfaction out of it. *(pause)* You know what I really can't stand about a situation like this? The stench. The filth.

NICKI I don't suppose they like it much themselves.

BREEN No, but they bring it with them, don't they. Anyway, you think this is bad, it's about to get worse.

NICKI Well, aren't you the cheerful one! How?

BREEN Kigali's been overrun.

NICKI Finally! When?

BREEN Two days ago. Don't they tell you people anything?

NICKI Well, that's good, isn't it?

BREEN Depends which side you're on. Probably means the fighting's just about over.

NICKI I thought I heard shooting earlier this evening.

BREEN We figure it's units of the RPF.

NICKI Tutsi guerrillas?

BREEN Not anymore, thank you ma'am! As of yesterday, they're the government army.

NICKI   They can't be coming here, can they?

BREEN   Who knows?

NICKI   Well, I mean, *can* they?

BREEN   Legally they shouldn't cross the Tanzanian border, but there's fuck-all around here to stop them. What's left of the old government forces are on the run, pushing most of the Hutu population along with them. Who are now totally shit-scared, by the way. As well they might be, 'cause right now the RPF are pretty bloody-minded.

NICKI   Christ. What happens if they come into the camp?

BREEN   The Ghanaians have secured the airstrip, if we have to pull out…

NICKI   I mean to the refugees? We're just going to leave all these people…

BREEN   …to the tender mercies of Tutsi soldiers who are still finding out what the Hutu did to their brothers and sisters. And nothing we can do about it.

NICKI   Jesus, what a bloody nightmare!

BREEN   You ain't kidding. Nicki, listen. If the shit hits the fan, we're going to have to get out of here real fast. You can't *save* anybody, know what I'm saying? You get on that plane, and you go.

NICKI   I hear you.

BREEN   I just want you to know, I'll be looking out for you, making sure you're okay.

NICKI   *(guarded)* That's very chivalrous of you.

BREEN   You know what I'm saying?

NICKI   Yes. I know.

BREEN   *(after a pause)* So what do you think?

NICKI   About what?

BREEN   You know.

NICKI   Do I?

BREEN   Come on, don't be cute. We're too old for that.

NICKI   Speak for yourself.

BREEN   So…?

NICKI   So?

BREEN   So, do you want me to come by later?

NICKI   Better not, don't you think?

BREEN   Do I think? No, I don't think.

NICKI   Larry. I don't know.

BREEN   What don't you know?

NICKI   It doesn't make sense.

BREEN   Makes more sense than most things.

NICKI   You would think that.

BREEN   Bit of comfort. Bit of company.

NICKI   Yes. I know.

BREEN   So.

NICKI   There's so much wretchedness. It's so *hot*. I'm exhausted.

BREEN   These aren't reasons.

NICKI   No. I suppose not.

BREEN   So what then?

NICKI   Well… *(lifting his ring hand)* What about this? Mm?

BREEN   What about it?

NICKI   You tell me.

BREEN   Same one as yesterday. *(beat)* I thought you were okay with it.

NICKI   So did I.

BREEN   So?

NICKI   Larry, I'm sorry…

BREEN   Sure, sure…. Fine. I get the message.

NICKI   Do you?

BREEN   *(briskly)* I'd better go. Got to see the Ghanaian C.O. Beef up the security around the compound. Some rough characters out there.

NICKI   Larry, you're a gent. I'm not kidding.

BREEN   Sure. So. You going to be okay then?

NICKI   I'll be fine. I've been in places like this before you know.

BREEN   Because if there's anything you need…

NICKI   …I have this. *(the cell phone)* Actually, what I need is sleep. Don't you ever sleep?

BREEN   Nah. Given it up. *(pause)* Okay, well, goodnight, I guess.

NICKI   Good night, Larry. And thanks, you know?

BREEN   Really. *(He goes.)*

Alone once more, NICKI relaxes, sits at the table, plays another McGarrigle's track "Tell My Sister" (Kate McGarrigle/Garden Court Music ASCAP), unbuttons her shirt, puts cream on her face, gets a nearly empty 40 of scotch from the cupboard and pours a rationed shot into a plastic cup, takes a sip, shuts her eyes.

NICKI   *(matter of factly)* Our father or mother, whichever you prefer, who art in heaven, hallowed be thy name, thy kingdom come, thy will be done on earth as it is in heaven. Give us this day our daily bread, and forgive us our trespasses as we forgive them that trespass against us. Lead us not into temptation, but deliver us from evil – if it's not too much to ask.

In the shadows behind the tent, a figure is moving. An African MAN, raggedly dressed in shirt and shorts, bare feet, dirty, emerges from the darkness and approaches NICKI cautiously. She is drifting into sleep again, but a movement startles her, and she jerks awake to see the intruder crouching a few feet away.

(panicky) What do you want? What are you doing here? I'm sorry but you can't come inside the compound. *(He stands, moves towards her; she tries to button her shirt.)* Please! We open at seven in the morning. There's nothing here. *(He comes closer.)* Get away from me! *(She grabs the cell phone and starts to punch in a number. He leaps forward and grabs the phone.)* Aaaah!

MAN   *(urgently)* Veronica?

NICKI   What?

MAN   You don't recognize me.

NICKI   *(She does.)* Oh my God!

MAN   Nicki.

NICKI   Patrice? *(It is.)* Oh my God.

PATRICE   You didn't recognize me.

NICKI   *(buttoning her shirt)* I… I didn't… I'm sorry…

PATRICE   I am making you nervous.

NICKI   No, I mean, I'm just… you scared me. Christ!

PATRICE   I'm sorry. I will go.

NICKI   No! Of course you can't *go!* Back out there? *(pause)* Patrice. You're alive. You're here.

PATRICE   I'm here. *(a beat)* Are you happy to see me?

NICKI   Yes! Of course! It's just…

> PATRICE *is reaching out to touch her, when* BREEN *enters abruptly. He grabs* PATRICE *in an armlock, checks him for a weapon, seems about to rough him up.*

BREEN   How the hell did he get in here? *(loudly)* What are you after? Huh? Huh? You don't come in here! Do you understand? *Peux pas entrer ici, compris?*

NICKI   Larry, it's all right!

PATRICE   *Oui, je comprends.*

BREEN   Ah. *Vous parlez français?*

PATRICE   Or English, as you wish.

NICKI   It's all right, Larry.

BREEN   It's not all right! No refugees inside the compound! I don't know what the hell you're think you're doing, but you're coming with me.

NICKI   No, really, Larry…

BREEN   *(forcing PATRICE to his knees)* Did he attack you? If you laid a finger on this lady, I'll smash your brains out.

NICKI   Larry… I know him!

BREEN   What?

NICKI   He's a… friend.

BREEN   *(registering this)* A friend? A friend of yours?

PATRICE   As Doctor Olsen says.

NICKI   Oh not "Doctor Olsen" for God's sake!

PATRICE   As Veronica says.

BREEN   Where from?

NICKI   His name is Patrice Umbiwimana…

PATRICE   *(hastily cutting her off)* Patrice Nkongoli.

NICKI   This is Captain Breen.

BREEN   Whatever. He's not supposed to be inside the compound. None of them are. How did he get in?

NICKI   Larry, please! Let him go!

BREEN   How did you get in here?

NICKI   There's nothing to worry about! He's not… I mean… I take responsibility.

PATRICE   *(still on his knees)* She takes responsibility.

NICKI   Larry, stop this.

BREEN Some of these people are armed. From the militias, the Interahamwe.

NICKI I know, but this is different. Larry, let him go!

BREEN *(reluctantly releasing PATRICE)* He can't stay here, you know that.

NICKI Yes, I do know that!

BREEN So make sure he's out of here…

NICKI All right, already!

BREEN I'm giving you twenty minutes, then I'm coming right back.

NICKI Yes! All right! Just… go, okay?

BREEN *(a warning)* I'm right here if you need…

NICKI That's fine. That's great.

BREEN So don't try anything, okay? *(BREEN goes. There is an awkward pause.)*

NICKI *(She is extremely agitated.)* Oh God, this is so crazy. What are you *doing here?* Well, I mean, obviously you're… you've come from Kigali? Are you all right? Are you, I mean, hungry?

PATRICE What do you think?

NICKI The trouble is, I don't have anything…

PATRICE Veronica…

NICKI It's all locked up. I've got this. *(the chocolate bar)*

PATRICE Veronica.

NICKI Yes?

PATRICE Is that whisky?

NICKI Oh. Yes, it is. I probably shouldn't, I mean, in the middle of all this, but it's nearly gone and…

PATRICE Yes?

NICKI Well, it was duty free.

PATRICE *(with slight irony)* So that's all right.

NICKI I've only got these plastic cups…

PATRICE If I could…?

NICKI Of course! *(He pours himself a shot and drinks.)* Patrice! You're shivering! Here! *(She wraps a blanket around him.)* Are you all right? Do you want to… tell me…?

PATRICE *(noticing)* You are wearing glasses. They make you look…

NICKI Older, I know.

PATRICE   More severe.

NICKI   I can't keep contacts in, not with all the dust. *(pause)* You're in the camp?

PATRICE   Yes. I am in the camp.

NICKI   How long…?

PATRICE   Two days.

NICKI   And you came… from there? From Kigali? On foot? Your family, are they…?

PATRICE   They are alive.

NICKI   Oh thank God! I'm sorry. That sounds so trite. *(pause)* How did you find me? What gave you any idea…?

PATRICE   There is a CANAID mission.

NICKI   Yes, but…

PATRICE   I heard there was a Canadian lady…

NICKI   And you thought…

PATRICE   I thought, why not? It is possible.

>   *There is a distant burst of automatic weapons fire. NICKI and PATRICE both tense in alarm.*

NICKI   Oh shit, what are they doing?

PATRICE   They are on the other side of the river.

NICKI   The RPF? *(The gunfire sounds again. They listen.)*

PATRICE   And you, how long are you here?

NICKI   Oh God, an eternity. Twenty-three days, I think. They just keep coming and coming.

PATRICE   "They?"

NICKI   There's so little we can really do.

PATRICE   But you are doing something. Feeding the hungry. Christian charity.

NICKI   Patrice. Why did you lie to Captain Breen?

PATRICE   Lie?

NICKI   Your name. You said…

PATRICE   …is a well-known Hutu name. It is not good to be a Hutu now. My name is a death warrant.

NICKI   You were there, in Kigali, during the…?

PATRICE   *(suddenly guarded)* I was there.

NICKI   Larry was there too, in the first few weeks, before they were pulled out. He won't talk about it. *(pause)* Do you want to sleep here?

PATRICE   You know I cannot do that. "Larry" said so.

NICKI   But where do you…?

PATRICE   In the dust when it's dry, in the mud when it rains. *(beat)* Do you have washing water?

NICKI   Oh, I do! *(She grabs a plastic canister and a bowl.)*

PATRICE   I have not washed myself for… many days.

NICKI   They give us twenty-five litres a day. It's a disgraceful luxury. But I'm more or less dirty all the time anyway. You tend to stop bothering. *(noticing)* Oh God, your feet… they're all cut up! *(She starts to wash his feet.)*

PATRICE   I wore shoes for too long. Like a civilized person.

NICKI   Patrice. Why did you never write to me?

PATRICE   I wrote to you!

NICKI   A postcard, from Nairobi.

PATRICE   I wrote letters.

NICKI   When?

PATRICE   You didn't receive them?

NICKI   I've had nothing from you for over a year.

PATRICE   This is our shitty postal service. The clerks take the stamps off and resell them.

NICKI   You didn't have to use the post office. You could have faxed, you could have used the diplomatic bag, you could have *telephoned* me!

PATRICE   How could I…?

NICKI   You were Minister for Economic Development, for Christ's sake! I know! I read *Africa Report*. You think I didn't try and find out everything I could?

PATRICE   It was difficult…

NICKI   How difficult could it be? You never tried.

PATRICE   Veronica…

NICKI   What?

PATRICE   Please. Will you help me? *(pause)* You said I could sleep here?

NICKI   You must be exhausted.

PATRICE   I have not slept in a bed for… a while.

NICKI   It's only a cot.

PATRICE Where will you sleep?

NICKI I'll be all right. Here, have the blanket. It gets quite cold by dawn.

PATRICE *(ironically)* Really?

NICKI Of course. Stupid of me.

PATRICE Nicki, you are very good.

NICKI Yes, I know. I'm a relief worker.

PATRICE Nicki.

NICKI Yes?

PATRICE I'm afraid.

NICKI It's all right. You're safe here. Sleep.

> *PATRICE composes himself to sleep. NICKI plays tape "Talk to Me of Mendocino" (Kate McGarrigle/Anna McGarrigle) and sits beside him. When he appears to be asleep, she leans over and kisses him. She gets up, pours the last few drops of scotch, and drains the glass. She sits again at the table, lowers the volume on the tape, turns the lamp down, takes a couple of pills, cleans her teeth, rests her head on her arms. After a while, Larry BREEN enters.*

BREEN *(abruptly)* Has he gone?

NICKI Ssssh.

BREEN What?

NICKI He's exhausted.

BREEN Nicki, you know he can't…

NICKI SSSSSH! I said he could.

BREEN But…

NICKI He's been on the road for God knows how long.

BREEN So have all the others.

NICKI Larry, I can't turn him away.

BREEN Who the hell is he? Where do you know him from?

NICKI He was my… student.

BREEN He was *what?*

NICKI My student. Grad student. At Concordia.

BREEN Rich, then?

NICKI Oh yes. Quite, I gather. Or he was. His family were…

BREEN   What?

NICKI   Well, quite prominent.

BREEN   In the previous regime.

NICKI   Yes.

BREEN   I see. A prominent Hutu. *(beat)* Your student?

NICKI   He was doing his Master's. *(beat)* I was his supervisor.

BREEN   Oh really! His "supervisor." You "supervised" him.

NICKI   What are you suggesting?

BREEN   I'm not suggesting anything.

NICKI   Yes you are, you're accusing me…

BREEN   I'm not accusing you…

NICKI   …of having a relationship with him.

BREEN   Not at all.

NICKI   Well it's true. I did.

BREEN   I see.

NICKI   No, you don't see.

BREEN   That sort of thing okay is it? In the university?

NICKI   It's none of your business.

BREEN   A bit young, don't you think?

NICKI   For what?

BREEN   Well…

NICKI   I'm a bit old, that's what you mean.

BREEN   Is he the reason you came here?

NICKI   I didn't expect to find him. How could I imagine…?

BREEN   All the same, you…

NICKI   Yes! I wondered about him.

BREEN   You must be relieved.

NICKI   Of course I'm relieved! God knows what he's been through!

BREEN   God knows indeed! *(beat)* And now what?

NICKI   I don't know. I haven't thought.

BREEN   He can't stay here.

NICKI   So you keep saying.

BREEN Well he can't! All right?

NICKI All right! *(beat)* Listen, I don't care what you say, or what the official rules are, I can't just…

BREEN What else do you have in mind?

NICKI He's a *person*, for God's sake!

BREEN Let's hope so.

NICKI What the hell do you mean by that?

BREEN I was *in* Kigali. I was *there*, right? You know what I'm saying?

NICKI Larry, this is someone I *know*.

BREEN Sure, you were his "supervisor."

NICKI Don't be such a shit.

BREEN Listen, no business of mine. *(leaving)* I hope you know what you're doing.

NICKI *(calling after him)* Larry! Don't be like that. Oh shit!

Silence. The crickets are loud in the night.

PATRICE *(suddenly)* So what *are* you going to do with him?

NICKI Oh my God. I thought you were asleep.

PATRICE You will send me back out there.

NICKI Patrice!

PATRICE You have to.

NICKI We'll have to hide you. That's all there is to it. *(She looks around her meagre tent ironically.)* Well I don't know! God, I wish I had more scotch.

PATRICE I'm sorry.

NICKI In the stores shed or somewhere. At least during the day.

PATRICE He'll be looking.

NICKI It's none of his business.

PATRICE He wants to have you for himself.

NICKI Oh ridiculous.

PATRICE It's true, I can see it.

NICKI He's a married man.

PATRICE And that makes a difference?

NICKI It does to me.

PATRICE Nicki, I am in very big danger here, you know that.

NICKI   Here?

PATRICE   In the camp.

NICKI   This is a safe area.

PATRICE   The RPF are coming. They're just across the river.

NICKI   But why should they come here?

PATRICE   They are looking for leading Hutu. To kill them. For revenge.

NICKI   God help us.

PATRICE   Especially Hutu from the old elite. If they find me, they will kill me.

NICKI   *(decisively)* Then we have to get you away.

PATRICE   Where? Into Tanzania? They don't want us. Into Kenya? How do I get there?

NICKI   Well you can't just sit here! You can't!

PATRICE   *(beat)* You could take me to Canada.

NICKI   Patrice – how could I?

PATRICE   Yes, you could.

NICKI   How?

PATRICE   As a refugee.

NICKI   But I can't... there's a whole process... you know that. I mean, you have to claim refugee status, and be vetted, and I don't even know...

PATRICE   You could sponsor me. If you wanted to.

NICKI   Oh Jesus.

PATRICE   Veronica. If I am found I will be killed. *(pause)* You can vouch for me. Identify me.

NICKI   What do you mean?

PATRICE   I have no papers, no passport, nothing to say who I am. You can identify me.

NICKI   Patrice, you don't understand. I can't...

PATRICE   Nicki, my life is in your hands.

NICKI   Don't say that.

PATRICE   I have a lot of money, you know. In Switzerland.

NICKI   It's not about money!

PATRICE   Your government likes immigrants with money. *(beat)* Nicki, if you bring me to Canada, we could be like we were before.

NICKI Could we?

PATRICE Do you want that?

NICKI What *were* we like... before?

PATRICE I think you were happy.

NICKI Is that what I was? Happy?

PATRICE You were my woman.

NICKI Oh God, I can't deal with this!

PATRICE You have a man now, in Canada?

NICKI *(a beat)* No.

PATRICE *(urgently)* I am in your hands, Veronica. Do you see that?

NICKI *(faintly)* Yes.

PATRICE I have wanted you very much.

NICKI I looked, every day...

PATRICE Nicki. Have you wanted me?

NICKI Yes. All the time.

PATRICE Here. Come. Lie down with me. There is room for two.

NICKI No, Patrice, I can't. Not here. Not like this.

PATRICE Nothing will happen. We shall lie together. We shall make ourselves very thin. Come. I shall keep you warm. Like before.

The sound of the crickets in the African night rises and fades again, as the scene ends in a blackout.

Scene Two

Morning light, already strong, streams into the tent. NICKI is sitting on the edge of the cot, painfully putting in contact lenses. Sporadic gunfire can be heard in the distance. Larry BREEN arrives.

BREEN *(heartily)* Good morning, campers. Another lovely morning in the heart of Africa! High expected today about thirty-three under sunny skies. Maybe it'll rain like hell later in the day, maybe it won't.

NICKI Please! Knock it off!

BREEN Are you okay?

NICKI I'm okay.

BREEN It's after six.

NICKI   I know.

BREEN   Are you going over to the commissary?

NICKI   Couple of minutes.

BREEN   So.

NICKI   So?

BREEN   So where's your "student?"

NICKI   He's not here.

BREEN   I can see that. Where did he go?

NICKI   Back. Out there. Before dawn.

BREEN   He slept here?

NICKI   He slept on the cot. I slept on the ground. Okay?

BREEN   Did I ask?

NICKI   No.

BREEN   And you told him to go?

NICKI   I didn't have to.

BREEN   Are you all right?

NICKI   What do you mean? Why shouldn't I be?

BREEN   You're upset.

NICKI   What's all that shooting about?

BREEN   It's mostly in the air.

NICKI   *Mostly?*

BREEN   A lot of noise. To show who's boss. An RPF forward column crossed the river during the night.

NICKI   They're here? They're in the camp?

BREEN   Putting the fear of God in the bloody Hutu.

NICKI   God, it could be a massacre!

BREEN   I don't think so, actually. Right now, the RPF are the good guys. If they're smart, they won't want to blow it.

NICKI   What if they're not smart?

BREEN   *(matter-of-factly)* It'll be a fucking bloodbath.

NICKI   You say that so calmly.

BREEN   *It'll be a fucking bloodbath!* Is that okay?

NICKI   Can't anyone do something?

BREEN   Me?

NICKI   The UN force.

BREEN   Like what? Like get in the way? Form a human shield around the Hutu?

NICKI   That's what you're here for, isn't it?

BREEN   We're here to protect the relief operation, period.

NICKI   But you can't just sit back and…

BREEN   Period. Can't do anything else. Seriously, what do you imagine "peacekeepers" can do? We don't have the numbers and we don't have the mandate. *(a beat)* And I'll tell you something else. Your Hutu stud had better lie very low indeed.

NICKI   Don't call him that!

BREEN   Sorry – your "student." He's in one hell of a lot of danger! Eh? Rich family, government connections…. The RPF aren't going to ask too many questions. Why should they? After what those savages did in Kigali.

NICKI   Larry!

BREEN   *(very intense)* I said savages, I mean savages. Don't get all liberal-correct! This isn't a race thing. This is about savagery. This is about hacking people into pieces, can you picture that? Going for a woman with a baby, and grabbing the baby, with the mother right there, and like hacking it up, I've *seen* this, the mother is screaming and shaking, and these *savages* are hacking up her baby with these fucking great machetes that aren't even sharp…

NICKI   Stop it!

BREEN   And they have these sticks, like clubs, with nails sticking out of them…

NICKI   Stop it!

BREEN   And some of them are like hammers, ordinary hammers like you use at home, only the handles are longer…

NICKI   Why are you doing this?

BREEN   And when they've finished hacking up the baby, so it's just smashed up pieces, and blood everywhere, they start in on the mother, and she's screaming and screaming, and I'm *seeing this happening* and there's not a damn thing I can do about it, and all I can think of is getting an M-16 and blasting them all to hell, every last fucking one of them, shooting in their grinning faces, blowing their heads to bits, fucking savages.

NICKI   *(shaken by his rage)* And what good would that do?

BREEN   *(matter-of-factly)* I don't know. It would make something right.

NICKI   Like what?

BREEN   Like retribution, like wiping them out, I don't give a shit, you know?

NICKI   What if some of them are innocent?

BREEN   What's innocent? Nobody's innocent. Not the Hutu. Hutu men. Boys. Kids, some of them. And now you want me to protect them? Savages. Exterminate them.

    Silence.

NICKI   Larry. You're sick.

BREEN   Yep. That's right. I'm sick.

NICKI   You should leave.

BREEN   I can't leave. Not yet. I have a job to do.

NICKI   You're crazy.

BREEN   I'm not crazy. I'm sick, but I'm not crazy.

NICKI   You can't do any sort of a job like this.

BREEN   Look at me – I'm doing it. I'm not sure what the hell my job *is*, but I'm doing it. I'm walking around in a blue hat. Good Canadian guy, nice policeman, helping little girls find Mummy and Daddy at the fairground

    There is a long burst of gunfire, rather too close.

NICKI   *Jesus Christ!*

BREEN   You're not kidding! Get down flat.

NICKI   What are they doing?

BREEN   Fucked if I know, but right now I wouldn't go out and ask.

    They wait. After a few moments, an African soldier, MAJOR K, strides in – tall, lean, in combat fatigues, boots, maroon beret, wearing dark glasses, carrying a small automatic assault rifle. BREEN carefully gets to his feet. The intruder swings around to face him. There is the click of the safety catch being released.

MAJOR K   *(He is hard, intense, very controlled.)* Qu'est-ce que vous faites ici? What are you doing here?

BREEN   *(confrontational)* I was going to ask you the same thing.

MAJOR K   Huh?

BREEN   What do you want?

MAJOR K   What is this? This place? This is your place?

BREEN   Relief agency personnel. CANAID.

MAJOR K   France? Belgique?

BREEN   Canada.

MAJOR K   Ah, Canada. You are Canadian?

BREEN   Captain Larry Breen. UN Protection Force.

MAJOR K   Ah.

BREEN   *(helping NICKI to her feet)* And this…

MAJOR K   *(alert again)* Huh?

BREEN   …is Miss Veronica Olsen.

MAJOR K   Canadian?

NICKI   Yes.

MAJOR K   *(to BREEN)* Again, you.

BREEN   What?

MAJOR K   Your name.

BREEN   Captain Larry Breen.

MAJOR K   French.

BREEN   No, I told you. Canadian.

MAJOR K   To hell with the French!

BREEN   If you say so.

MAJOR K   *(indicating himself)* Major Joel Kanyemera.

BREEN   I see.

MAJOR K   *Major* Kanyemera.

BREEN   Yes. I got that.

MAJOR K   RPF. Rwanda Patriotic Front. You know what that is?

BREEN   I know what it is.

MAJOR K   We are in charge now. We have no more need for the UN. You can go now.

BREEN   You're not in charge *here!*

MAJOR K   We are in charge. You can go now.

BREEN   You are on Tanzanian territory, Major. You have no authority here. *(He punches a number into his cell phone.)*

MAJOR K   You! You are on African territory. What are you doing here? What are you doing in Africa? To stop the Black men killing each other? Who made Hutu,

Tutsi hate each other? Who? Do you know this? Let me tell you. Before the Whites came, Tutsi and Hutu lived together. No fighting, no hatred…

BREEN Yeah, okay, Major, I have to make this call…

MAJOR K Now the Hutu have massacred the Tutsi, many, many of them, perhaps one million. And we will find them, and we will execute them, the guilty ones, the *genocidaires*.

NICKI And what happens then? There are thousands of people here, scores of thousands, with nothing, sick, dying, children starving…

MAJOR K We will look after them.

BREEN They're terrified of you. *(He starts to talk into cell phone.)* It's Captain Breen, sector seven. Who am I talking to? Okay, sergeant, listen carefully…

NICKI *(to MAJOR K)* They came here to get away from you.

MAJOR K They are Hutu.

NICKI Not all of them.

MAJOR K *(to BREEN)* What are you doing? You! Who are you talking to?

BREEN …Take this down. Report Colonel Lapointe. Urgent. RPF units crossed the river in force, sector seven, violation of Tanzanian sovereignty. Suggest Colonel contact UN command, re. General Kagame, order immediate pull-back. You got that?

MAJOR K You stop that! Are you listening to me? *(He knocks the cell phone out of BREEN's hand.)*

BREEN Fuck you, my friend! *(He moves to retrieve cell phone. The MAJOR puts his foot on it.)* You give me that phone, Major! *You hear what I'm saying? (MAJOR K makes as if to use his weapon.)* And don't even think about that! *(This is quite a tense confrontation. BREEN is trembling with suppressed rage.)* Don't even think about shooting a UN officer, or you will be so badly fucked, you won't be able to sit down for a month? You get it? *(The MAJOR is sufficiently overawed to take his foot off the cell phone. BREEN picks it up.)* Thank you, Major.

MAJOR K *(bitterly)* Protecting Hutu! Oh yes! Where was UN protection in Kigali? Where?

BREEN You want to know? *You want to know?* Our general, our Canadian general, was *begging* for more soldiers, begging, pleading, send us five thousand men or there's going to be a bloodbath. What did they do? They pulled us out.

MAJOR K Because we are Africans. Africans want to kill each other? Let them! But rescue our White people! Oh yes, we must save them!

BREEN I'm telling you, General Dallaire did everything he could to…

MAJOR K And now you protect the Hutu butchers. Huh? Feed them. Care for them. Huh?

NICKI *(fiercely)* Major, they are starving women and children, children without parents, hundreds are dying every day, there is cholera, there is typhus…

MAJOR K You listen to me! There are many bad men out there. Very bad men. We know them. They dress as women, oh yes, now they are poor, crying, they rub dirt on their bodies, but we know them! We know their names. Very bad men. Devils.

NICKI If there are people here guilty of atrocities, they will be brought to justice. It's no good…

MAJOR K *Do you know what is justice?* Do you? I know what is justice. The man who kills your wife, kills your children, your mother, your father, burns your house, you find him, you kill him. That is the justice. You don't tell me.

NICKI It's just another massacre…

MAJOR K It is execution. We find the guilty ones – we know who they are – we shoot them. Shoot them, that is all! We do not burn them, we do not cut them up, we do not cut off their sex and put it in their mouth…

NICKI Oh God!

MAJOR K Because we are not like them. *(a burst of gunfire)* We are not like the Hutu.

NICKI If there are guilty ones among the refugees…

MAJOR K We know who they are! They have come here from Kigali. We have followed them.

BREEN You'll never find them in that mob!

MAJOR K We know their names. Everyone knows them. The big names, the big families. *(He numbers them on his fingers.)* Pascal Simbikangwa. Andre Sebatware. Patrice Umbiwimana. Tharcisse Renzaho. Leaders of the Interahamwe. Now they don't have their bodyguards, their Mercedes, their servants, their women. Now they are naked, with bare feet. But we know them. And we will find them. *(He calls out an order in Kinya-Rwanda, the Rwandan language, and receives a reply. He prepares to leave.)* Captain!

BREEN Major?

MAJOR K *(saluting him)* Not French?

BREEN *(returning the salute)* Canadian.

MAJOR K Okay. *(He strides out.)*

BREEN Welcome to the new order. Thank Christ we're not French, eh? Listen, I've got to get over to the command centre, figure out where the hell we stand. You want me to walk you across?

NICKI You go ahead. I'll be another couple of minutes.

BREEN Listen, Nicki, be real careful, do you hear what I'm saying? This is a bad situation. Stay cool, and don't stare at anyone with a gun, you know what I mean? And be ready to move. I guess we keep going for now, but if shit starts we may be out of here in a hurry. You all right?

NICKI Yes, Larry, I'm all right!

BREEN God, I hate this place!

> *BREEN leaves. NICKI is immobile. There is the sound of a heavy aircraft coming in to land. A big shadow passes over. She looks up, shielding her eyes. She begins to speak, as if to herself.*

NICKI He said your name. He said your name! That man, the RPF major, he named you. *He named you, Patrice.* What does that mean?

> *She opens the tent flap. PATRICE has been crouching in the cupboard, and now comes out.*

PATRICE It means I am a dead man. You see what these people are like?

NICKI But how does he have your name?

PATRICE My family was very well known. My father was…

NICKI But he named *you*. Patrice Umbiwimana. He said your name. Why?

PATRICE Who knows where he got it? It is my uncle's name also. They are ignorant, these people. Uneducated.

NICKI What about the other names? Did you recognize them?

PATRICE I know… some of them. One or two.

NICKI Who are they? Are any of them here?

PATRICE They are not here. They got away.

NICKI Were any of them… I mean… is he right about them, what he says?

PATRICE You can't believe him. He knows nothing. He wasn't there.

NICKI And what about you? *(a beat)* You were there. In Kigali.

PATRICE Yes, I was there.

NICKI What were you doing?

PATRICE What are you asking? If I did what he is saying? If I *could* do such things?

NICKI No, I don't know, of course I don't – but you were *there*.

PATRICE   I was there.

NICKI   And you saw… things.

PATRICE   You cannot understand.

NICKI   No. I can't.

PATRICE   Nicki… *(He moves to put his hands on her shoulders. She flinches.)*

NICKI   I have to get over to the canteen. They stop serving at seven.

PATRICE   Nicki.

NICKI   I'll try and bring something for you.

PATRICE   *(desperately)* What am I to do?

NICKI   You have to stay hidden. I don't know.

PATRICE   How many days?

NICKI   You have to. With *them* here. What else can I do?

PATRICE   You have to get me out of here. This one – he will kill me.

NICKI   Not if you haven't done anything.

PATRICE   You want them to catch me? You want to see how they will "question" me? *(He mimes being brutally beaten and crying out from the blows.)* You are Patrice Umbiwimana? Aah! You are Hutu? Aah! How many Tutsi you kill? Aah! How many Tutsi? Aah! How many? How many? How many? You tell us before we kill you! *(in his own voice)* I did not kill Tutsi. *(in Tutsi voice)* You a liar! Aah! You a fuckin' liar! Aah! We goin' fuckin' kill you! We goin' chop your hands! We goin' chop your balls! We goin' chop your head! *(He is on hands and knees, covering his head with his hands.)*

NICKI   *(PATRICE has obviously seen something similar to what he has just enacted.)* Patrice…

PATRICE   You want to see this?

NICKI   *(looking anxiously at her watch)* Patrice, I have to go.

PATRICE   They are not even real Rwandans. They are rebels, bandits. Kagame's people. From Uganda.

NICKI   Patrice, I have to go to work. I'm in charge of a relocation centre. They're waiting for me.

PATRICE   A what?

NICKI   A relocation centre. I'm in charge of it.

PATRICE   In charge? You are in charge?

NICKI   Yes, in charge. I'm not new at this, you know!

PATRICE Then get me away from here. Relocate *me*. On the planes. Where do they go?

NICKI They come in from Nairobi mostly.

PATRICE Nairobi is good! I will be safe there.

NICKI Yes, but I can't do it! I can't just go out onto the airstrip and say to the pilot, "Oh, excuse me, I have a friend who needs to get out of here."

PATRICE Your captain says you may be taken out.

NICKI Only if we can't work any longer. If it gets too dangerous.

PATRICE If it gets too dangerous for *you*. *(a beat)* And you would go? *(He takes hold of her hand.)*

NICKI Look, it's not going to happen. The RPF don't really want us to leave. They shouldn't be over this side.

PATRICE They don't go back with empty hands.

NICKI *(A siren is heard.)* Patrice, I have to go. You have to stay hidden for now.

PATRICE In here?

NICKI I know it's awful, but what else is there? I *will* figure something out. The UNHCR is trying to get the Tanzanians to resettle some people…

PATRICE I don't want to go to Tanzania!

NICKI You may have to! Patrice. I have to go. Please, I'm not going to abandon you.

> *They look at each other. Another heavy aircraft flies over, taking off this time. Blackout.*

Scene Three

> *Mid morning, very hot and bright. NICKI is standing at a display map on an easel, giving a briefing to a group of relief workers, constructed as the audience. She wears a Blue Jays cap and carries a cell phone. Larry BREEN stands by protectively. MAJOR Kanyemera looks on with obvious suspicion. NICKI looks repeatedly towards her tent, where PATRICE is in hiding.*

NICKI Okay. Can you all hear me? We've finally got permission from the authorities in Ngara to set up a longer-term refugee facility in the Lumavimbi area up here. *(She points to the map. Sound of a heavy aircraft flying over.)* The site is about twenty kilometres from here, by road, so it means we're going to have to move up to fifteen hundred people every day. And when they get to the site, they're going to have to make their own shelters. UNHCR is bringing in several thousand tarpaulin sheets, like this *(displaying one)*, but the frames to support them will have to be made from scratch. It's better, we think, if we move people up in batches by truck, rather than have them straggling along the road on foot. This *should* be fairly straightforward – famous last words! – so long as we're not hindered in the process. *(MAJOR K abruptly stalks off. NICKI looks after him anxiously.)* But we have to move fast, because there's another wave of refugees, mostly women and children, coming from the Mundu region. Which is going to put a hell of a strain on the services we're able to provide, a hell of a strain on the, on the services we're able to...

> *NICKI is having a hallucination. She "sees" MAJOR K going to her tent and finding PATRICE, hauling him out of hiding, beating him, and dragging him off. At the same time, the light gets hotter and brighter, and there is an intense buzzing sound, rising in volume. NICKI seems to stagger and lose her balance. BREEN springs forward to support her. The light and buzzing fade down to normal.*

BREEN   What's the matter?

NICKI   I'm okay.

BREEN   You look lousy.

NICKI   I didn't have any breakfast. Stupid of me.

BREEN   You're not getting sick? *(He feels her forehead.)*

NICKI   I'm fine.

BREEN   You're hot.

NICKI   Of course I'm hot! You're hot. Everybody's hot. Just give me a minute. *(to her audience)* I'm sorry. The sun is really getting to me, I guess. No big deal. Where was I? Yes. Um.... The point is, we have to get the movement from here up to Lumavimbi rolling smoothly before the next wave hits us. Or we're going to be just swamped. So we need to be organizing groups of about sixty men to go ahead as the advance party. And be sure to explain *really clearly* what the plan is, because people are going to panic if they think that, if they think, they're going to panic if they...

> *As before, NICKI is overcome by an hallucinatory vision of MAJOR K finding PATRICE and dragging him brutally away. The light once again increases in intensity, and the buzzing sound rises to a painful level. NICKI is on the verge of collapse, but BREEN catches her in his arms. The vision disappears, and the light and sound fade down rapidly.*

I'm sorry, people, I don't think I can...

BREEN   *(offering her water from a bottle)* Okay, that's it! You're taking it easy!

NICKI   *(rejecting his bottle, drinking from her own)* I'll be fine! I just need...

BREEN   You need a break. You need to eat.

NICKI *(apologetically, to the audience)* I'm afraid I do have to… take a little time. It's nothing serious. Excuse me, everyone. André, would you take over?

BREEN You should lie down. I'll get you back to your tent.

NICKI No, really! I'll be just fine.

BREEN Bullshit. You'll collapse on the way.

NICKI That's stupid! There's nothing wrong with me. I'll just go and lie down for half an hour.

BREEN I'm coming with you.

NICKI No! I don't need that! *(a beat)* Thank you. I'm not an invalid.

> *She crosses rapidly to her tent. PATRICE is nowhere to be seen. She calls urgently in a half whisper.*

NICKI Patrice! *Patrice!* Are you here?

PATRICE *(entering)* I'm here.

NICKI Shit, I was so scared. I was sure something had happened.

PATRICE What could happen?

NICKI That RPF guy…

PATRICE Did he ask you again?

NICKI He was there, watching me.

PATRICE Did he follow you?

NICKI He went away. I was afraid he had…

PATRICE Why did you come back? I thought you were going to…

NICKI I got faint. I nearly passed out.

PATRICE You're sick?

NICKI Just nerves. And hunger, I guess. No breakfast.

PATRICE *(ironically)* You are hungry?

NICKI I know, I know, I'll try and get you something.

PATRICE And some water.

NICKI *(giving him her water bottle)* Here, take it. I can get more.

PATRICE I am becoming a burden. The white woman's burden.

NICKI No! No, you're not. I'm sorry. I'm just… I'm under a lot of strain. Okay? I'm trying to figure out how to get you away. You can't stay here. It's too dangerous. There's a stores shed in the compound. We keep it padlocked. I think you'd be safe there for a couple of days. And then I can get you away in one of the trucks going up to Lumavimbi…

PATRICE What is Lumavimbi?

NICKI It's a new camp, away from the border. Better organized. We're going to…

PATRICE You're shipping me off to a camp? How long do I stay there? Months? Years? What do I do? Make baskets? Eat millet cakes? Shit in a hole in the ground?

NICKI Look, Patrice, I don't know! We're trying to deal with thousands of people, tens of thousands… I can't… it's not… I can't put you ahead of all the others just because…

PATRICE What? Just because what?

NICKI *You know what I mean! (a beat)* I'll do what I can.

PATRICE Where is this stores shed?

NICKI I'll take you there.

PATRICE Now?

NICKI It won't be very comfortable, I'm afraid. It's made of corrugated metal…

PATRICE It is an oven. You want to cook me?

NICKI Of course I don't! I want to get you safely away from here. Somewhere we could…

PATRICE *(reaching to touch her)* What?

NICKI I don't know. I can't think about it. *(gunfire, several short bursts)* Oh Jesus!

PATRICE What is that?

NICKI I don't know. *(gunfire again)*

PATRICE That is an Uzi. What the RPF use.

NICKI How do you know?

PATRICE I know.

> *There is another burst of firing. NICKI punches in a number on the cell phone.*

NICKI Larry? What the hell was that? What's going on? *(BREEN appears with cell phone.)*

BREEN Where are you?

NICKI At my tent. What's happening?

BREEN Summary justice. Tutsi style.

NICKI Jesus Christ.

BREEN They've found some guys they claim were in the Interahamwe killing squads…

NICKI   And they're…

BREEN   If they put up any kind of resistance.

NICKI   *Can't you do anything about it?*

BREEN   Like what? Ask them to please stop? I kind of doubt Major Whatsit would take much notice, do you? Maybe it's the best thing anyway.

NICKI   They're just picking up people at random…

BREEN   Oh believe me, it's not random. They seem to know what they're doing!

NICKI   And how many…? *(gunfire)* Mother of God!

BREEN   Yeah! *(urgent)* Listen, Nicki. Your student…

NICKI   Yes?

BREEN   What did you say his name was?

NICKI   *(a beat)* Why?

BREEN   Fine. Put it this way: is his name something like Umbiwani? *(a beat)* Are you there?

NICKI   I'm here.

BREEN   Because if it is, he's in very deep shit. I'm serious. Our friendly Major is convinced he's here. One of the men they've shot claims he saw him in the camp. And they think he's very big. One of the ones they really want. Apparently he was a *minister* in the last government. Did you know that? *(beat)* Okay, no comment. Anyway, they say he was mixed up in some very nasty stuff indeed. He should have gotten away to Kenya like the biggest bastards did, but he stayed around too long. According to the Major, his wife and kid are safe in Nairobi, but he's still on the run, and they're pretty damn sure he's here. Nicki?

NICKI   Yes?

BREEN   Don't stick your neck out too far for this guy.

NICKI   What do you mean?

BREEN   These people aren't fooling around.

NICKI   No.

BREEN   Are you okay? Do you want me to come over?

NICKI   No!

BREEN   Is he there now?

NICKI   What?

BREEN   Is he there? Your friend.

NICKI   No.

BREEN   Where is he?

NICKI   I don't know.

BREEN   Okay, play stupid. But he isn't worth it. I'm telling you, as a friend. Get rid of him while you can. Over and out.

Silence; another short burst of gunfire.

NICKI   They're looking for you, Patrice.

PATRICE   He told you that?

NICKI   They know you're here.

PATRICE   They can't know that.

NICKI   People say they've seen you.

PATRICE   People.

NICKI   Ones they've caught.

PATRICE   They would say anything. To save themselves.

NICKI   They know you.

PATRICE   They are shit. They know nothing.

NICKI   They say…

PATRICE   What do they say?

NICKI   They say… that you are one of the guilty ones.

PATRICE   Do you think that?

NICKI   Patrice…

PATRICE   Do you think that?

NICKI   I don't…

PATRICE   Do you think that?

NICKI   You were there…

PATRICE   So I am guilty. All those who were there are guilty.

NICKI   You were important. You were…

PATRICE   So you had better tell the Major. You want Patrice Umbiwimana? You looking for him? I've got him locked up in a little shed.

NICKI   Patrice, you know I wouldn't…

PATRICE   Why not? You think I am guilty. "You are a Hutu. You were important. You were there." *(beat)* Veronica, you know me. You *know* me.

NICKI   Do I? What do I know?

PATRICE   When a woman takes her pleasure from a man, she knows him.

NICKI   Yes, I did think that.

PATRICE   But now you believe that…

NICKI   *(abruptly)* Patrice! Why do you want to go to Nairobi?

PATRICE   Why?

NICKI   Why Nairobi?

PATRICE   It is safe there.

NICKI   No.

PATRICE   It is safe there. For a Hutu.

NICKI   That's not it.

PATRICE   What are you…?

NICKI   You have a wife there. And a child.

PATRICE   What?

NICKI   In Nairobi. You have a wife and child.

PATRICE   Who is telling you this?

NICKI   It's true. Isn't it! All that time, that whole time, you had a wife…

PATRICE   It is not true…

NICKI   …and a child. *I know you did. Don't lie about it. I know!*

PATRICE   You don't know. You can't know. It's a lie.

NICKI   I know it.

PATRICE   Nicki…

NICKI   Don't. Don't!

PATRICE   I swear by God…

NICKI   *Don't!*

PATRICE   The RPF Major? He knows nothing. Nothing.

NICKI   It's true. You know it. I know it. I've known it all along.

PATRICE   What are you talking about?

NICKI   I knew. Back then. I just didn't know that I knew. God, I was such a stupid, stupid fool. Did you laugh at me? Did you tell your wife? About your "mistress"? When you were writing to her, and she was sending you the kid's drawings? About your mistress? Your "supervisor." Christ, what a joke. "There's this old lady who can't get enough of it, and I have to keep on screwing her, because she can screw me if I don't." *Was that it? (a beat)* How old is your child? Boy or girl? Boy, I would guess, I don't know why. Ours would have been a boy.

PATRICE You told me that…

NICKI Don't say anything. Don't say anything! It was a boy. They don't tell you. But I knew. *(a beat)* I wanted it.

PATRICE You said…

NICKI Never mind what I said! I wanted a child. I wanted your child. Even if you were going away. And you wouldn't let me. You wouldn't let me. So I didn't. What the fuck right did you have? What fucking right did you have? Were you afraid I'd have a claim on you? *(pause)* And now it's too late.

PATRICE It's not…

NICKI It's too late! It's too late! Do you know how old I am? I'm forty-two. Surprise! I told you I was thirty-six.

PATRICE Thirty-five.

NICKI So what? So bloody what? Thirty-five, twenty-five…

PATRICE You lied to me.

NICKI Yes, I did. I lied to you. How about that!

PATRICE *(a beat)* I knew. I saw your passport.

NICKI Ah. *(pause) Do* you have a wife and child in Nairobi?

PATRICE Yes.

NICKI Is it a boy?

PATRICE Girl. Nicki…

NICKI Don't say anything. I don't want to hear. Just go. Away from me.

PATRICE Where shall I go?

NICKI I don't give a shit. Just go.

PATRICE Where?

NICKI Go to hell. Go back where you came from, see if I give a shit! I hope they catch you!

PATRICE Nicki…

NICKI *Just get away from me and go to hell! (Silence; a very long burst of gunfire; blackout.)*

Scene Four

In a hot bright light, accompanied by a fierce electronic buzzing sound, PATRICE kneels, blindfolded, at the front of the stage, his hands tied in front of him. MAJOR K stands behind him, a pistol against the back of his head.

MAJOR K Patrice Umbiwimana, for the crime of genocidal massacre against the Tutsi people of Rwanda, you are sentenced to death by shooting. Do you have anything to say?

NICKI *(from the surrounding shadows)* Patrice!

MAJOR K Patrice Umbiwimana, do you have anything to say? Do you wish to express remorse for your part in these crimes, and to ask forgiveness of the Tutsi people?

NICKI Patrice! Say something!

MAJOR K The prisoner has declined to make any statement. Veronica Olsen, do you have anything to say in defence of the prisoner?

NICKI I... *(She is unable to speak.)*

MAJOR K What have you to say in defence of the prisoner?

NICKI I...

MAJOR K There is no statement in defence of the prisoner. Captain Breen, what do you have to say?

BREEN *(from another part of the stage)* Exterminate all the brutes.

MAJOR K Repeat your statement, please.

BREEN Exterminate the brutes!

MAJOR K The sentence will now be carried out. *(click of the safety catch of his pistol)*

NICKI *No!*

There is a single shot; a change of light; the electronic buzz diminishes, indicating that the preceding scene has been a nightmare of NICKI's, who now startles into wakefulness, lying on her camp cot.

Oh Jesus!

BREEN *(beside her)* Nicki?

NICKI What have I done?

BREEN Are you okay?

NICKI *Jesus, what have I done?*

BREEN You were dreaming.

NICKI Larry, what have I done? I told him to go to hell.

BREEN Well, if there's any justice in the world, he just might.

NICKI Don't say that!

BREEN Christ, Nicki, the man's a killer. Face it, he's a killer.

NICKI We don't know that.

BREEN He lied to you.

NICKI So what? I lied to him. I lied to myself.

BREEN He used you. Took advantage.

NICKI "Took advantage?" I'm not a child!

BREEN Took what he wanted.

NICKI So did I.

BREEN Nicki, he took part in the butchery.

NICKI We don't know that. It's just an allegation.

BREEN The Major seems pretty damn sure.

NICKI Larry, I *know* him, for God's sake!

BREEN What did you know? What did you know? Did you know he had a wife and child?

NICKI It's not the same. Lots of men lie about that.

BREEN I didn't. Just for the record.

NICKI No. You didn't. You get a gold star.

BREEN Listen, let him go! Get out of here. I can get you on a flight to Goma, in Zaire.

NICKI I don't want to go to Goma! It's worse than here, for God's sake. I came to work with CANAID. I've got a job to do.

BREEN Well you're not in much of a shape to do it right now.

NICKI I could have hidden him. I could have gotten him away.

BREEN You've given him as much of a chance as he deserves.

NICKI Larry...

BREEN Just get the hell away from here.

NICKI *I have to find him.* I have to get him out. Help me to do that.

BREEN What the hell do you expect me to do? There's forty or fifty thousand of the bastards out there, and a whole lot more on the way. *(a beat)* Uh oh! Spoke too soon.

NICKI *(uncomprehending)* What?

> *PATRICE, bloody, obviously beaten, his hands tied in front of him, stumbles into view, roughly shoved by MAJOR K, who carries with him a machete. The MAJOR forces PATRICE to his knees in front of NICKI. PATRICE doesn't look at her, or show any sign of recognition.*

MAJOR K Captain Green…

BREEN Breen.

MAJOR K Miss Olsen. I am looking for a man here. You know him. His name is Patrice Umbiwimana.

NICKI *(rigid)* I don't know anything about him.

MAJOR K Identify him, please.

NICKI What are you talking about?

MAJOR K You have been with him. *(to BREEN)* Yes?

NICKI Larry! What did you tell him?

BREEN Nicki, you don't know about him! Ask the Major what he did in Kigali.

MAJOR K Miss Nicki, if I can call you, this man Umbiwimana is a murderer, one of the worst. We know this. We have witnesses, people who *saw* him.

NICKI What did they see?

MAJOR K He has killed little children. *(pause)* He has done this. There are many people who have seen him. They will swear to it.

NICKI He ordered the killing of children?

MAJOR K Not order. Kill them himself. You can ask him. *(a beat)* This is the man we are looking for?

NICKI No!

MAJOR K This one is not Umbiwimana? But he knows where he is. *(hauling PATRICE to his feet and preparing to drag him violently away)* Let us see what he knows.

NICKI Oh God! *(to the MAJOR)* Please… don't…

MAJOR K Why do you care for this? This man is nothing to you. *(He shoves PATRICE brutally.)*

NICKI Larry, for God's sake…!

BREEN What do you want me to do?

NICKI Make him stop this!

MAJOR K *(bluntly)* This is the man? I think so, yes?

BREEN   That's your guy.

NICKI   You bastard.

MAJOR K   *(formal declaration)* Patrice Umbiwimana, you are a prisoner of the Rwanda Patriotic Front. *(He forces PATRICE back to his knees.)*

BREEN   There's no need for that, Major.

NICKI   *(as PATRICE kneels)* Patrice, don't!

MAJOR K   Patrice Umbiwimana, you will answer for your crimes against the Tutsi people.

NICKI   Say something!

MAJOR K   You have nothing to say? *(He seems to be about to shoot PATRICE.)*

BREEN   Don't do it, Major!

MAJOR K   This is not a matter for you.

BREEN   You're on Tanzanian territory.

MAJOR K   This is for him and for me.

BREEN   You can't shoot an unarmed man in cold blood!

MAJOR K   What is cold blood? The blood in Kigali is not cold. The blood is on his hands. *(He puts the machete in PATRICE's bound hands.)* You see? You see this? *(to PATRICE)* You remember this?

NICKI   Patrice, say something!

PATRICE   What do you want?

NICKI   Do you know what he says?

MAJOR K   I say Patrice Umbiwimana is a leader of the *genocidaires*. He is a butcher of children. *(He forces PATRICE's head to the ground.)*

NICKI   Stop it!

BREEN   All right, Major, that's enough!

MAJOR K   That's enough? That's enough? For this man, what is enough? Do you know what they have done? You say, "Oh yes, we know." You say, "Oh yes, they have killed some of your people. *C'est la guerre.* You people are always going crazy, killing each other." No, you don't know! *(pause)* When we come to Kigali we find everywhere the dead, in the street, in the houses, in the bush. Some of them are without hands, without feet. And this man, he is one of those who showed the way. What should be done with him? You… *(to NICKI)* What should be done with him?

NICKI   Patrice. Is it true? What he says. That you killed… a child? Children?

PATRICE   What he says! What he says! What does he know? Nothing.

NICKI Did you kill children?

PATRICE What kind of man do you think I am?

NICKI I don't know. I don't know. *(pause)* You did. *(silence)*

PATRICE They came to my house. The Interahamwe. They said to me…. They said to me, "If you do not kill a Tutsi child… if you do not kill a Tutsi child, we will kill your child." They said to me, "You do not hate Tutsi. We know you. You are Tutsi in your heart. You must show us. You are a big man. We will kill your child if you do not show us."

NICKI You believed them?

PATRICE Oh yes. In front of my eyes they would kill my child. I have seen this.

NICKI And so… you killed a child?

PATRICE They would have killed her anyway.

NICKI Her? *(a beat)* Did you know this child?

PATRICE Her mother was my servant.

NICKI Where was she, the mother? She was there, when you killed her child?

PATRICE Of course she was there! What do you think? She had to see. She had to cry. Then we kill her too. *(silence)*

MAJOR K He tells this to make you sorry for him.

NICKI No.

MAJOR K Of course he makes his excuses! The Hutu are all liars. He killed many people. Raped the women.

NICKI You killed others?

PATRICE In the next days…

NICKI Other children?

PATRICE …there was madness.

NICKI You raped women?

PATRICE There was madness. It was like a passion. Like dreaming. This thing is happening. A helpless thing. You are out of yourself, running, crying, why are there so many of them? Crawling, screaming…

MAJOR K "There was madness. It was not my fault. There was madness." No! You must not believe this. In madness, you can kill for a day. A thousand people. They kill a million!

BREEN This thing was planned. Everyone knew what was coming.

MAJOR K On the radio, Radio Mille Collines, we can hear them, every day. "Brothers, the Tutsi are your enemies, there is no more time, we must kill them, kill all the cockroaches, kill the women and the children, kill them until there are no more Tutsi, then Rwanda is a clean place."

NICKI Did you hate them so much?

PATRICE You do not kill them because you hate them. *You hate them because you are killing them. (pause)* And then it is finished. You are empty. Your soul is empty.

> *Silence.*

NICKI And your child?

PATRICE She is alive. She is in Nairobi.

NICKI With her mother. *(pause)* Patrice… how old is she?

PATRICE She is a baby. Six months.

NICKI *(NICKI digests this.)* What is her name?

PATRICE You know, I think.

NICKI Tell me.

PATRICE Her name is Veronique. *(He is crying.)*

MAJOR K Oh yes, he has made you sorry now. He is very sad. He is alone. He is afraid. He tells you, "It is not my fault. They would kill my child."

PATRICE What would you have done? You, Captain. *What would you have done?* Do you know? *(to NICKI)* Do you know?

> *Long pause.*

NICKI Not that.

PATRICE What, then?

NICKI Not that.

PATRICE What, then? What, then? Let them kill you? That is easy! I would let them kill me. Do you think I would not? I am not a monster. But they don't want that. One more body is nothing. They want my soul. "Kill for us. You are with us in blood. Guilty with us. Or we kill your child. Choose." What, then? You. *(to BREEN)* You have children? What do you know? All that you know is, that this could never happen. Never, never. Not in Canada. Not in your whole life. Never will they come to you, your people, and say, "Show us how you hate them. Kill this child, or we say 'he does not hate them, he is one of them, we will kill his child.'" What do you know in here *(touching his own head)*, in here *(his heart)*, that you can say, "I would not do this"? Do you know this? *He* knows this. *(indicates the MAJOR)* He can kill me now, but he knows this.

BREEN Oh, man!

MAJOR K Oh yes! Oh yes! Now you have the sympathy for him. You say, "Oh, he is not one of the guilty ones. The other ones, they are guilty." Who *is* guilty for this?

PATRICE I am guilty for this.

NICKI Yes.

PATRICE I killed a baby girl in Kigali. I killed others. His people. I killed them!

MAJOR K He is making a comedy for you. Do you see? He is beating his breast for you. Crawling on the earth, "I am a bad man. I am a sinner. Shoot me, please!"

NICKI Patrice, stop this!

MAJOR K You are going to say to me, "Let him go! He is not a bad man." You do nothing when the Hutu try to kill my people, now you say, "Oh, he is sorry, *il est triste*, you must set him free…"

NICKI No! I'm not saying that! I'm not saying that!

BREEN Nicki, what *are* you saying?

NICKI I'm saying, I'm saying that nothing is made right by killing him. Not for him, not for you, not for the people in Rwanda…

MAJOR K You think it is too much to pay with his life? For what he has done?

NICKI I think it is not enough. *(She addresses PATRICE.)* How can you atone for this? Is it possible? The mother whose child you killed – what does she ask from you? If you were on your knees in front of *her*. What would she ask, for the death of her child. For taking her baby from her arms and… *(She cannot say it.)* What can atone for that? *What can atone for that?* Does she want to kill you? Is that enough? No. I don't think so. What is that to her? You are dead. That is nothing. *(pause)* To kill *your* child, your Veronique? Could she ask for that? Could she? To make you *know*. The helpless anguish. "Give me the blood of his child." No. Not to kill her. But never to see her again. Your Veronique. To grieve for her, suffer for her. But never see her again. Is that what she would want?

PATRICE The mother is dead. I killed her.

NICKI But others are alive. In Kigali. What can you say to them? Can you face them?

PATRICE You would send me back there? The only one? To be the scapegoat for all the others, the ones who laughed as they were killing?

NICKI To atone. To seek forgiveness.

BREEN *(wearily)* Jesus, turn the poor bastard loose, and have done with it.

NICKI Turn him loose? *You're* saying turn him loose?

BREEN Who appointed you some kind of Solomon here? It's not our business.

NICKI I'm not trying to…

BREEN   You want to crucify the guy now?

NICKI   I'm saying if he wants to save his soul…

BREEN   Oh for Christ's sake!

MAJOR K   This is not a choice for him! "To save his soul." I am taking him back to Kigali, to prison there. He will be put on trial, with the others. He will have a fair trial. He brings his witnesses. Then we judge.

PATRICE   Veronica. You don't know. I know. He takes me to Kigali. This is a very big thing for him. He says, "See who I have here! I have Patrice Umbiwimana! Look! I catch him. Hutu big devil. He kill your mother, your father, your children." You think I would get from the truck to the jail alive?

MAJOR K   *(impatiently cutting him off)* He will have a fair trial! There has been a very great crime done. The need of the people is to see that the men who did these things, the leaders, are tried by the law. Do you see? We must bring back the law to Rwanda. If he is guilty and he accepts his punishment, that may be good for him. For that he may recover his humanity.

PATRICE   *(to NICKI)* You said to me, "Go to hell!"

NICKI   I did. I know.

PATRICE   This would be hell.

NICKI   But it might be the way…

PATRICE   You think it would be like the justice in Canada?

NICKI   Of course I don't think that.

PATRICE   There is just one thing…

NICKI   Yes?

PATRICE   Nicki…

NICKI   Yes? *(She guesses what he is going to say.)* Oh my God.

PATRICE   You know, I think…

NICKI   Say it.

BREEN   What? What are we talking about?

NICKI   Say it.

PATRICE   If you would come there with me…

NICKI   To Kigali?

BREEN   Jesus, fuck! *(to NICKI)* Don't even *think* about it!

NICKI   If I could be a witness?

BREEN Oh for God's sake…! You think you owe him something? You don't owe him!

NICKI *(She is considering.)* Who can say what we "owe?"

MAJOR K *(intervening decisively)* No! We will not consent to this! That you will come to "monitor" our justice, as you say it. It will be very hard for us, oh yes! We have no courts, no judges, almost we have no lawyers. But we will do it without you! *(challengingly)* Shall we come to Canada to "monitor" your justice? I am taking Patrice Umbiwimana with me now back to Kigali, as a prisoner. He will have the chance to defend himself, when the time comes.

PATRICE *(equally decisive)* No.

MAJOR K Come. It is time.

PATRICE I am not going there.

NICKI Patrice!

PATRICE *(taking up the machete in his tied hands and brandishing it threateningly)* I will not go back there, to prison, tied like a dog, dragged through the streets, the people spit at me, stone me, beat me with sticks, screaming, "Kill him, kill him!" *(pause)* Let him shoot me here!

NICKI No, Patrice! What about your family, your child?

PATRICE I am dead to them already. *(He continues to threaten the MAJOR with the machete. The MAJOR aims his pistol at PATRICE's head.)*

BREEN Don't do it, Major!

MAJOR K This is not for you! This is for him and me.

NICKI Patrice!

> *The MAJOR fires a single shot. PATRICE falls. The lights intensify rapidly to a blinding glare, accompanied by a fierce electronic buzzing sound, then fade rapidly to black and silence.*
>
> *End.*

THE DERSHOWITZ PROTOCOL

The Dershowitz Protocol was first produced in the Toronto Summerworks Festival, in August 2003, with the following company:

JACK McCALL	Marvin Hinz
JANE COSENTINO	Niki Landau
RANDAL WATKIN	Paul de la Rosa
IQBAL AZIZ	Ravi Steve Khajuria
Direction	Mark Cassidy
Set and Props Design	Leslie Wright
Sound Design	Peter Cassidy
Stage Management	Angie Stillitano

The play was subsequently produced by the Downstairs Cabaret Theatre (producing director Chris Kawolsky) in Rochester, New York, in June 2006, with the following company:

JACK McCALL	Richard St. George
JANE COSENTINO	Ruth Childs
RANDALL WATKIN	Reuben Josephe Tapp
IQBAL AZIZ	J. Simmons
Direction	Jean Gordon Ryan
Set and Lighting Design	Jay Moscowitz
Costume Design	Meredith Van Scoy
Stage Management	Lynette Wilson

CHARACTERS

JACK McCALL, FBI Interrogator, 42. A New Yorker. His aim is to extract information from the subject regarding a suspected terrorist plot, of which there is reason to believe the subject has detailed knowledge.

JANE COSENTINO, US Justice Department lawyer, 38. Appointed as judicial "Monitor" charged with ensuring that the Protocol is strictly observed. The Monitor shares dual control of the procedure, and is empowered to call a halt to the proceedings at any time.

DR. RANDALL WATKIN, Administering Officer, 47. One of a small and strictly-recruited team trained and empowered to administer torture under the Protocol. A senior academic in the field of criminology, on the faculty of a university in the southern US. Watkin is Black.

IQBAL AZIZ, Syrian-American journalist, 37. The subject under interrogation, who has resided legally in the United States for twelve years. As the action begins, he is already hooked up to the pain-administering device, his physiological functions being recorded and monitored. He is not visible to the audience, but can be heard over the intercom whenever it is open. A flashing red light indicates his desire to communicate.

SETTING

An interrogation facility in an FBI building, consisting of a suite of two adjoining rooms, somewhere in the United States.

One of the rooms is a soundproof cell, in which the subject of the interrogation is attached to a specially devised and calibrated instrument for the administration of pain directly to the central nervous system. This room is invisible to the audience.

The other room – the stage – is a control room from which the pain stimulus is administered, and from which the subject of the interrogation can be questioned by the interrogator, via a two-way intercom. This intercom can be switched off by the interrogator, rendering the subject inaudible. The condition of the subject and all exchanges between the subject and the interrogator are monitored and recorded by video feed to a remote location. A large wall map of the US dominates the room.

The graduated administration of pain is applied electronically, by means of a computer to which only the mandated Administering Officer, operating under a special warrant, has the access codes. This computer and its functions can in turn only be activated with the compliance of the Justice Department-appointed "Monitor," who has a dual access code.

All stages of the interrogation procedure, which is strictly governed by a Presidentially-authorized protocol, are registered by the computer, so that an exact record of the process, including the intensity and duration of the applications and read-outs of the subject's physiological responses, can be preserved for subsequent judicial scrutiny.

The torture process – to give it a rather blunt name – has been designed to be as sterile, clinical and impersonal as possible, to minimize abuse and arbitrariness and provide full accountability. As long as the protocol is strictly observed, the participants are guaranteed immunity to any personal liability.

The action which follows is the first occasion on which the procedure, known as "rigorous interrogation," with its attendant protocol, has been put into operation.

THE DERSHOWITZ PROTOCOL

At rise, Jane COSENTINO has just arrived in the interrogation control room. Jack McCALL is impatient to begin the process, which cannot commence until all three of the participating team are present. There is a coffee urn and a tray of muffins. McCALL would like to smoke, but there is a prohibition sign.

COSENTINO *(taking in the room)* So this is it?

McCALL Excuse me?

COSENTINO Room 201? "What a dump!"

McCALL And who the hell are you?

COSENTINO Do you want to try that again?

McCALL Oh, I'm sorry. *(with elaborate politeness)* "I don't think I've had the pleasure…"

COSENTINO *(assertively)* Jane Cosentino, Justice Department.

McCALL Jane what?

COSENTINO *(indicating her identity badge)* Cosentino. And you are…?

McCALL From Justice?

COSENTINO That's right.

McCALL Oh. So you're the whatsitcalled?

COSENTINO Monitor. I will be acting as Monitor. Yes.

McCALL *(checks clipboard)* But you're not…?

COSENTINO I am not Mr. Erickson. Very observant of you.

McCALL *(prompting her)* So…?

COSENTINO Mr. Erickson is sick. He cannot be here.

McCALL Sick? He's sick? I see. And you're… pinch-hitting, are you?

COSENTINO You could say that.

McCALL Right. Stepping up to the plate.

COSENTINO I am Mr. Erickson's assistant. He has deputed me to attend in his place.

McCALL Is that a good idea?

COSENTINO What's that supposed to mean?

McCALL Well, you know…

COSENTINO What?

McCALL Do you have any idea what we're about to do here?

COSENTINO *(reading his identity badge)* Captain McCall…

McCALL Jack.

COSENTINO *(ignoring this)* I helped draft the Protocol. *(She dumps a document on the table.)*

McCALL That's not what I asked.

COSENTINO I know exactly what we're here to do.

McCALL I hope so.

COSENTINO Are you thoroughly conversant with the Protocol?

McCALL I've got the general idea.

COSENTINO A general idea is not good enough.

McCALL Let's say I know the rules.

COSENTINO Good. And you *understand* them? *(a beat)* So. The subject…?

McCALL We've been questioning him for thirty-six hours straight. We're not getting anywhere.

COSENTINO So you think…?

McCALL I don't think we have any alternative.

COSENTINO Where is he?

McCALL *(indicating)* He's in there. Wired up. Ready to go. As stipulated in your Protocol. *(The red light is flashing, indicating that "the subject," AZIZ, in the adjoining, soundproof room, wishes to speak)* Oh, speak of the devil! *(opening the intercom)* Listen, my friend, why don't you save us all a lot of unpleasantness, and just tell us what we want to know?

AZIZ I'm telling you, I don't know anything…

McCALL You want to do it the nice way, or you want to do it the hard way?

AZIZ I don't know anything!

McCALL We've heard this! We've heard this!

AZIZ You've got to believe me. You've got the wrong person.

McCALL I don't think so.

AZIZ You've got the wrong person. You're wasting your time.

McCALL I'll decide that, okay? *(He closes the intercom.)* He's right. We're wasting time. This thing is ticking! I can hear it! *(a beat)* Where the hell is The Man? Going to tell me he's sick too!

COSENTINO I understand he's on his way.

McCALL How long can it take? It's three in the fucking morning!

COSENTINO They're bringing him in a helicopter. *(pointing upward)* Right to the roof.

McCALL What do you know about him?

COSENTINO He's a research criminologist, apparently.

McCALL No kidding. *(The red light is flashing again. He opens the intercom.)* You got something you want to tell me?

AZIZ What can I tell you? I don't know anything.

McCALL Just can it then! *(closes intercom)* Don't call us, we'll call you. Fuck! Listen, why don't I just go in there and beat the living crap out of him? Huh?

COSENTINO Captain McCall…

McCALL Jack…

COSENTINO That is precisely what I'm here to prevent.

McCALL Okay! Okay!

COSENTINO This is going to be done properly, or it's not going to be done at all!

McCALL I'm kidding, For Christ's sake! Jeez, lighten up! You're not going to be a pain in the ass about this, are you? *(a beat) What are we waiting for?* These sons-of-bitches have got a fucking nucular [sic] gun to the head of the United States of America, and we're here fiddling with our dicks – saving your presence – 'cause Mr. Big isn't here to start the ignition. Christ, I need a smoke. *(pause)* You've got the codes to this thing, right?

COSENTINO What do you mean?

McCALL The codes. You've got them.

COSENTINO One of them. It's dual access. He's got the other one.

McCALL Oh, right. Joined at the hip.

COSENTINO It's in the Protocol.

McCALL 'Til death do you part.

COSENTINO Let's hope it doesn't come to that.

McCALL Hell, give me the good old third degree! We'd be getting somewhere by now, let me tell you! *(The phone trills.)* Here we go again! *(He takes the call.)* McCall. Nothing. Nada. He's not here. Yes, I know that. Listen, tell the President, if it was up to me, I'd have the fucker's *cojones* in a vice right now, and he'd be singing like an angel. No, not the President! *(to COSENTINO)* Fuck! *(to the phone)* Very funny. So what are they telling the media? Good, keep it that way. And get his ass down here as soon as the wheels hit the roof. *(He hangs up.)* They're just shitting themselves up there. What are they going to do? Take a chance on an American city going up in a mushroom cloud? Or issue a general alert, and have a hundred and fifty million people in a screaming fucking panic, killing each other to get out of every town bigger than Mudhole, Arkansas? *(opening intercom)* Tell us where it is, or we're going to hurt you so bad you'll wish you'd never been born! *(closing intercom)*

COSENTINO   Get a grip.

McCALL   Yeah, right. *(pouring himself coffee)* What kinda of muffins you reckon these are?

COSENTINO   *(taking a look)* Blueberry.

McCALL   Jeez, I hate squishy pieces of fruit in a muffin!

COSENTINO   The other ones are carrot.

McCALL   That's not much better. *(He takes a bite.)* So where the hell is it? *(the device)*

COSENTINO   If it's anywhere.

McCALL   It's somewhere. Believe me. This one is real.

COSENTINO   *(sarcastically)* So were the others.

McCALL   This one's real. It's got the right smell.

COSENTINO   Hunches. Rumours.

McCALL   Information. Intelligence gathering. You think we're stupid?

COSENTINO   I think you may be unnecessarily alarmist.

McCALL   You want to gamble? Look at 9/11. There was more than enough to go on, if anyone had put it together.

COSENTINO   *(staring at the large wall-map of the United States)* Could be anywhere.

McCALL   Could be fucking anywhere. In a shipping container, on a flatbed, in the middle of some godforsaken truckstop, in… where? *(He too stares at the map.)* Where would it really, really hurt? Houston? San Francisco? Seattle? Chicago? Ten bucks, it's Chicago.

COSENTINO   Why not Washington?

McCALL   That, my friend, is the one place it isn't. You couldn't sneak a firecracker into Washington these days.

COSENTINO   New York.

McCALL Nah, they've done New York. Chicago, I'm telling you. Ten bucks. You wanna take it?

COSENTINO I'm from Chicago.

McCALL Ah. Well then.

COSENTINO And you people seriously think that guy in there knows something?

McCALL "You people?"

COSENTINO Your department.

McCALL Oh no! We just went out into the street and picked him up at random! Of course we think he knows something! Pity the poor bastard if he doesn't! Listen. He's what we've got. Him and the other one.

COSENTINO They've got three more in Buffalo.

McCALL Yeah, well, we figure ours are better.

COSENTINO "Better?"

McCALL Been watching them a long time. Surveillance. Wiretaps. They're hooked into a network. Look, we know stuff, a *lot* of stuff. We've got tabs on thousands of these people. We get information. There are people plotting things, and we're trying to get to them, and stop them. 9/11 *happened*, for Christ's sake, and before it happened there were people who knew about it! And we didn't get to them.

COSENTINO *(evenly)* Unless some people had an idea it was going to happen, and decided to let it.

McCALL Why the fuck would anyone…?

COSENTINO Because no-one would have dreamt such a thing could happen. And now we know it could. Right?

McCALL We'd let planes hit the World Trade Center? The Pentagon? Could have been the White House? When we could have prevented it? Let three thousand Americans die…?

WATKIN I will not believe that. *(Randall WATKIN has arrived. He is Black. This surprises them.)* I *will* not believe that. That the government of the United States is cynical and unscrupulous and indifferent to the loss of human life. I will not believe that.

COSENTINO Why not?

WATKIN Because it's unthinkable.

COSENTINO There are people who think it.

WATKIN It *has* to be unthinkable. We can't…. We cannot live like that. *(a beat)* The terror threat is real. It exists. There are evil people out there.

COSENTINO   "Evil?"

WATKIN   What would you call them? *(decisively)* Let us be clear. We are in an emergency situation. There is a clear and present danger. *(a beat)* I have here a warrant issued by a Federal Court judge. It authorizes the rigorous interrogation of persons suspected of possessing information pertinent to a Code Red emergency as defined by the Homeland Security Act. Such interrogation to be conducted under the Dershowitz Protocol, as established by the Attorney General of the United States. *(pause)* I am Dr. Randall Watkin, authorized Administering Officer.

McCALL   You're a doctor?

WATKIN   I have a PhD. I am not a medical practitioner.

McCALL   *(a beat)* Right. Well. Let's play ball! Jack McCall, FBI, Interrogating Officer.

WATKIN   Mr. McCall.

McCALL   Captain.

WATKIN   Captain McCall.

COSENTINO   Jane Cosentino, Justice Department, Monitor.

WATKIN   *(disconcerted)* I was given to understand…

COSENTINO   Mr. Erickson is sick.

WATKIN   I see. *(pause)* And the… subject?

McCALL   In there. Ready when you are, Doctor.

WATKIN   He… understands the situation… the procedure?

McCALL   I think he pretty much gets the picture.

WATKIN   And he persists in refusing to divulge…?

McCALL   He claims to have no information.

WATKIN   But you believe…?

McCALL   I… we believe he does.

WATKIN   Yes.

McCALL   *(a beat)* Do you mind me asking, have you done this before?

WATKIN   *(guardedly)* Done what?

McCALL   This. What we're doing.

WATKIN   I have not.

McCALL   Makes three of us.

COSENTINO   Four.

McCALL *(it takes him a moment)* Oh, right!

WATKIN We are establishing a precedent. We have a grave responsibility.

COSENTINO Absolutely.

McCALL Yes, well... *(pause)* Do you want coffee or a muffin or something? Juice?

WATKIN Thank you, no. *(expectant pause)* Well, then.... Shall we, ah, proceed?

McCALL Just say the word. *(There is obviously a general reluctance to get started.)*

WATKIN *(a formality)* Ms. Cosentino, I must ask you, as Justice Department Monitor, are you satisfied that a rigorous interrogation is warranted in this instance?

COSENTINO Well... *(They look at her.)* As Justice Department Monitor, I am obliged to say that I have serious misgivings, I'm afraid.

McCALL Give me a fucking break!

WATKIN Captain McCall! *(to COSENTINO)* Misgivings about the interrogation of this subject...?

COSENTINO It is a descent into barbarity.

McCALL For Christ's sake...! 9/11 was the descent into barbarity!

WATKIN Ms. Cosentino, your appointment as Justice Department monitor, and your presence here tonight, presume your acceptance of the necessity of this extraordinary... exercise.

COSENTINO Of course. Yes. I realize that. But I wish to put on record...

WATKIN You understand that, as Administering Officer, I cannot proceed without your specific and periodically renewed assent?

McCALL Fuck's going on? Every minute counts here! There's a nucular fucking device out there! Let's go already! *(opening intercom)* Don't worry, brother – we haven't forgotten you!

AZIZ Please, I am telling you... *(McCALL closes intercom.)*

WATKIN *(abruptly)* Captain, I must ask you to refrain from profanity.

McCALL *(uncomprehending)* Whaa?

WATKIN Your language... is offensive to me.

McCALL Jesus! *(correcting himself)* "Good Grief!"

WATKIN Ms. Cosentino, are you prepared to enter the access codes, to enable initiation of the procedure?

COSENTINO "Initiation of the procedure"?

McCALL Let's get a move on here!

COSENTINO   We're about to torture a man...

WATKIN   Please, Ms. Cosentino...

COSENTINO   ...who may not have any information to give us.

WATKIN   That is the risk we run. That is the consideration we weigh.

COSENTINO   Does that not concern you?

WATKIN   Of course it "concerns" me! What do you imagine? It concerns me very much that we have been driven – by our enemies! – to a gross violation of everything America stands for. That concerns me! But this is an unprecedented situation. Historically unprecedented. People who know something this critical...

COSENTINO   *(interjecting)* If they do...

WATKIN   ...must be *compelled* to divulge it. The debate is over. The public accepts it.

McCALL   Seventy-three per cent in favour.

WATKIN   We do not undertake this action lightly. We undertake it under strict safeguards and clear guidelines – which it is your responsibility to maintain at all points. That is why you are here.

The phone trills again. McCALL answers it.

McCALL   McCall. *(angrily)* No, not yet. Soon! We're still going through the formalities. The Whoozit Protocol. I know that. You think I don't know that? Over and out. *(hanging up)* They're getting just a wee bit impatient up there.

WATKIN   Ms. Cosentino, I am going to enter my access codes, and I am asking you to do the same. I remind us that once the procedure has been initiated, every operation will be monitored by the medical attendant and recorded. As will every communication between us, and with the... subject. Every ten minutes the Protocol requires us to re-enter the access codes to continue with the procedure. *(WATKIN addresses himself to a computer terminal, and proceeds to enter some commands and passwords. He turns to COSENTINO.)* Ms. Cosentino? *(no response)* Ms. Cosentino, I have to ask you...

COSENTINO   *(fiercely)* All right! *(She sits at an adjacent terminal and enters her own access codes.)*

McCALL   Attagirl!

COSENTINO   Don't!

WATKIN   Thank you. We are now operational.

McCALL   Okay!

WATKIN   A moment. I would like to commence by offering a short prayer. *(They look at him in astonishment.)* O Lord, we ask for your guidance and wisdom in our undertaking here tonight. Give us the strength and the resolve to do what is required of us, and the... restraint and... compassion to... ah... do no more than is absolutely necessary. Forgive us, as we hope to be forgiven. Amen. *(He looks expectantly at the others.)*

McCALL   Amen.

COSENTINO   *(uncomfortably)* Amen.

McCALL   So let's go already!

WATKIN   I will now address the subject. Please open the communication channel, Captain McCall. *(McCALL opens the intercom. AZIZ begins to protest immediately, but WATKIN ignores him.)* Mr.... *(He consults a paper.)* ...Aziz. I have been appointed by judicial warrant to act as the Administering Officer in the exercise of a rigorous interrogation, under the Dershowitz Protocol. I am accompanied by an official of the Federal Department of Justice, acting as judicial monitor. Mr. Aziz, will you state your full name please?

AZIZ   *(He has been protesting frantically.)* You know my name!

WATKIN   Please state it for the record.

AZIZ   My name is Iqbal Aziz, I am a journalist, legal resident of the United States, I have no knowledge of...

WATKIN   That will be sufficient, thank you.

AZIZ   ...any terroristic activity...

WATKIN   Mr. Aziz, do you understand the nature of a rigorous interrogation? *(silence)* Mr. Aziz...?

AZIZ   You are going to torture me.

WATKIN   *(carefully)* You will be asked a series of questions. If you refuse to answer these questions in a satisfactory manner, a... physical... stimulus will be administered.

AZIZ   *(hysterically)* I don't know anything! I can't tell you anything! What can I do?

WATKIN   Captain, go ahead please.

McCALL   Mr. Aziz. Mr. Aziz! *(He closes the intercom for a moment.)* This ain't gonna to be easy. *(He re-opens intercom and speaks firmly over AZIZ's protests.)* Mr. Aziz, credible information has been received by the United States government that a nucular device has been planted in a major US city, timed to detonate within the next *(checking watch)* seven hours. We have reason to believe, from information received, that you have material knowledge of the whereabouts of that device. Will you tell us now where that device has been planted?

AZIZ   I don't know! I don't know! I don't know!

McCALL I'm giving you a second chance…

AZIZ I don't know anything. Please – don't do this…!

> *They look at each other. McCALL nods briefly, and indicates with his hands: "Ten seconds, Level one."*

WATKIN *(at the keyboard, and speaking for the record)* I am entering a Level One application, ten seconds duration. Close the intercom, please.

McCALL *(doing so)* Closing it. *(Captain Picard voice)* Engage, Number One!

WATKIN Commencing… now.

> *The lights dim slightly and a faint hum is audible. All three flinch involuntarily. Ten seconds elapse. The light brightens, the hum ceases. They breathe. McCALL is about to re-open the intercom, to resume questioning.*

McCALL Okay, let's try again.

WATKIN Please! Give him a little… recovery time.

COSENTINO *(confused)* What are we doing to him? What…? It's not an electric shock…?

McCALL I thought you knew "exactly" what we're doing.

WATKIN It connects directly to the central nervous system.

COSENTINO My God. So it's…

WATKIN Pure. Very intense. Pain.

COSENTINO But, I mean… what does it… feel like?

WATKIN What are you asking?

COSENTINO How much…?

WATKIN It produces a sensation of acute agony. Believe me.

COSENTINO How do you know?

WATKIN *I know! (The implication is that he has had to experience it himself. They look at him in shock.)* You were unaware of that?

McCALL So you've, like, had it…?

WATKIN It was a requirement. Of the authorization.

McCALL Holy cow! *(a beat)* Excuse me.

WATKIN *(wryly)* "Holy cow" is okay. *(a beat)* Shall we continue?

McCALL *(opening the intercom)* Mr. Aziz…?

AZIZ *(traumatized, trembling)* Oh my God, oh God, oh God…

McCALL Mr. Aziz!

AZIZ Oh God, oh God…

McCALL I'm going to ask you again…

AZIZ Please, please, oh God…

McCALL Where is that device planted?

AZIZ I don't know, I don't know.

McCALL You refuse to tell me?

AZIZ I don't know anything! Please! I don't…

McCALL Okay! Maybe this will help. *(McCALL signals to WATKIN: "Fifteen seconds, Level one.")*

WATKIN I am entering a Level One application, fifteen seconds duration. Close the intercom, please. *(McCALL closes the intercom, and signals that he has done so.)* Commencing… now.

> As before, the lights dim slightly and the faint hum is heard. Fifteen seconds elapse.

McCALL *(loosening collar)* Is it just me, or is it hot in here? *(He opens the intercom. AZIZ can be heard emitting a kind of high, wheezing panting.)* Okay, are we ready yet? *(no answer)* Aziz, I'm serious about this. And I don't have all night.

AZIZ Don't do this! I am begging, don't do this to me!

McCALL *(patiently)* Just tell me where it is. There's a nucular bomb…

AZIZ I don't know! I would tell you! These people who do this, they are not my people…

McCALL What people?

AZIZ Who do these things.

McCALL You know these people?

AZIZ No! I don't know anything!

McCALL Where is that device?

AZIZ No! Please…!

> McCALL shuts off the intercom and holds up two fingers to WATKIN.

WATKIN Level Two application, fifteen seconds. Commencing… now.

> The lights dim slightly, the faint hum is heard. Abruptly the phone rings. McCALL grabs it.

McCALL *(hoarsely)* Not now, for Christ's sake! Because… because we're… busy! Yes, I know! *(He slams down the phone.)*

The fifteen seconds are over. The light brightens, the hum ceases. There is a general exhalation and wiping of brows.

My God, I need a drink.

COSENTINO   *You* need a drink?

McCALL opens the intercom. AZIZ is wailing shrilly.

McCALL   *(fiercely)* Listen, Ik-ball, just tell me where that thing is! Okay? Okay? We've got to know where it is. So tell me, you stupid fuck, and get this over with! Where is that nucular device?

AZIZ continues to wail hysterically.

COSENTINO   Dear God, I can't take this any longer…

McCALL   Whaa?

COSENTINO   The word is "nuclear." "NU-CLE-AR"! Jesus Christ.

McCALL   That's what I…

COSENTINO   You keep saying "nucular."

McCALL   Well I'm sorry!

COSENTINO   It's just so ignorant!

McCALL   Well fuck you, lady!

WATKIN   Language. Please.

McCALL   *(to the intercom)* Where is it, Ik-ball? Is it in Seattle? *(AZIZ continues to wail.)* Houston? San Francisco? Chicago?

AZIZ   *(shrilly)* Chicago!

McCALL   Chicago? Did you say Chicago? *(more wailing)* It's in Chicago?

AZIZ   I don't know, oh God, oh God…

McCALL   Okay, buddy, you asked for it!

AZIZ   Chicago! Chicago!

McCALL   *(singing)* "That toddlin' town!" All right, now we're getting somewhere!

COSENTINO   We're not getting anywhere!

McCALL   *Where* in Chicago?

AZIZ   I don't know!

McCALL   Oh dear! I thought you were going to help us. Okay, here we go again.

AZIZ   No! Please! Please!

McCALL   Let's go to a level three.

COSENTINO   I don't think…

McCALL   *(urgently)* Level Three! Let's go! *Let's go!*

WATKIN   Level Three application, fifteen seconds. Commencing… now.

> *An awful horrible animal screaming fills the space. McCALL has forgotten to close the intercom.*

(hysterically) Jesus fucking Christ!

McCALL   *(closing the intercom)* Language, reverend!

WATKIN   I'm sorry. I apologize. I beg your pardon.

McCALL   Forget it. *(There is a tense silence, as they wait out the fifteen seconds.)*

COSENTINO   *(after a pause)* This is… we can't go on… it's barbarous. We're savages.

WATKIN   We are not savages!

COSENTINO   What are we doing? Listen to that!

WATKIN   It is… difficult.

COSENTINO   Difficult?

McCALL   *(still urgent)* Let's get on with it! We're getting somewhere. I can smell it.

COSENTINO   We're not getting anywhere! The man doesn't know anything.

McCALL   That's for me to decide! *(opening intercom)* Aziz! *(There is a sound of desperate, child-like crying.)*

COSENTINO   My God. *(to the intercom)* Listen, Mr. Aziz, this is Jane Cosentino, Justice Department. Please, for God's sake, if you know anything at all, just tell us now, and get this over with!

WATKIN   *(urgently)* Wait! Close it!

McCALL   *(closing the intercom)* Fucking hell!

WATKIN   *(to COSENTINO)* Don't ever do that again!

COSENTINO   What are you talking about?

McCALL   Give your name!

WATKIN   Don't ever do that! It's a total breach of the Protocol.

McCALL   "Just so ignorant!"

WATKIN   Never, ever, reveal your identity, or the identity of anyone engaged in this operation. Do you understand?

COSENTINO   *(abashed)* You're right. I… I apologize.

WATKIN   Ms. Cosentino…

COSENTINO   No, you're right. I shouldn't have. Article 14, paragraph 2.

WATKIN Ms. Cosentino. *(pause)* Ten minutes have now elapsed since the system was activated.

COSENTINO What?

WATKIN Under the Protocol, in order to proceed we are obliged to re-enter our access codes.

COSENTINO *(The power relations are suddenly reversed.)* No. I'm sorry.

WATKIN Ms. Cosentino… Jane…

COSENTINO No! I'm not doing it. We're not going on.

McCALL *(urgently)* Come on! Don't wimp out on us, for Christ's sake!

COSENTINO I'm not wimping out! This is unforgivable.

McCALL You're wimping out.

COSENTINO It's sickening.

McCALL You know, I didn't want to say this…

COSENTINO Oh, I'm sure you didn't.

McCALL …but I really don't think this is a job for a woman.

COSENTINO And why is that?

McCALL Because you don't have…

COSENTINO The balls?

McCALL Your word, not mine.

COSENTINO And what is your word?

McCALL The "intestinal fortitude."

COSENTINO The balls.

McCALL The will. You can't wimp out just because you feel bad!

COSENTINO And you're… what are you… getting off on it?

McCALL Pardon the expression, but I've got a job to do.

COSENTINO So do I. And I'm doing it. I'm saying "No." Period.

McCALL And what are you saying "Yes" to? A hundred thousand dead?

WATKIN *(evenly)* Ms. Cosentino, you have the right and the power to say "No," according to the Protocol…

McCALL Which you helped write, I believe…

COSENTINO *(replying to WATKIN)* Yes, I do!

WATKIN Yes. But only on procedure! You know that! You have a sworn obligation not to impede the interrogation.

COSENTINO   I have an obligation to prevent abuse. This is abuse.

WATKIN   It is not an abuse of the Protocol.

COSENTINO   It's an abuse of that man!

McCALL   Of course it's an abuse of that man! What did you expect, for Christ's sake?

WATKIN   It's not for us, at this point, to question the legitimacy…

COSENTINO   Right. Just following orders.

WATKIN   Nobody ordered you. You agreed.

McCALL   It's a huge fucking concession having you here at all!

COSENTINO   *Concession?*

McCALL   To let you people in on this.

COSENTINO   Who's conceding to whom here?

McCALL   I knew it was a mistake.

COSENTINO   My presence is the condition that makes this possible!

McCALL   Typically fucking liberal, to tie one hand behind our backs.

COSENTINO   Typically liberal, thank God, to impose some constraints!

McCALL   We could have done this quick and dirty, and no-one the wiser. We do it "properly," and you're screwing us around.

COSENTINO   I'm saying it's utterly barbarous. I will not be a party to it.

WATKIN   *(carefully)* It is not… barbarous. You don't know barbarous.

COSENTINO   What?

WATKIN   This is clean. This is humane.

COSENTINO   You're crazy.

WATKIN   It's humane.

COSENTINO   To have a man in there screaming like an animal?

WATKIN   You don't know barbarous. What we are doing here is, finally, bearable. *(pause)* What is unbearable is the terror of mutilation. If this goes on too long you'll be blinded. Your testicles crushed. Your hands smashed. Your rectum burned out.

COSENTINO   For God's sake…

WATKIN   And having to watch it happening to others. Your wife. Your child. *(COSENTINO is sickened.)* You think it doesn't happen? It happens. Our enemies do it all the time.

McCALL   So do our "friends." On our behalf. Quick and dirty. Don't ask, don't tell.

WATKIN And I may tell you, it works.

McCALL It works. Better than this.

WATKIN I've told you. This is bearable. Even the maximum application. If you're a saint or a fanatic, this is bearable.

McCALL Which this guy isn't.

COSENTINO It could kill him.

WATKIN *(matter of fact)* That is true, it could. But they are monitoring his vital signs.

COSENTINO It could traumatize him for life.

They are at an impasse.

McCALL Look. Give me one more period, okay? Another ten minutes. You wanna say no after that, fine.

COSENTINO He doesn't know anything!

McCALL He may not.

COSENTINO You *know* that!

McCALL But if he does, another ten minutes will get it. Listen, I don't like doing this. It's not my idea of a good time. You think I'm some kind of a psycho? I'm a good guy. I've got two kids.

WATKIN Ms. Cosentino?

COSENTINO Why is it up to me? *(no answer)* Ten minutes?

McCALL It's all I ask.

COSENTINO And then…?

McCALL And then we try the other one.

WATKIN I'm entering the codes.

McCALL Jane?

COSENTINO Do *not* call me Jane!

McCALL There's a ticking bomb here, for Christ's sake! You want it to go off, because you're too fucking *sensitive*?

COSENTINO *(a tense pause)* One more time! *(She too enters the codes.)* God help him.

WATKIN God help us all.

McCALL Amen to that, Brother Man! *(opening the intercom)* Aziz. Aziz? *(no response)* Come on, we know you're in there.

COSENTINO For God's sake…!

McCALL Aziz. I'm talking to you. *(AZIZ can be heard whimpering or praying in Arabic.)* Listen. This can be over with as soon as you like. Okay? Are you hearing me? There's a *(carefully)* nu-cle-ar device out there. Either you know where it is, or you know people who do. *(no response)* You know what's going to happen, right? It's your choice, okay? Here's a little reminder, all right? *(closing intercom)* Give him a quickie, level one, seven seconds.

WATKIN I'm entering a Level One application, seven seconds. Commencing… now.

> *McCALL closes the intercom. As usual, the lights dim slightly, and the faint hum is heard.*

McCALL *(opening the intercom without any delay, and talking very fast over AZIZ's cries)* Okay. Aziz? Remember that? That's what I can do. That's what I'm going to do. Only more so, okay? I've got my hand on this dial, it goes from one to five. That was number one you got just there. I don't get what I want, I'm going to number five, and I'm leaving it there. We can't hear you out here, you know that? Is that what you want? 'Cause that's what I'm going to do. I'm not bullshitting. So don't you bullshit me! *Where is that device? Aziz! Where is that device? Where is that device? Where is that device?*

AZIZ *(babbling frantically)* I don't know, I don't know, I don't know…

McCALL Okay, my friend, you've asked for it. Here it comes. *(closing intercom)* Level five, thirty seconds.

COSENTINO No!

McCALL *(to WATKIN)* Do it! Level five!

WATKIN I'm entering a Level Five application, duration thirty seconds. Commencing… now.

> *Intercom is closed. Lights dim, faint hum. The thirty seconds seem interminable. McCALL, with deliberate nonchalance, pours himself a coffee, and gestures an offer to do the same for the others. There is quite a long silence, following the end of the thirty second "application," during which the three avoid looking at each other. After a sufficient time has elapsed, McCALL opens the intercom. AZIZ can be heard whimpering faintly.*

McCALL *(almost gently)* Where is it, Ik-ball? Just tell me, and it's all over. *(AZIZ is crying like a child.)* It's in Chicago, isn't it? Is it in Chicago?

AZIZ *(whimpering)* Chicago.

McCALL Yes. Now just tell me *where* in Chicago, and it's all over. Okay? Where in Chicago?

AZIZ *(faintly)* I don't know, I don't know…

McCALL Ik-ball, where in Chicago?

AZIZ   I don't know.

McCALL   Do you need a reminder?

AZIZ   No!

McCALL   I think you do. What shall we say? Another thirty seconds?

AZIZ   No! No!

McCALL   So where in Chicago?

AZIZ   *(faintly)* The train station.

McCALL   The train station? Which train station? *(off-mike, to Jane COSENTINO)* What's the main train station in Chicago?

COSENTINO   Just… Union Station.

McCALL   *(on mike again)* Is it Union Station? Ik-ball? Is it Union Station?

AZIZ   Yes.

McCALL   Say it for me.

AZIZ   Union Station.

McCALL   *(satisfied)* That's my boy. Thank you, Ik-ball. That's it. You've been very helpful. You're through. *(He picks up the phone, dials a three-digit number.)* McCall. Yeah. For what it's worth: Chicago. Union Station. *(pause)* Yeah, sure. Give him a few minutes, then send someone to get him, will you? Take him to recovery. *(an afterthought)* Be nice to him, okay? He's had a bad time. *(He hangs up.)* Well. That didn't take very long at all! I thought we'd be here 'til breakfast time.

   Silence.

COSENTINO   Now what?

McCALL   *(gesturing upwards)* Now it's up to them. *(He seems drained.)*

COSENTINO   It's not worth a pinch of shit, you know that.

McCALL   I don't know that.

COSENTINO   We all know that.

McCALL   Yeah?

COSENTINO   It's crap. He'll tell you anything he thinks you want to hear.

McCALL   *(wearily)* Maybe. You got a better idea you want to try? *(He picks up the phone again, dials the same three-digit number, and talks.)* So! It's all yours. *(in response to a question)* I don't know. Could be. Your guess is as good as mine. *(pause)* I'm saying "could be." *(pause)* Do what the hell you want. Your call. *(pause)* Me? I'd do a search. Clear the place. Tear the fucking building apart. Go through every container. Call it an anthrax threat or something. Start evacuating. Just don't say the nuke-word. *(beat)* 'Cause you can't take it back, that's why. *(He hangs up.)* Okay. I'm going for a smoke. You're on your own, guys. Don't do anything I wouldn't do. *(He leaves.)*

COSENTINO *(after a pause)* It's not worth anything, is it?

WATKIN Isn't it?

COSENTINO Come on! You heard what happened!

WATKIN I heard.

COSENTINO So? You think the guy knows anything at all? He's screaming desperate. He'd say anything.

WATKIN I am not in a position to assess that. *(He too seems drained.)*

COSENTINO I guess not.

WATKIN I'm not the investigator.

COSENTINO No. You just get to push the buttons.

WATKIN That's right. That's what I do.

COSENTINO *(pressing)* And how do you feel about that?

WATKIN I beg your pardon?

COSENTINO How does it make you feel, doing this?

WATKIN Why are you asking?

COSENTINO I want to know. I want to know what we're doing here.

WATKIN It's a task. I'm performing a function.

COSENTINO I know that! I'm asking what you *feel* – when you "administer" your fifteen seconds, level three.

WATKIN Please! Ms. Cosentino!

COSENTINO I want to know! How you do it. Does anyone *know* you do it? Does your wife know?

WATKIN My wife?

COSENTINO That's a wedding ring, isn't it? What does she think of your "function"?

WATKIN My wife…

COSENTINO Does she say, "Have a good day, dear!"?

WATKIN …worked on the ninety-third floor of the World Trade Center. The second tower to be hit.

COSENTINO Oh.

WATKIN I saw the plane go in. I saw it burn. I saw the tower go down.

COSENTINO I see.

WATKIN No, you don't.

> *They look at each other. McCALL abruptly reenters. He is extremely agitated.*

McCALL Did they come and get him yet?

COSENTINO No.

McCALL *(He opens the intercom and immediately addresses the not-visible AZIZ.)* You bastards! You bastards! You fucking evil bastards! You've done it. Oh my God. You fucking bastards. We're sitting here wasting our time with this little fucker, and they've gone ahead and done it. Oh my God.

COSENTINO What?

McCALL *(still addressing AZIZ)* This is *it*, you know? They're going to be stringing you people up in the streets. It's going to be open season on you people. You thought it was bad after 9/11? This is going to be *bad*.

COSENTINO What, for God's sake?

McCALL *(intercom still open)* They've hit Denver. Some kind of a nuke. Some kind of a dirty, half-assed fucking nucular device has gone off in Denver, Colorado. *Jesus Christ!* How many? God knows. God knows. Tens of thousands? Hundreds of thousands? It's a fucking inferno. *(to the intercom)* What do you have to say, my friend? What do you have to say? Are you happy? Huh? Are you happy? Are you happy now? Are you praising God? *I'm asking you!*

AZIZ *(bewildered)* Denver?

McCALL You evil bastards…

AZIZ But…

McCALL …you ain't seen nothing yet! So you were fucking with me, Ik-ball. Eh? Oh dear. That's too bad. You had me fooled there. You're a clever guy. You're a brave guy. I'm impressed, you know that? Chicago, huh? Stringing me along. Oh Ik-ball, you're going to be sorry for that. Denver's an inferno, and you're in here, and you told me Chicago. Now you tell me why I shouldn't put this thing on full, and walk away and leave it? Why not? *(without bothering to close the intercom)* Give him a little buzz. Couple of seconds. Do it!

WATKIN *(fast)* Level One, two seconds, now.

> *AZIZ screams.*

COSENTINO *(desperately)* You can't do this!

McCALL Just watch me!

COSENTINO You're gratuitously punishing him.

McCALL I can do what the fuck I like with this little shit.

COSENTINO *(to WATKIN)* You can't go along with this. The Protocol…

McCALL Fuck the Protocol! *(to WATKIN)* Give him another buzz! *(WATKIN does so, without the preliminary formula.)*

    AZIZ screams.

You clever fucking weasel! Are you listening?

AZIZ No! Please! I didn't…

McCALL You could have given me Denver. What do you people *want*? You were lying to me. You were fucking with me. You told me Chicago.

AZIZ I didn't…

McCALL You told me Chicago, Ik-ball. You had me convinced, Ik-ball.

AZIZ I thought…

McCALL Why did you do that to me, Ik-ball?

AZIZ I thought…

McCALL What did you think, Ik-ball? You thought it *was* Chicago? Oh sure! Give him another buzz, give him number five!

AZIZ *(frantically)* No! Please…

WATKIN *(throwing up his hands)* I've timed out!

McCALL You weren't bullshitting me, Ik-ball?

AZIZ *(desperately)* I swear to God!

McCALL *(quietly)* Do you? Do you swear to God? Well, well. *(He closes the intercom. He is silent. He gets out a cigarette, puts it in his mouth. COSENTINO makes the beginning of a gesture to the "No Smoking" sign. He glares at her, but makes no move to light up.)* It's Chicago. Like I said.

COSENTINO But…

McCALL You heard. I told him Denver, he was surprised.

WATKIN But…?

McCALL Denver's fine. Nothing's happened to Denver. The point is, our boy here believed me that a bomb had gone off. It was only Denver that was wrong.

COSENTINO *(taking this in)* Okay, but that still doesn't prove…

McCALL What the fuck do you want? You're not going to get proof. This isn't science. You get *leads*.

WATKIN *(after a pause)* Captain McCall, I congratulate you. *(He shakes McCALL's hand.)*

McCALL *(self-disparagingly)* Yeah, well, you know…

WATKIN   I sincerely mean it.

McCALL   Thank you, Doctor. And thank you for your cooperation.

WATKIN   A privilege. *(COSENTINO's silence is deafening.)*

COSENTINO   *(finally)* Well done, I guess.

McCALL   Yeah, sure!

COSENTINO   Clever.

McCALL   *(ironically)* Thank you, ma'am.

WATKIN   Ms. Cosentino, you also did your job.

COSENTINO   *(witheringly)* Did I? Did I really?

McCALL   *(Bogart voice)* You did okay, sister. *(normal voice)* Seriously. "The record will show…"

COSENTINO   Yes? What?

WATKIN   The record will show that you conducted yourself appropriately under the Protocol.

COSENTINO   "Under the Protocol." We have done something unspeakable "under the Protocol."

McCALL   *(He picks up the phone again, punches in the three-digit number.)* McCall here. Listen. I just want to confirm previous conclusion. New information *strongly* suggests Chicago…. What? *(longish pause)* Jesus Christ! *(pause)* When? *(pause)* Jesus. Oh my God. Oh my God.

>   *McCALL appears stunned. WATKIN and COSENTINO look at him expectantly. Fade to black.*
>
>   *End.*

photo by Patrick Fothergill

Born in England in 1941, and educated at Downing College, Cambridge, Robert Fothergill came to Canada in 1963 to pursue graduate work at McMaster University and the University of Toronto. His PhD dissertation was published as *Private Chronicles: a Study of English Diaries* by Oxford University Press in 1974. After teaching for many years in the English Department of Atkinson College at York University, he joined the Department of Theatre in the Faculty of Fine Arts in 1994, serving as Chair for five years. An early play, *Something To Do*, won a prize in a one-act play competition at the U of T in 1965, but for a number of years he was more involved in film, founding the Canadian Film-makers' Distribution Centre in 1967, with Lorne Michaels and David Cronenberg, and making the controversial TV news simulation, "Countdown Canada," in 1970. Peripheral involvement in theatre over the years has included old geezer roles in Theatre@York productions, as well as three recent visits to India to direct Canadian plays with students at the Universities of Baroda and Jaipur. He was reluctantly retired from York in 2006, but continues to teach there as though nothing had happened. He is married with two grown sons, and lives in Toronto. (e-mail: robf@yorku.ca)